NIGERIAN PENTECOSTALISM AND CHRISTIAN SOCIAL RESPONSIBILITY

NIGERIAN PENTECOSTALISM AND CHRISTIAN SOCIAL RESPONSIBILITY

Edited by

Babatunde Aderemi Adedibu · Benson Ohihon Igboin

Rotimi Alabi Oti · Isaac Deji Ayegboyin

GALDA VERLAG 2021

Bibliografische Information der Deutschen Nationalbibliothek
Die Deutsche Nationalbibliothek verzeichnet diese Publikation in der Deutschen
Nationalbibliografie; detaillierte bibliografische Daten sind im Internet über
https://dnb.de abrufbar.

ISBN 978-3-96203-161-9 (Print)
ISBN 978-3-96203-162-6 (E-Book)

TABLE OF CONTENTS

Introduction   vii

Chapter 1:   Corporate Social Responsibility
             and Christian Social Responsiveness
             – Benson Ohihon Igboin   1

Chapter 2:   Propositioning Elisha's Prophetic Ministry as a
             Template for Pentecostal Prophets' Civic Roles
             and Corporate Social Responsibility in Nigeria
             – Michael Ogunewu and Deji Ayegboyin   31

Chapter 3:   Targeted Evangelism and Knife Crime in London:
             A Case of Corporate/Church Social Responsibility by
             Migrant Pentecostal Churches in the United Kingdom
             – Bisi Kleevat   49

Chapter 4:   Centrifugal and Centripetal Mission Approaches:
             Studies in the Corporate Social Responsibility (CSR) of
             Pentecostal Churches in Nigeria with Emphasis on RCCG
             – Walnshak Alheri Danfulani and
             Umar Habila Dadem Danfulani   73

Chapter 5:   Sustainable Development in Nigeria:
             The Interventionist Approaches to Healthcare Delivery
             of the Redeemed Christian Church of God, Nigeria
             – Babatunde Aderemi Adedibu   103

Chapter 6:   Ministering Beyond the Pulpit: An Examination
             of the Impact of Redeemed Christian Church of
             God (RCCG) on Healthcare Delivery in Nigeria
             – Samuel Kehinde Fabunmi and
             Olumuyiwa Olusesan Familusi   125

Chapter 7:   Nigerian Pentecostalism and Corporate Social
             Responsibility: The Case of Christ Against Drug
             Abuse Ministry of RCCG in Lagos State
             – Alaba Rotimi Oti   139

Chapter 8:   Nigerian Pentecostalism, Civic Roles and
              Corporate Social Responsibility
              – Gabriel Oyevesho Akinlade-Daniel   151

Chapter 9:   An Examination of the Catholic Social Teaching
              – Deborah Doyinsola Adegbite   163

Notes on Contributors   169

Introduction

In 2018, the International Conference on African Pentecostalism's (ICAP's) theme centred on probity and accountability in the church, especially African Pentecostalism. Many participants at the conference expressed disapproval of some Pentecostal church leaders' ostentatious lifestyles as well as their utter neglect of their poor and impoverished members. They argued that African Pentecostal leadership's emphasis on prosperity does not translate to prosperity for all; it is a prosperity whose locale restricts to the topnotch of the Pentecostal hegemony. It is prosperity for the leaders, from the members to the leaders. Paradoxically, prosperity theology, if it qualifies to be so referred, creates prosperity for the wealthy and poverty for the poor. In addition, they accused the Pentecostals of lack of probity and accountability in their dealing; they evade accountability by shrouding it in divine clout, claiming to be solely responsible and accountable to God. Accountability should have first and foremost been to members, and ultimately, God. The final point that resonated at the conference is that due to lack of accountability and openness in the leaders' transactions, members are continuously and blindly exploited.

Some other participants viewed such criticisms as baseless and out of tune with the reality within the Pentecostal circle. Although none would rationally object to the glaring opulence of some Pentecostal leaders; that, they argued, did not suggest that Pentecostal leaders have not impacted and continue to intervene in the broader sphere of Africa's development. The anxiety to have space to ventilate the interventions of Pentecostals in development strides in the continent led to the 2019 ICAP's theme: African Pentecostalism and Corporate Social Responsibility. This present volume is, therefore, a compilation of some of the papers presented at the conference.

Ordinarily, the Christian mission to most people until recently is to convert the whole person and tailor them towards heaven. The converts are not only transformed through rupturing of the past by faith in the atoning work of Christ, their moral life and social relationship are also transformed to conform to the moral mandate enshrined in the Scriptures. This distinctive experience is not only a spiritual badge worn for social recognition, but also moral imprint, which for the converts makes them world-rejecting. The world-rejecting Christianity that expected an imminent blast of the final trumpet, an end of the world event, in the course of time began to shift focus to intervene in the social, moral, political and ecological disaster that is about to thunder. This shift towards world-affirming Christianity, a major trajectory of neo-Pentecostalism, is oftentimes classified within the remit of Progressive Pentecostalism.

Progressive Pentecostalism, as missiologists view it, is referred to as the third wave of Pentecostalism; the first being the classical Pentecostalism associated with the events of Asuza Street in 1906 and the second, the rise of charismatic brands within the mainstream Christian denominations in the 1960s. Progressive Pentecostalism as the third wave has its peculiar frames because it is not just world-affirming, it is more critically interested and involved in a whole developmental trajectory of the society. It thus alters the economic and theoretical dynamics of Western developmental leanings when it situates the cause of poverty and under-development in spirituality. Poverty and under-development are generally viewed in material and quantitative terms and could be caused by natural and systemic structure, which must be addressed in order to remedy them. But Progressive Pentecostalism docks them as a devil-inspired affliction that requires, and in fact, demands, spiritual machine gun to dismantle. Consequently, Progressive Pentecostalism claims that it is inspired by the Holy Spirit and the life of Jesus to intervene in physical, social, spiritual and economic life of society. It is this holistic view of development that many Pentecostal churches and their leaders are keying into, in their attempt to address the developmental deficiencies in Africa.[1]

Even though Progressive Pentecostalism perceives under-development as a spiritual problem that requires spiritual antidote, it does also concretely or physically intervene to transform, change or chart a new course of action in Pentecostal sphere of influence and beyond. For the most part, however, this volume examines Pentecostal interventionist strategies and actions, not in relation to spiritual cause, but as a conscious effort to better the life of society in general. Of course, as some of the contributors have argued, there are underlying spiritual interests and motives in their corporate/Christian social responsibility.

---

[1] Frederick Kakwata, "The Progressive Pentecostal Conception of Development within an African Context of Poverty," *Stellenbosch Theological Journal*, 3/1 (2017): 159-183.

Several arguments abound as to what the Christian/Pentecostal social interventions should be called. Should it be referred to as corporate social responsibility in relation to multinational corporations' corporate social responsibility? Are the Christian bodies incorporated in the same way as the multinationals to then qualify them to be called corporate? Or, should it be termed Christian social responsibility to give it a distinctive finesse? If it is Christian social responsibility, does it not give it the toga of corporate social responsibility that is generally believed to have been instigated by corporate social irresponsibility? If Christian social actions are interventionist, does it make sense (or nonsense) to consider it as Christian social responsiveness since it is not compelled to act as the corporations are? Are the goals of corporate and Christian social actions the same? Should it be Christian corporate social responsibility as some have posited? Despite these questions, there is a clear agreement that Christians, Pentecostals in this instance, have contributed immensely to the development of their societies.

Thus, in Chapter One, Igboin engages the concept of corporate social responsibility and Christian social responsiveness. He argues that corporate social responsibility is a sly concept whose origin is shrouded in controversies. It is viewed as an act of philanthropy, which also requires stewardship. Since corporations are first and foremost interested in profit making without regard to other stakeholders, it becomes imperative to push corporations to recognise the rights of stakeholders and the environment within which they operate. This then suggests that corporate social responsibility is a consequence of corporate social irresponsibility, that is, the deliberate neglect of the welfare and well-being of stakeholders and the ecosystem. The push for corporate social responsibility also garnered some recognition because of the realisation that non-renewable resources being depleted by corporations have consequences for human continued existence both now and in the future. But whether or not the principles of corporate social responsibility are enacted practically is debatable. But Igboin argues that corporate social responsibility has become a wheel of corruption by both national and multinational corporations to enrich themselves to the detriment of the masses and the environment. Therefore, he evinces that it is reasonable to think that there is Christian social responsiveness since the goal of their intervention goes beyond the popular and mundane objective the corporate world and government have failed to meet.

In Chapter Two, Ogunewu and Ayegboyin contend that Pentecostal Christianity is grounded in prophetism and as such, its corporate social responsibility must also be guided by prophetic template as exemplified by Prophet Elisha. Although Pentecostal Christianity constantly claims to be a product of the New Testament, its utterances and actions are indisputably situated in Old Testament form of prophetic action. Consequently, Ogunewu and Ayegboyin argue that Prophet Elisha's ministry is a quintessence and standard for any contemporary Pentecostal ministry if its corporate social activities will be meaningful. Elisha maintained a sterling moral standard and administrative openness that was geared towards enhancing lives, contributing to personal and community development, advancing socio-economic and political development of his time. All of these were done altruistically. The Pentecostal Christianity that prides itself in exploitation, self-aggrandisement, opulence and arrogance is antithetical to the spirit and letter of biblical prophetism. They also pointed out that there are certain criteria and checks that Elisha set and operated within that should mark the personalities and operations of contemporary Pentecostal prophets in Africa.

Kleevat maintains that "Churches are already involved, and it is important their involvement in social action is brought to national attention and that their capacity is improved as much as possible." Since no one lights a candle and puts it under a bushel, it is high time Pentecostal churches showcased their interventions in societies as evidence against the caustic critics who posit that they are self-centred. She understudies the Salvation Proclaimers Anointed Church, a migrant church in London that wholly devotes its resources and time to ministering to knife criminals. Although the church has no formal evangelism prospectus, it, however, believes that results are more crucially important than format. Its unorthodox strategy of converting the street urchins may not be unrelated to Paul being a Jewish to the Jews, Greek to the Gentiles and yet faithful to Christ in order to win all to Christ.

The next four chapters concentrate on the Redeemed Christian Church of God's (RCCG's) Christian social responsibility. "The Redeemed Christian Church of God (RCCG) is the longest Pentecostal franchise in Africa. On account of its size, wealth, long history, and self-definition as a successful spiritual-economic corporation, many other Pentecostal churches see it as a trendsetter and a paradigm of power and copy its theology, rituals, and practices."[2] The church has received formal recognitions and praises from secular authorities for its corporate/Christian social responsibility just as it has attracted avalanches of criticisms. Blazing the trail, Danfulani and Danfulani examine the RCCG from the ambit of centrifugal and centripetal missional approach. Centripetal missional approach denotes a centre-seeking church that, in the course of time, becomes docile and passive unlike the centrifugal one that stretches out to reach those at the peripheries or margins of existence. Historically, the RCCG was a world-rejecting mission that harped on holiness and sanctification, consecration and heaven as its goal. However, it has come to stoke both world-rejecting and world-affirming ethos, a shift towards Progressive Pentecostalism that claims inspiration from the Holy Spirit to intervene in human social order in order to ensure a holistic development for all irrespective of religious and social affiliation. The RCCG's Christian social responsibility is multi-prone, straddling health, education, empowerment, humanitarianism, sports and so forth. With these stark interventions, Danfulani and Danfulani opine that the RCCG counterbalances its centripetal position with centrifugal activities.

Adedibu examines Sustainable Development Goal 3 in the context of RCCG's health intervention in Nigeria. He empirically demonstrates that the RCCG has counterbalanced its pneuma-diaconal approach to mission. Although many have argued that Progressive Pentecostalism views reality from metaphysical or spiritual angle and thus emphasises a spiritual solution to every problem, Adedibu argues that the fact that miracles take place and the church also establishes many health care facilities does not contravene any biblical mandate, nor does it raise any paradoxical question. For instance, how would the Redemption Camp where sick people troop to for divine healing house many modern health care facilities? Leveraging on the SDG 3, he explores how the RCCG has, as part of its Christian social responsibility, invested immensely in health sector across the country and beyond. These modern health facilities are a melting and meeting place of medical expertise and spiritual intervention as part of Progressive Pentecostal conception of wholesome development both of persons and systems. He concludes that with the massive intervention of the RCCG in health care system, it would be unreasonable to think that social capital can be divorced from any strategy aimed at meeting the target of SDG 3.

---

[2] Asonzeh Ukah, "Prosperity, Prophecy and the COVID-19 Pandemic: The Healing Economy of African Pentecostalism," *Pneuma*, 42 (2020): 456.

Fabunmi and Familusi do not agree less with Adedibu when they argue that spiritual or Pentecostals' interest and intervention in health system despite their claim to divine healing is critical to achieving the SDG 3. "The RCCG commitment to Christian Social Responsibility especially in the area of health care delivery demonstrates the fact that the church recognises that it is part of society and as such, it needs to be part of the progress of society, which it has demonstrated and it is still demonstrating by ministering to the health of the people as complement to faith/divine healing." They note that the RCCG, in its bid to contribute to global health, liaises and collaborates with international bodies and governments on health matters. The RCCG's glocal health protocols involve building and contributing to local health system and stimulating international intervention in meeting health challenges. This was most clearly demonstrated during this COVID-19 pandemic lockdown, when the church donated medical items to government health facilities. This focus, they point out, situates the church as an epicentre of modern development within the Nigerian landscape.

Oti specifically examines the RCCG's Christ Against Drug Abuse Ministry (CADAM). Just like Kleevat argues that Salvation Proclaimers Anointed Church is critically concerned with converting youths involved in knife crime, Oti posits that the RCCG pays attention to drug addicts as part of its Christian social responsibility. "CADAM is set up to rescue drug addicts so as not to inflict the rest of society with the malaise. In the same vein, the RCCG is performing her moral obligation to society and extending the frontiers of evangelism in setting up this rehabilitation programme." He espouses that medical-spiritual modus operandi is utilised in restoring health to the addicts. In order to ensure that there are no relapses, patients are given skill development and acquisition programme and empowered thereafter to live a productive life.

Akinlade-Daniel underscores that other Pentecostal churches also involve in some form of Christian social responsibility. The RCCG, Deeper Life Bible Church, Christ Embassy and so on are intervening in development projects because either the government has failed and thus unable to fulfil its mandate or the churches are just interested in filling in some obvious gaps in order to contribute to whole development. But he argues that Christian social responsibility is more of the former than the latter. Even at that, it cannot be completely claimed that Christian social interventions are altruistic because they have evangelistic undertone, and also to be relevant in the places where they are situated. Expanding their scope of intervention, he concludes, would ensure a better world for all.

Finally, Adegbite grounds Christian social responsibility in the Catholic Social Teaching. The cardinal goals of the CST are human dignity and common good. The principles of CST lay responsibility on everyone in society and thus require that both humans and the system also respond to the challenges facing humanity. Solidarity and subsidiarity guide the demand for rights as well as the duty. Once these are ingrained, we do not only think about the poor and the needy, but also consider their dignity in the community of inter-related persons. Herein lies the core and call to corporate social responsibility.

B.A. Adedibu, B.O. Igboin, R.A. Oti, I.D. Ayegboyin

Chapter 1: Corporate Social Responsibility and Christian Social Responsiveness

Benson Ohihon Igboin[1]

Introduction

At first thought, corporate social responsibility (CSR[1]) appears to be geared towards business corporations and their responsibilities of charity and stewardship to their host communities. This formative understanding undergirds the expansion of the application of corporate social responsibility principles by both national and multinational corporations worldwide. The level of compliance of businesses and corporations with CSR[1] to stakeholders, social space and the environment has been a matter of intense debate. Although many scholars and theorists have concentrated on corporate social responsibility, there seems to be little awareness of corporate social irresponsibility (CSI), which naturally would have been the ground for the consciousness and rise of corporate social responsibility. "Naturally" is deliberately used here because as with classical capitalists and business owners, the quest for profit and its maximisation is the primary motive for business establishments. This human inclination towards profit more often than not undermines even the very source or means of profit-making ventures itself. In this sense, the earth, for instance, is not strictly viewed as a capital, but as an impersonal resource that is assumed can infinitely result in profit, no matter the intensity of exploitation. But recently, such view has come to be questioned as it has been realised that ecological and environmental degradation means that business establishments are already 'eating' their profit and capital as well as jeopardising the future of the unborn. This chapter will argue that it is corporate social irresponsibility (CSI) that gave rise to the notion of corporate social responsibility (CSR[1]), and the level of CSR[1] to Corporate Social Responsiveness (CSR[3]) is a matter of intense controversy, but one that requires the Christian social responsiveness (CSR[2]) to mediate in order to stem the tide of social irresponsibility.

---

[1] Benson Ohihon Igboin is an Academic Associate of the Research Institute of Theology and Religion, University of South Africa, Pretoria, South Africa.

Corporate social irresponsibility (CSI) calls for responses and actions that should redirect the profit-inclination to general well-being of the capital, the environment and stakeholders. Here, arguments have been raised on how best to define CSR[1] that encapsulates the charity and stewardship principles in dealing with the environment. While some would argue that ethic does not direct human actions but prescribes limits, there is a sense in which Christian ethic can, and indeed, has been able to introduce principles and practices that can, and should, guide a new attitude towards CSR[1]. The ethical issues involved in human rights abuse and environmental depletion and degradation by corporations have become increasingly pervasive that they cannot be conveniently neglected without adverse consequences. Of course, these human and environmental abuses are more pronounced in developing countries where weak and corrupt governments suffuse, and corporations of developed countries latch on the lapses and weaknesses to maximise profit at the detriment of the host communities. Rapacious profit orientation which is given vent by capitalism has had more negative impacts on human and ecological well-being than systems that consider a more holistic approach to doing business. The ethic of safer business in a safer environment becomes imperative, which can be guaranteed by socially responsible actions. There is, therefore, no serious basis to continuously hold the belief which has hitherto been pushed by rugged capitalists that business decisions and ethical decisions are perpetually at variance. Ethical and moral standards that will ensure we have safer business and safer environment cannot be divorced from the teachings of religions and cultures; hence, religion, particularly Christianity in this context, has critical roles to play in social responsibility discourse and praxis.[2]

From the outset, therefore, it must be stated very clearly that CSR[1] is not easy to encase in one box. The case is also true of previous scholarship as regards Christian social responsibility (CSR) and Christian social responsiveness (CSR[2]). The Christian social responsibility has also generated different formats of thought, but when viewed together, they present some more intelligible rationale to engage CSR[1]. In this regard, I will examine what has been referred to as faith-based social responsibility (F-bSR) which tends to view how different religions and even denominations within particular religions have understood and pursued the principles of

---

[2] Heribert Schmitz, "The Business in Society: Can Companies save the World?" In Bartholomew Okonkwo (ed.), *Christian Ethics and Corporate Culture: A Critical Viewpoint on Corporate Responsibilities*, Cham: Springer, 2014, 5-7. See also Stefano Zamagni, "Setting up the Dialogue Between CST and CSR: The Challenges of Clashing Theories." In *Christian Ethics and Corporate Culture*, 10.

CSR[1]. One fundamental question to ask is whether CSR[1] or F-bSR can be classified as business establishment, and if not, how does it carry out its responsibilities differently from CSR[1]? This is where this essay is critically intervening. Rather than argue for Christian social responsibility, I shall argue for Christian social responsiveness (CSR[2]) because the former concentrates on prescriptive principles of what to do, while the latter responds to proximate and remote needs that Christian organisations are actively involved in. In what follows, I shall examine each of these concepts and show how they can better be utilised for optimal benefits to humankind, and how Christian social responsiveness (CSR[2]) has keyed into it using the contextual approach.

Corporate Social Responsibility (CSR[1])

In order to understand CSR[1], there is the need to have a brief historical background. As we shall see shortly, there are many definitions of CSR[1] just as there are controversies shrouding its emergence. What many scholars have done over the years to research into CSR[1] from cultural/national contexts is to examine and delineate the historical development of CSR[1] in order to explain the various tortuous engagements with such controversies of origin. As credible, and even reasonable, as this detour may be, the question of the history or evolution of CSR[1] has not been rested. While the management concept of CSR[1] took shape in 1950s in Europe, the history, as an authority states, dates back to the 1800s during the Industrial Revolution, which ignited avid concern for the welfare and well-being of workers rather than profit of the organisations. Increasing criticisms and unrest associated with factory conditions and working system, employment of women and children were cannon fodders for the owners of businesses to begin to think, at least, responsibly. Because businesses could only grow and maximise profits in a peaceful environment, business owners had to also begin to think creatively on how to ensure labour rest rather than incessant labour unrest. Such attempts resulted in what is today referred to as integration of "humanitarianism and business acumen."[3] This implies that business owners are no longer going to be exclusively concerned about their businesses but also about the workers and other stakeholders who directly or indirectly contribute to the successes of their businesses, whose actions could also mar the fortunes of their businesses.[4]

---

[3] Business & Industry, "A Brief History of Corporate Social Responsibility (CSR)," *Business & Industry*, 25 September, 2019 https://www.thomasnet.com/insights/history-of-corporate-social-responsibilty-/ (accessed 1st July, 2020).

[4] Business & Industry, "A Brief History of Corporate Social Responsibility (CSR)

Corporate social responsibility then was not a formal commitment to stakeholders; it came in the form of philanthropy whose altruism is still highly debated. As some have argued, to associate altruism with CSR[1] is to misrepresent the hidden or core agenda of corporations. What corporations present as acts of sacrifice must be subjected to scrutiny, and can only be so accepted if and only if they are not inimical to their growth and sustenance or a Greek gift to the stakeholders.[5] However, Andrew Carnegie is said to be the first to use the term CSR[1] by his very generous acts of philanthropy. Carnegie had made great fortune from steel business and donated humongous amounts of money "to education and scientific research." John D. Rockefeller who was an oil magnate also donated to religious, educational and scientific projects.[6] According to Carnegie,

> The problem of our age is the administration of wealth, so that the ties of brotherhood may still bind together the rich and poor in harmonious relationship. The conditions of human life have not only been changed, but revolutionized, within the past few hundred years. In former days there was little difference between the dwelling, dress, food, and environment of the chief and those of his retainers…. The contrast between the palace of the millionaire and the cottage of the laborer with us to-day measures the change which has come with civilization.[7]

From this classical point of view, CSR[1] harped on conscious and guided distribution of excess profits that organisations made over a period of time. These excess profits were directed towards social development that extended beyond the frontiers of the organisation; it was indeed a way of distributing values. Thus, Carnegie in his work, *The Gospel of Wealth* (1889), discusses two critical principles in relation to CSR[1] namely, charity and stewardship. For him, corporations are "stewards of their property" not only to benefit themselves, but also the whole society.[8] These two components of social responsibility of corporations influenced how wealth was conceived by those who were given to philanthropy. In other words, philanthropy was a moral obligation. It is in this light that we can understand John Maynard Keynes' classical thought that "When the accumulation of wealth is no longer of high social importance,

---

[5] Peter S. Gawu and Husein Inusah, "Corporate Social Responsibility: An Old Wine in a New Gourd," *Journal of Philosophy and Culture*, 7/1 (March 2019): 1-6.

[6] Business & Industry, "A Brief History of Corporate Social Responsibility (CSR)

[7] Engelbert C. Pasag, "Corporate Social Responsibility: Business Philosophy in Global Times, *Filosofia: International Journal of Philosophy*, 17/1 (2016): 1.

[8] Pasag, 1.

there will be great changes in the code of morals. We shall be able to rid ourselves of many of the pseudo-moral principles which have been with us for two hundred years, by which we have exalted some of the most distasteful of human qualities into the position of the highest virtues."[9] Keynes points out that there was indeed immoral and irresponsible attitude to wealth and profit accumulation, an act which undermined the well-being of employees and also threatened the corporate existence of stakeholders as well as the environment. Thus, for Zamagni, philanthropic acts shrouded in distribution of wealth as Carnegie posits, does not immediately suggest that "good business is good ethics."[10] Where methods of doing business are less ethical and profits from it are geared towards philanthropy, there is a covert self-serving interest. Intention is more important than consequence in considering ethical behaviour. Therefore, even though philanthropy is a positive development, it should not serve as an instrument of further deprivation and oppression of the recipients.

The principle of charity and stewardship can further be understood as: compassion and respect for humanity, sense of, and respect for community, and recognition and protection of ecology: the environment. Compassion here could mean helping others without expecting anything in return, an altruistic action geared towards the poor and helpless in society. It is compassion if and only if it is done in respect, and not to disparage the status of the poor or make them feel further helpless. It is for this reason that Carnegie argues and also insists that the poor should not be helped to be poorer by giving them fish, but they could be helped to be helpers of other poor people by teaching and enabling them to fish. In order to ensure this, Carnegie ensured that processes and intermediaries that could obstruct or tamper with the donations to the poor were removed so that the target poor could access the donations. In our contemporary experience, it is common for government to announce palliatives for the poor and they end up in the pockets of the rich and influential politicians, thus weaponising and reinforcing poverty in society.

An unsavoury example is the recent #EndSARS protest in Nigeria, which was eventually hijacked by obviously sponsored hoodlums. The hoodlums, having done with attacking the peaceful protesters, like monsters, turned to attack some politicians' houses and government warehouses where COVID-19 palliatives meant for the people were shamelessly hoarded. A politician would

---

[9] Pasag, 1.
[10] Zamagni, 10.

say that he kept the palliatives to be distributed on his birthday. He would have appeared to be involved in philanthropic act when distributing them to the people who would not have known that the palliatives were theirs in the first instance.

Two, community provides enabling environment for the thriving of corporations. In other words, corporations cannot do well if the community of its localisation becomes hostile as in the case of the Niger Delta of Nigeria, which I will shortly elaborate on. Corporations cannot operate in isolation of the community they are situated because their decisions and operations have direct and indirect impacts on the community. To neglect this very important responsibility is to court reactions which in the course of history have not been positive in many instances. Three, corporations have critical social responsibility to the ecology – environment – within which they operate. Of course, there are renewable and non-renewable natural resources that reasonable corporations must take important note of. The depletion of non-renewable resources, which eventually results in extinction of some natural endowments, has led to agitation, hostility and revolt as I shall also discuss later. That is why CSR[1] was thought to encapsulate "The Triple Bottom Line" – "Profit, People and Planet" if it must be meaningful and relevant especially in a globalised world.[11]

However, Chaffee historicises the emergence of corporate social responsibility within the remit of the ancient Roman Laws that emphasised social component in corporate behaviour. Those Roman Laws gave rise to the creation of asylums, homes of the poor, the aged, hospitals, orphanages and so on. These social facilities were to ensure that those at the margin of society were not completely neglected as they contributed to the well-being of society. These thoughts on corporations were carried on with the English Law to the Middle Ages as part of academic discourse. It was expanded by the English Crown in the sixteenth and seventeenth centuries, and understood as instruments for social development.[12]

According to Agudelo, Johannsdottir and Davidsdottir, Howard Bowen is the father of modern corporate social responsibility for his far-reaching perception. Bowen's pioneering effort as the first academic who devoted his volume specifically to discourses of CSR[1] is worthy of note. Bowen clearly

---

[11] Irina-Eugenia Iamandi, "Corporate Social Responsibility and Social Responsiveness in a Global Business Environment: A Comparative Theoretical Approach," Romanian Journal of Economic Forecasting, 23 (June 2007): 4.

[12] E. C. Chaffee, "The Origins of Corporate Social Responsibility," University of Cincinnati Law Review, 85 (2017): 347-373.

outlines the businessmen's social responsibilities to the stakeholders and the principles they need as guidance in fulfilling them. Thus, Bowen defines social responsibility as "the obligations of businessmen to pursue those policies, to make those decisions, or to follow those lines of action which are desirable in terms of the objectives and values of our society."[13] Nevertheless, the continuous interest in CSR[1] after Bowen depended and still depends on the changing social expectations and social behaviour of stakeholders in a business environment. Responses to the foregoing appear in ethical and legal legislations to ensure that the principles of CSR[1] are faithfully adhered to.

The definitional constructs of CSR[1] have also been a matter that evolves through different phases as different epochs presented different challenges in business environment. For instance, Christine Mallin defines CSR[1] as "the ways in which a business seeks to align its values and behaviour with those of its various stakeholders."[14] This definition entails that the business has the onerous task of striking a balance between its values and the ever-evolving and changing demands of stakeholders. Honestly, attempts at balancing these extremes require deft strategies, and if successful, result in harmonious relationship, trust being the token. But as we have noted earlier, corporate social responsibility extends critically to the environment, the space taken together. Lack of encapsulating the environment makes this definition limited in scope, and if pursued, might give the leeway for corporations to continuously exploit the environment without replenishment. That is why DesJardins' definition becomes helpful when he prospects that in the twenty-first century, global business concern should countenance being economically puissant to address the needs of the billions of people living in the planet, ecologically sensitive and proactive so that the earth and its resources are not used in such a way as to diminish support for life now and in the future, and yet ethically responsible so that human dignity is not sacrificed on the altar of profit.[15]

Osemeke, Adegbite and Adegbite argue that although corporations are supposed to cater for the communities within which they operate, studies have shown that CSR[1] is either mere prescriptions or image-making protocols for

---

[13] Mauricio A. L. Agudelo, Lara Johannsdottir and Brynhiidur Davidsdottir, "A Literature Review of the History and Evolution of Corporate Social Responsibility," *International Journal of Corporate Social Responsibility*, 4/1 (2019): 4.

[14] Christine A. Mallin, "Introduction and Overview." In Christine A. Mallin, (ed.), *Corporate Social Responsibility: A Case Study Approach*, Cheltenham: Edward Elgar Publishing Ltd, 2009, 1.

[15] Joseph R. DesJardins, "Doing Well by Doing Good: Distinguishing the Right from the Good in Theories of Corporate Social Responsibility." In *Christian Ethics and Corporate Culture*, 101.

many corporations. In other words, the expected commitment of corporations to the CSR[1] is significantly lacking in many respects. Corporations often see themselves as not duty-bound to implement the terms of corporate social responsibility. As a result, they define CSR[1] as "the voluntary provision or contribution of a business' resources beyond their fiduciary responsibility, aimed at satisfying the various internal and external stakeholders."[16]

Recently, the notion of CSR[1] being voluntary has been severely criticised because of the impact it has on socio-economic, political and environmental community. As a result, CSR[1] is conceived as an anti-corruption issue; and thus, it involves both binding and non-binding rules that corporations obey in order to be socially responsible. Adefolake Adeyeye avers that CSR[1] has critical roles to play in combating international corruption. According to her, "the role corporations play in fuelling the engine of corruption is best addressed under CSR."[17] The importance of focusing on CSR[1] as an antidote to corruption is that international corruption is much more easily carried out in the guise of corporate social responsibility through multi-national corporations. "Although MNCs are vehicles of development, they are also seedbeds of corruption. They are the chief participants in the supply side of corruption, giving bribes. They are involved in making facilitation payments to public officials to grease the wheels for speedy receipts of contracts; though much has been written about whether they in fact 'grease' or 'sand' the wheels."[18] In other words, offering bribes to access contracts and other facilities may pay off for the bribe-giver and oils the pockets of the receiver, it does ultimately crack the wheel of development for the generality of the community. This, in fact, is the core of MNCs as agents of anti-corruption – preventing corruption. She posits that developing countries are most adversely affected by international corruption. The responses of the developing countries to international corruption, as developed countries have done, are to promulgate appropriate laws to combat international corruption facilitated by MNCs. For example, some provisions in Nigeria's Corrupt Practices and Other Related Offences Act (2000) and Economic and Financial Crimes Commission relate directly with dealing with international corruption orchestrated and perpetrated by MNCs. In 2003, some ministers in Nigeria were charged to court by the Independent Corrupt Practices Commission for

---

[16] Louis Osemeke, Stephen Adegbite and Emmanuel Adegbite, "Corporate Social Responsibility Initiatives in Nigeria." In Samuel O. Idowu (ed.), *Key Initiatives in Corporate Social Responsibility: Global Dimension in CSR in Corporate Entities*, Cham: Springer, 2016, 362.

[17] Adefolake O. Adeyeye, *Corporate Social Responsibility of Multinational Corporations in Developing Countries: Perspectives on Anti-Corruption*, Cambridge: CUP, 2012, 1.

[18] Adeyeye, 44-45.

taking bribes of various sums from a French firm, Sagem SA. However, the excuses and manner with which the charges were withdrawn with the promise of filing fresh charges which never took place are a clear testimonial of how developing countries are susceptible to pressure from developed countries. Several other examples depict the fact that developing countries are weak in many occasions to determine how corporate social responsibility should be exercised in their domains. In addition, inveterate corruption among public officials in developing countries has undermined legal and political processes of demanding corporate social responsibility. The judiciary in many of the developing countries is not only not independent, but also very corrupt: this has adversely affected prosecution of international corruption. Despite the fact that Nigeria has laws and legal bodies established to fight national and international corruption, it lacks "the political will to implement the laws."[19] In fact, after examining the Nigerian corruption index, Robert Rotberg concludes that dealing with her corruption requires more than a political will.[20] Ngozi Okonjo-Iweala adds that although political will is a good virtue, it is not enough to deal with Nigeria's peculiar corruption status; it requires stubborn commitment to fighting corruption.[21] The "anti anti-corruption forces" in Nigeria are complex; they are made up of those who claim to fight corruption and also involve the cluster of those who are fought for their involvement in corrupt practices. These forces have been active in MNCs, customs and excise duties.[22] The anti-corruption fight in CSR[1] can be fought within and without: it has to do with the political will and unwavering commitment of the MNCs themselves and the other agencies involved in anti-corruption processes. "The company's top management must be personally committed in the fight against corruption."[23]

Osemeke, Adegbite and Adegbite further posit that in order to properly examine the level of compliance or otherwise with CSR[1] by corporations, there is need for contextual studies, that is, studies that focus on regional or national scale. Afterall MNCs are situated within a particular geographical place. The

---

[19] Adeyeye, 69.

[20] Robert Rotberg, *The Corruption Cure: How Citizens and Leaders can Combat Graft*, Princeton and Oxford: Princeton University Press, 2017.

[21] Ngozi Okonjo-Iweala, *Fighting Corruption is Dangerous: The Story Behind the Headlines*, Cambridge: The MIT Press, 2018.

[22] Benson O. Igboin, "The Faces of Corruption in Nigeria: A New Thinking in the Reverse Order." In Chris Jones, Pregala Pillay and Idayat Hassan (eds.), *Fighting Corruption in African Contexts: Our Collective Responsibility*, England: Cambridge Scholars Publishing, 2020.

[23] Stefania Giavazzi, Francesca Cottone and Michele De Rosa, "The ABC Program: An Anti-Bribery Compliance Program Recommended to Corporations Operating in a Multinational Environment." In Stefano Manacorda, Francesco Centonze and Gabrio Forti (eds.), *Preventing Corporate Corruption: The Anti-Bribery Compliance Model*, Cham: Springer, 2014, 126.

advantage of this is that it helps to monitor and assess the performance of corporations more closely by those who understand the terrain better, and generate data for comparative studies at a global level.[24] These suggestions and approaches are critical to this present work as we have seen in the case of Nigeria.

In Nigeria, the agitation for CSR[1] arose from derelictions of the multinational corporations operating in the Niger Delta region of the country, on the one hand, and the failure of government to provide social amenities for the communities, on the other hand. The oil sector of the Nigerian economy has been the mainstay of resources for the country. Nigeria is one of the highest oil-producing countries of the world and has also suffered most from environmental degradation caused by oil exploration over the years. Niger Delta may not have been faced with thermonuclear weapons, but the eco-crisis that it has faced over the years has curried international attention and intervention. Despite the agitation for a better response to the ecological disaster waiting to explode beyond its present escalation, 'exploitation' and neglect of the environment have been a recurring decimal. Oil spillage and gas flaring, for example, have adversely affected the means of livelihood of the host communities to the multinational oil corporations. Since the communities can no longer fish in their rivers or farm on their lands, hostilities could not be nipped in the bud, especially when government and the corporations paid deaf ears to the suffering and lamentation of the communities. It is pertinent to add that rivers used to be the major sources of drinking water for the majority of the communities in the absence of potable water. Thus, the rivers being polluted by oil spillage means that the communities will not have access to drinking water.

As a result, several pressure groups naturally sprang up to demand better treatment of the environment. The height was in November 2005 when the General Sani Abacha military regime executed the environmentalist Ken Saro-Wiwa. His execution, despite appeal from international bodies, resulted in sanctions on the country. But it also drew greater attention of the multinational corporations to the danger of unconscionable neglect of the communities. It must be added that one of the resultant effects of the neglect of the environment is abduction of oil workers. As a social condition then,

---

[24] See also Adebimpe Lincoln, Oluwatofunmi Adedoyin and Jane Croad, "Fostering Corporate Social Responsibility among Nigerian Small and Medium Scale Enterprises." In Samuel O. Idowu (ed.), *Key Initiatives in Corporate Social Responsibility: Global Dimension in CSR in Corporate Entities*, Cham: Springer, 2016, 377-397.

abduction of oil workers was meant to call attention of government and the corporations to the grubby conditions of their environment. In other words, they were calling attention to corporate social responsibility. But gradually and steadily, the social condition slipped into social problem, and today, abduction or kidnapping has become a criminal activity that is difficult to fight in Nigeria, adding to the index of insecurity.

Corruption and poverty go hand in hand. The Niger Delta crisis exemplifies this twin concept. Money for investment in the area was diverted by individuals who manned the commissions set up to cater for the yearnings of the people. That did not stop the masses to continue their activities which they labelled 'freedom' agitation. In the course of time, the youth organised themselves into groups pressurising government and the multinationals to respond to their environmental demand. In no time, acquiring dangerous weapons, these groups started blowing up oil installations which cost the government billions of naira daily. This led to the declaration of amnesty, when government failed in its military campaigns against them. The amnesty programme itself became corrupted along the line, and sparks of agitation have continued to spring up in the area, all geared towards 'responsive' corporate social responsibility.

I have gone this far to give this background to the issue of the Niger Delta because of the neglect of CSR[1] of the multinational oil companies. Like I stated earlier, the environment is crucial to business establishments, and its neglect helps in understanding the psychology of their owners. This presupposes that there are principles of corporate social responsibility that are not implemented. It is not that there are no environmental laws that ought to guide the use of the environment, it is that the laws are flagrantly disobeyed even by those who ought to by virtue of their positions obey them.[25] Osemeke, Adegbite and Adegbite argue along this line that, in Nigeria, CSR[1] lacks strategic implementation; rather it is based on such cultural factors as religion, ethnicity, traditions and so on. As a result, what is mainly practised is donations or philanthropy, which in actual sense are not CSR[1] but cosmetic response to deep-seated environmental and social problems. Such philanthropic gestures include beautification of places, provision of boreholes without sustainable electricity to power them, constructing school buildings without

---

[25] Aniefiok E. Ite, Usenobong F. Ufot, Margaret U. Ite, Idongesit O. Isaac and Udo J. Ibok, "Petroleum Industry in Nigeria: Environmental Issues, National Environmental Legislation and Implementation on International Environmental Law," *American Journal of Environmental Protection*, 4/1 (2016): 21-37.

personnel and instructional materials, hospitals without medical personnel and kits, youth empowerment that involves giving bikes, tricycles that do not essentially empower them and so on. Government failure to provide amenities has steadily shifted responsibilities to non-governmental organisations that in turn carry out these responsibilities at their whims and discretions.[26] This demonstrates that, in Nigeria, CSR[1] arose from irresponsibility and unconscionable corruption of government and negligence of corporations to human and environmental issues.

Corporate Social Irresponsibility (CSI)

From the foregoing analysis of corporate social responsibility, we can glean that corporate social irresponsibility (CSI) is the rationale for the emergence of the principles of CSR[1]. Clearly, CSI is the opposite of CSR[1]. CSR[1] is the expectation that corporations would act ethically and be socially responsible to the stakeholders. CSR[1] implies that corporations would act in such a way that what they say they would do is exactly what they did eventually. Since CSR[1] is a testament of what the stakeholders are to expect from corporations, it, therefore, follows that any deviation is a breach, hence acting irresponsibly. Acting right and being a good corporate citizen put corporations in good light and attract tremendous positive attention to their image. But to act otherwise is to curry criticisms, litigation and pressures that end up in blacklisting and other punishments.

CSI is the immoral or unethical decisions corporations make towards their stakeholders, failure in acting responsibly, acting in a socially unacceptable manner or "as a decision to accept a choice that is less moral than its alternative."[27] That is, corporations may focus their CSR[1] on doing good, but not actually avoiding doing bad.

While it is possible that corporations may not be breaking any known laws, they can act irresponsibly by not taking full responsibility of their actions. Corporations can act irresponsibly intentionally or unintentionally. The intentional acts of irresponsibility are those things corporations consciously do to present scorecards or actions that do not reflect actual state of affairs. Those acts may include bribing or avoiding taxation or influencing the media to give favourable image contrary to what practically obtains. Unintentional

---

[26] Osemeke, Adegbite and Adegbite, 373.
[27] Veronica Jonsson and Josefine Steen, "Corporate Social Irresponsibility (CSI): Everything you say, or not say, can be held against You," Bachelor Thesis, School of Health and Society, Kristianstad, 2016, 7.

acts of irresponsibility occur when corporations' activities indirectly cause small- or large-scale harm like earthquake.[28]

As stated earlier, CSI could be the precursor to CSR[1], and it can also be its aftermath. In this case, corporations that act irresponsibly do not have strategic plans to act ethically or responsibly ahead of time; they act reactively or retroactively depending on the amount of pressure stakeholders mount on them. With the increasing activities of whistleblowers, many corporations that have been actively irresponsible have begun to re-think or rescind their decisions, conscious of the consequences that their corporations might face should they be exposed. The social media outfits, especially the Internet have helped to unravel several irresponsible actions of many corporations globally. The exposure of corporations makes meaning in comparing and contrasting their CSR[1] and CSI, where CSR[1] is what they say they would do, and CSI is what they fail to do eventually or do differently. While CSR[1] may show that a corporation is acting, CSI may reveal that it is acting poorly, reactively, retroactively, and not proactively, particularly when its actions are weighed against intentional or unintentional scale. In addition, a corporation may act in its own way with the intention to show goodwill as a demonstration of CSR[1], CSI exposes whether such actions are actually open and transparent. This makes CSR[1] an ideal and CSI the real.[29] In other words, CSR[1] is a theoretical construct that aligns with the aspirations of stakeholders, while CSI aligns with shareholders' model of evaluation. CSI questions the ideal that corporations hold on to. Accordingly,

> It should not be forgotten that CSI can impact on and harm companies' bottom line and it is primarily for this reason that a conspiracy of silence pervades organisations and workplace cultures where irresponsible practices exist.... Regarding their social responsibility practices a CSI-CSR audit can help businesses identify areas of strength and areas for improvement.[30]

Jonsson and Steen posit that in determining the impact of CSI, one has to be contextual in one's approach and analysis. In response to this, George, Kuye and Onokala examine the basis of the crisis in the Niger Delta region of Nigeria where multinational corporations have been exploring oil since

---

[28] Jonsson and Steen, 8.
[29] Jonsson and Steen, 9-11.
[30] Brian Jones, Ryan Bowd and Ralph Tench, "Corporate Irresponsibility and Corporate Social Responsibility: Competing Realities," *Social Responsibility Journal*, 5/3 (2009): 308, 300-310.

1951. According to them, while the corporations declare billions yearly as profits, little attention is paid to the environment: "the MNCs have behaved irresponsibly towards the host communities through their philanthropic gestures rather than behaving responsibly by genuinely holding and treating the communities as real stakeholders."[31] They argue that the consequences of their irresponsibility are avoidable; if the corporations had behaved in a manner that reflects respect for the humanity of their host communities, the rise of violence and general insecurity that have become pervasive in the region would have been nipped in the bud. "The multinational oil companies brought this on themselves and the country through their social irresponsibility."[32] Osemeke, Adegbite and Adegbite corroborate that these corporations' social irresponsibility has contributed to environmental degradation, global warming, climate change, abuses of human rights whose consequences are visibly noticeable in the violent reactions of the host communities. It seems that these irresponsible acts are done deliberately, without respect for the rights of the host communities, actions which the corporation would not dare in their home countries. They elucidate their point further:

> Concerns have been raised on the variance between the increasing environmental risks associated with the operations of the MNCs in developing countries and abysmal commitment to strengthening CSR for the economic transformation and social well-being of the host communities. As currently being practised by many MNCs and their local counterparts in developing countries, a business strategy which relegates CSR to the side lines as philanthropic gestures without the strategic provision of resources risk the prevalence of multifaceted challenges.[33]

Although we might think that CSI is theoretical in that it does expose what corporations ought to have done but did not do, corporate social irresponsiveness is an attitude that corporations put up to display their negligence to the plight of their host communities. It is in light of this that Pope Francis makes a clarion call to the Global North thus: "We should not forget the historic exploitation of the Global South that has created an

---

[31] Olusoji J. George, Owolabi Kuye and Uchechi C. Onokala, "Corporate Social Irresponsibility (CSI) a Catalyst to the Niger Delta Crisis: The Case of Nigerian Oil Multinational Companies versus the Militants of Niger Delta Region of Nigeria," *Journal of Management Research*, 4/2 (February 2012): 1.

[32] George, Kuye and Onokala, 1.

[33] Osemeke, Adegbite and Adegbite, 365.

enormous ecological debt, due mainly to resource plundering and excessive use of common environmental space for waste disposal."[34] In the following section, I will examine CSR[1] and CSR[3].

Corporate Social Responsibility (CSR[1]) and Corporate Social Responsiveness (CSR[3])

The ethic of responsibility as championed by Max Weber Weber entails that human decisions should countenance foreseeable consequences. He emphasises that the ethic of responsibility must characterise the "willingness to respond to the foreseeable consequences of one's actions."[35] In relation to CSR[1], stakeholders argue that corporations should not only as a matter of necessity put measures in place to adequately respond to foreseeable consequences, but also possible consequences. Corporations should act in such a way that consequences of their actions are in tandem with continued authentic human existence within society. The essence of expanding the Weberian ethic of responsibility from foreseeable to possible consequences in relation to CSR[1] can be understood from the fact that corporations increasingly and consistently generate unforeseeable consequences, which they cannot possibly deny.

The argument here is that corporations' CSR[1] tends to cover proximate consequences of their actions rather than their remote or ultimate consequences, which their actions or inactions have caused. It is, therefore, pertinent to concentrate on both as they have continued to make society unsafe by their corporate social irresponsibility. Corporate social responsiveness (CSR[3]) thus puts more pressing burden on corporations to anticipate and project beyond the proximate causes and effects that CSR[1] has been limited. Corporations' deliberate refusal to active proactively, respond to immediate need of their host communities, which in the first instance was directly and indirectly caused by them, is corporate social irresponsiveness. Corporate social irresponsiveness also means that the corporations have the responsibility, means and capacities to respond to a given situation particularly in their host communities but fragrantly refuse to intervene.

Accordingly, CSR[3] insists that "the firm must be in a condition to anticipate changes, carrying out programs and policies such that to minimize

---

[34] Claire Giangrave, "Pope Francis makes a Heartfelt Appeal for the Environment: 'Creation is Groaning,'" *Religion News Service*, 2nd September, 2020.

[35] Zamagni, 12.

negative effects that its own present and future activities may have in terms of social fallout, so avoiding to catalyze waves of complaint upon the firm."[36] Thus, CSR³ is action-oriented, dynamic, forward-looking and adaptable. CSR³ is concerned with actions and activities rather than concepts and debates about ethic of CSR¹. On the other hand, corporate social irresponsiveness would refer to deliberate acts of inaction or inactivity when corporations ought to have proactively responded to social need or social demand that could have prevented social and environmental crisis.

Within the contextual framework as it relates to the Niger Delta region, as a consequence of the hostilities that have engulfed the region for some time, oil companies have responded more actively and anticipatorily by setting up some credible community relations departments that are solely saddled with the responsibility of planning with the host communities in terms of projects and other development proposals. Such departments essentially combine two critical functions of CSR³ namely, determining the social issues to be responded to and how to dynamically respond to the identified social issues. Social action as social responsiveness thus includes managerial process of response, planning and forecasting, organising fitting social response, ability to control social activities, social decision making and social policy.[37] It, therefore, appears that social responsiveness is less coercive, more proactive, engaging and promising than CSR¹. But the major challenge is not well-crafted action plans, but the real, actual translation of the plans in concrete terms. Once a policy is not concretely deployed, it remains in the realm of theory, a proposal, and oftentimes, a deception, which results in social unrest and distrust as it is well known in Nigeria. The next section will focus on Christian social responsiveness (CSR²).

Christian Social Responsiveness (CSR²)

Thus far, we have seen that corporate social responsibility places much value on functionality rather than relationship. Its ethic has been prescriptive and corporations have not adequately demonstrated strong will to enact it practically without agitation from without. Agitation has been the precursor for the translation of CSR¹ to CSR³. Christian social responsiveness cannot wholly be said to have stemmed from corporate social irresponsibility or irresponsiveness. On the contrary, Christian social responsiveness is not only part of its mission to humanity or the universe as a whole, but also an interventionist strategy, which

---

[36] Giuseppe Argiolas, "The Social Vocation of the Firm." In *Christian Ethics and Corporate Culture*, 27.
[37] For details of these processes of social responsiveness, see Iamandi, 10-14.

at once fulfils that mission and calls to attention government and multinational companies' irresponsibility. One aspect of Christian social responsiveness is that unlike CSR[1] that considers profits and utilitarian satisfaction of customers as ultimate goals, and sometimes bends or circumvents ethical rules to ensure that profits are made, Christian social responsiveness focuses on the common good, which is to fully humanise the individuals.

There is a growing interest in scholarship delving into how faith-based social responsibility (F-bSR) or religions could be used to generate or intensify interest in CSR[1]. One of the arguments is that religions have virtues that can be appropriated to ensure that CSR[1] is deployed. Such virtues include honesty, faithfulness, transparency, fairness and integrity. Imbibing these virtues, it is argued, helps managers and workers in a corporation relate well with one another and environment. Christians have emotional attachment to their religion; they believe that their scriptures enjoin them to be charitable to others and the environment; they believe that there is an eschatological judgement in which their deeds would be evaluated and rewarded; they see their duties and responsibilities on earth as tasks accomplished not only for humanity, but also for God. These elicit their commitment to the corporations. This is why Christianity, as the argument goes, is critical to how CSR[1] can be implemented.[38] This is not to suggest that only Christian or religious people exercise these virtues in workplace. However, because they know their being and spiritual affiliation and relationship, there is the tendency for moral restraint where others might be involved in some morally reprehensive acts.

The turn of Christians to social responsibility was partly as a result of the growing moral failure of contemporary society. Although secularism emphasises separation of the church from the state, reliance on reason rather than faith, the immediate instead of ultimate, physical rather than metaphysical, the death of religion argument has not meant that it has ceased to influence human life and corporate system. The resurgence of religion in the twenty-first century in the West has helped to re-affirm the place of religion in contemporary society.[39] The Christian religious philosophy of the eighteenth and nineteenth centuries sharply responded to the moral failure of the time and pervasive poverty in Europe. This philosophical approach

---

[38] Lukman Raima, A. Patel, K. Yekini and A. Aljadani, "Exploring the Theological Foundation of Corporate Social Responsibility in Islam, Christianity and Judaism for Strengthening Compliance and Reporting: An Eclectic Approach," *Issues in Social and Environmental Accounting*, 7/1 (2013): 228-249.

[39] Bradley B. Onishi, *The Sacrality of the Secular: Postmodern Philosophy of Religion*, Columba University Press, 2018.

resulted in influential radical social action that is now considered as Christian social responsiveness. "The religious approach gave way to social reforms and to the Victorian philanthropy which perceived a series of social problems revolving around poverty and ignorance as well as child and female labor.... A clear case was the creation of the Youth Men's Christian Association (YMCA), a movement that began in London in 1844 with the objective of applying Christian values to the business activities of the time."[40] Explaining further the rationale for Christian social interventionist responsibility in corporate social responsibility, Hui says:

> There are still difficult moral issues separating people with different religious adherences in the world geographical landscape of the twenty-first century. And, the acts of strategizing with values that underlie the CSR principles are different from having knowledge of them. This calls for a novel perspective that grounds the existing CSR literature on faith systems to uncover some hidden views, which might be seminal, in explaining corporate sustainability.[41]

Is there a distinctive Christian social responsiveness or responsibility? No serious attempts have been made to define Christian social responsibility. Most literature on the topic use the corporate social responsibility contentious definitions in understanding, contextualising and applying Christian social responsibility. Just as there are various definitions and interpretations of CSR[1], so are there differences in conceiving and applying Christian social responsibility. For instance, the Evangelical movement had divergent interpretations of the Bible on how a Christian should respond to social issues. In 1974 at Lausanne, Switzerland, about 2700 representatives from 150 countries gathered to discuss what the position of the Evangelicals should be on social action in relation to evangelism. Of course, the responses from the Global North and Global South were different because of their different socio-political contexts and experiences. The radical group fervently argued in favour of social action in the socio-political situation they found themselves as part of God's purpose for the Christian. It argued for expanded intervention in human rights, political participation and freedom and social justice. But the conservative group prioritised evangelism over and above social action. For this latter group, the urgency of the Great Commission would be compromised if Evangelicals diverted their energy and resources to

---

[40] Agudelo, Johannsdottir and Davidsdottir, 3.
[41] Loi T. Hui, "Combining Faith and CSR: A Paradigm of Corporate Sustainability," *International Journal of Social Economics*, 25/6 (2008): 450.

social issues. At the end, the Lausanne Covenant had a kind of compromised positions that incorporated the feelings of both groups, a decision that was to later demonstrate the tension within the Evangelical movement as both groups interpreted the Lausanne Covenant to fit into their perspectives.[42]

Christian social responsiveness values relationship over functionality with regard to humans and the environment, and the care or stewardship of the environment ought not to be as a result of agitation. I argue that the Bible is the Christian social responsibility guide, which calls for responsiveness to the need of humanity and ecology. The ecclesial ethic does not interest itself in prescribing what should be done, but doing what has to be done. This markedly separates CSR[1] from CSR[2]. CSR[2] does argue for the respect of other creatures with whom human beings share the same command from God. For example, God blessed the animals in Genesis 1 and also blessed human beings He created and commanded both to be fruitful and multiply. In Genesis 6, God saved animals and Noah's family from the flood. In the New Testament, Jesus teaches about the providential supply of the need of animals as a demonstration of God's plan and care for them – His creatures, just as He miraculously fed multitude of people. Although the land was cursed in Genesis 3 because of the disobedience of Adam and Eve, in Romans 8:22ff the whole creation of God awaits redemption together. In other words, it is not only the human beings created in God's image that await redemption, but also every other creature of God. This exactly forms the basis of what scholars (for me) should refer to as Christian social responsibility; a theoretical understanding of the Christian social responsibility to other human beings and ecology. Although some Christians have interpreted the Scriptures to mean that the Old Testament is fulfilled in Christ's laying down His life for them to live, ritual slaughter of animal ceased on the cross, and now the animals have to lay down their lives for humans to live. Such theological and normative interpretation does not countenance the place of animals and by extension, the whole of ecology, in the right mode of ecclesial ethic. It is a consumerist interpretation. From the Old Testament to the New Testament, God has taken the ecology very dearly and in symbolic ways:

> [Christians] cannot ignore the fact that the water that is used to incorporate people into the church through baptism is the same water human beings pollute; that the bread eaten in Eucharist is

---

[42] Myung-Sahm Suh, "Glocalization of 'Christian Social Responsibility': The Contested Legacy of Lausanne Movement among Neo-Evangelicals in South Korea," *Religions*, 6 (2015): 1391-1410; doi: 10.3390/rel6041391

denied many in the world while others are overfed; that countries go to war over oil while Christians use it to anoint.... Every act of sacramental worship makes an ecological statement about the proper ends to which Christians put the resources of the natural world.[43]

In addition, the same water (flood) that was used to destroy the world in the Old Testament has become the water of baptism for the admission of people into God's kingdom. The food that Adam and Eve ate and forfeited the kingdom in the Garden of Eden has become the meal of redemption, as people who now believe participate in the Eucharist. The stinking oil (Eccl. 10:1) or lack of oil (Is. 1:6) has become the empowering anointing and presence of the Holy Spirit upon the believers. This redemptive transformation of the whole of creation is emphasised by Pope Francis when he also very emphatically talked about the inter-relatedness and inter-connectedness of creation. According to him,

We need constantly to remember that everything is interconnected. We have unbroken relationship with the Creator, with our fellow beings, and with the rest of creation. We need to heal the damaged relationships that are essential to supporting us and the entire fabric.... Today, we hear the voice of creation admonishing us to return to our rightful place in the natural created order – to remember that we are part of this interconnected web of life, not its masters.[44]

In the meantime, I shall examine how corporate social responsibility has been viewed in the light of Christian social responsibility.

One of the foremost attempts to systematise Christian social responsibility was done by the Catholic in what today is widely referred to as Catholic Social Teaching (CST). The CST is based on the Scriptures and traditions especially those of the patristic period, which brought to the fore the plight of the poor and the responsibility of the Church towards them. Pope Leo XIII's encyclical *Rerum Novarum* has been described as a radical and foundational document that affirms the rights of workers, charity to the poor and needy, advocating changes in socio-economic injustice, moving from individualism to a fundamental realisation and participation in equal creaturely status under God. The CST emphasises that the excess of what one has should be given to the poor. This teaching was sustained and reinvigorated by subsequent popes,

---

[43]   Samuel Wells, Ben Quash and Rebekah Eklund, *Introducing Christian Ethics*, 2nd ed., New Jersey: John Wiley & Sons Ltd, 2017, 390.

[44]   Giangrave, "Pope Francis makes a Heartfelt Appeal for the Environment.

but Pope John XXIII significantly altered the understanding and praxis of the CST. He moved the attention of the decision making from the rich concerning the poor to what the poor need to survive and thrive. Rather than consider the plight of the poor after the rich must have satisfied their needs, Pope John XXIII argued that the poor should be at the centre of the decision making. The Second Vatican Council further radically reinterpreted the CST to mean that the Church has the duty to change the system that makes people poor in the first instance. If Christians just preach about giving to the poor without actively participating in changing the system that made them poor, the system will continue to produce more poor people. Since the root of poverty is systemic, the cure must also be systemic. This is articulated in 1967 by Pope Paul IV when he states:

> It is not just a matter of eliminating hunger, or even of reducing poverty. The struggle against destitution, though urgent and necessary, is not enough. It is a question, rather, of building a world where every man, no matter what his race, religion, or nationality, can live a fully human life, freed from servitude imposed on him by other men or by natural forces over which he has no sufficient control.[45]

The Catholic teaching and emphasis on social justice is legendary. Pope Francis's second encyclical, "*Laudato Si*", calls global attention to the need for sustainable development and social justice.[46]

Christopher Marshall, writing from the Protestant viewpoint that is angled on postmodernism, calls for a fresh re-reading of the Pauline corpus in order to rediscover that Paul actually taught about Christian social responsibility, contrary to the gamut of theological interpretations that Paul was more concerned about righteousness as the *prima facie* of ultimate redemption. Marshall argues that though Paul correctly emphasises salvation and judgement, he also teaches about social justice which can be gleaned when his theology is carefully re-read. Paul, he notes, ingeniously talks about the common and corporate suffering and pain of the whole creation – both human beings and all other creatures – groaning together, and also in unison await the redemption, having borne together the consequences of sin and corruption. This common and corporate suffering and blissful hope for

---

[45] Rose Aspholm, "Catholic Social Teaching and the Christian Responsibility to the Poor," Master's Dissertation, Saint John's University, USA, 2017, 8.

[46] Giangrave, "Pope Francis makes a Heartfelt Appeal for the Environment.

redemption lays a heavy responsibility on human beings to care for all other non-human creatures of God.[47]

For Virginia Francis, it is clear, especially from South African experience, that the mainline churches played more critical roles in the struggle against apartheid than the Pentecostal and charismatic churches. This is not to suggest that the latter did not do anything significant in the cause for the struggle for independence. The prevailing socio-economic and political context provides ample basis for the re-reading and applying the Scriptures such that, for instance, the Bible can no longer be read and applied in the way it was read and applied during colonial era in Africa. The post-colonial period has its peculiar challenges that require the Bible to be re-read to address what the present African society faces. The thrust of the church, particularly the Pentecostal or charismatic churches, is to ensure that they "serve God and (South) Africa holistically."[48] Francis suggests that the church can fulfil this dual responsibility if she views herself as a corporation. Whereas business corporations are profit-oriented, the church as a corporation leans towards the spiritual well-being of the person. Her words are apposite:

> The church can be described as a 'corporation' – it has leader who drives a vision toward profit (in the case of the church that profit could be a 'whole' persons (sic) – spiritually, emotionally, psychologically and physically) …. As a result of the way that Pentecostal/ Charismatic Churches operate they could be likened to corporations. While corporations unquestioningly accept hierarchical structures, liberation theology… is positioned to deconstruct such notions of grandeur, promoting equal power and social relations, partnerships and mutuality.[49]

In fact, like corporations' CSR[1] that extends their care to the society and the environment, the church as a corporation has responsibility beyond the remit of her members; she has to be involved in the general welfare of the citizens and the environment by ensuring that social justice is dispensed properly. The holistic picture of Christian social responsiveness means that there is no neat separation between religion and development such as has observed in faith-based organisations (FBOs) or non-governmental organisations (NGOs) that

---

[47] Christopher Marshall, "Paul and Christian Social Responsibility," *ANVIL*, 17/1 (2000): 1-12.

[48] Virginia Francis, "Applying Corporate Social Responsibility to the Church: A Case Study of the Interface between the Indian Pentecostal/Charismatic Church in the Phoenix Community, Durban North (KwaZulu Natal) and Social Responsibility," an unpublished MPhil Dissertation, University of Stellenbosch, South Africa, 2008, 3.

[49] Francis, 19-20.

have championed developmental projects in several parts of Africa. Christian social responsiveness also ruptures the classical approach to development and instantiated a different dynamic that is at once social and spiritual.[50]

With particular reference to Pentecostalism generally and African Pentecostalism in particular, classical or holiness Pentecostal movement was somewhat ascetic, austere, world-rejecting, and bound to an eschatology of urgency expressed in aggressive evangelisation. In fact, it broke from the Protestant movement, which it thought had become cold and irresponsive to the urgency required to save the world from an impending judgement. As such, it had a stern position against social agenda of a world that was ending imminently. That eschatological fervour that characterised its teaching and relationship with the world could not result in serious involvement in improving the world. Members were taught and expected to endure social injustice as a mark of true disciple, and social action was prohibited. Pervasive poverty, social injustice, primordial corruption and other social vices that suffused the world made this movement passive and patiently looked for the immediate return of the Lord. Apart from this paralysing state of the movement, some other brands of Pentecostalism hold another extreme position that teaches that this present world is the scene of the fulfilment of the eschatological hope, and as such the kingdom of God can be built here on earth. This version overlooks personal and societal sins, teaching eternal security – that is, once someone is saved, salvation cannot be lost regardless of what they do.[51] The denial of evil, therefore, is a great challenge because evil that is not recognised or acknowledged cannot be fought. But the excessive preoccupation with evil is another extreme that has come to be associated with African Pentecostalism.[52] The over-spiritualisation of reality, even the social cause, also has a paralysing effect on the fight for social justice. The neo-Pentecostal movement is world-affirming. Its over-materialised contents and praxis have become both its boon and bane.[53]

---

[50] Dena Freeman, *Pentecostalism and Development: Churches, NGOs and Social Change in Africa*, Basingstoke: Palgrave Macmillan, 2012; Frederick Kakwata, "The Progressive Pentecostal Conception of Development within an African Context of Poverty," *Stellenbosch Theological Journal*, 3/1 (2017): 159-183.

[51] Roy Notice, "Social Responsibility and the Pentecostal Church," https://www.bethelbiblecollegecaribbean.edu.jm/ Accessed 9th July, 2020.

[52] Esther E. Acolatse, *Powers, Principalities, and the Spirit: Biblical Realism in Africa and the West*, Michigan: Wm.B. Eerdmanns Publishing Co., 2018.

[53] Benson O. Igboin and Babatunde Adedibu, "'Power Must Change Hands': Militarisation of Prayer and the Quest for Better Life among Nigerian Pentecostals," *Cyberjournal for Pentecostal-Charismatic Research*, 26, (February 2019) www.pctii.org (http://www.pctii.or/cyberj/cyberj26/Igboin Adedibu1.html); Babatunde Adedibu and Benson O. Igboin, "Eschato-praxis and Accountability: A Study of Neo-African Pentecostal Movement in the Light of Prosperity Gospel," *Verbum et Ecclesia*, 40/1 (October 2019), https://doi.org/10.4102/ve.v40i1.1987

A respectable Pentecostal social responsibility (PSR) has to deal with both extremes by returning to the teaching of Jesus namely, He, although fixed His eyes on heaven, yet fed the people, and leaves a social responsibility for His followers to care for the sick, give food to the hungry, clothe the naked, visit the prisoners, and as James 1: 27 summarises it: "pure or practical religion is defending the rights of the orphans and widows and remaining unspotted from the world." This simply means that Christians can intervene in the world without becoming worldly. Being a Christian, therefore, should actually move one to be interested and involved in what happens to others in their socio-economic and ethico-political situation and sphere.[54]

Christian social responsiveness is discursive in that it disrupts the privatisation and deprivatisation of religion in contemporary discourse. It is not focusing on mere concepts and conceptualisations, though they are important, it is interventionist in approach, consciously finding ways to intervene where public life is at its ebb. It intervenes where life is endangered; where meaning and meaningfulness of life are being eroded by public superstructure. It also intervenes in moral failure, especially in the face of massification of secularity. Thus, the constitutional walls separating the church and the state are being gradually pulled down, not by bulldozers or weapons of war, but by conscious, deliberate and interventionist actions geared towards making life more meaningful for all. The influences are thus clearly undeniable just as they are instruments of mobilisation for more active intervention. Political leadership all over the world has come to appreciate the strategic intervention and almost seamless mobilisation of adherents to a particular goal. Thus, political leaders have been displaying their private religious beliefs in their public assignments without necessarily violating the constitution. Their words and actions depict where their faith is in matters of public morality.[55] With the active Christian social responsiveness (CSR^2) in society, Christian organisations have become a toast for socio-political development. The blurring lines between privatisation and deprivatisation of religion are partly occasioned by the evidence of how religion generally is pragmatically shaping and being re-shaped by secular discourses, policies and social development. The Christian interest in politics has also shown how CSR^2 is re-shaping the political landscape across the globe. No serious political figure ignores the religious characterisation of political decisions,

---

[54] Notice, "Social Responsibility and the Pentecostal Church."
[55] Hui, 451.

particularly when they have to do with elections.[56] "Clearly, religion is not confined to the private sphere."[57]

Burgess, Knibbe and Quaas examine the interpenetration of the Redeemed Christian Church of God (RCCG) in the public sphere in Europe through CSR[2]. Encapsulated in what it calls God's love, the RCCG involves in social actions that have continued to re-world the religioscape in Europe. For the RCCG, love of God is not a theoretical or abstract concept waiting to be defined, but a call to act in ways that can unambiguously lead to the practical understanding of God's love, seen in concrete actions. Although Burgess, Knibbe and Quaas argue that there is no "coherent social doctrine," they find out that actions speak louder than words. The RCCG in Britain engages in social services: relief, charity, social development programmes, mentoring, business, politics, media, education and so on.[58] Thus, the RCCG's CSR Department defines Christian social responsibility as "a faith based obligation to meet societal needs through the demonstration of love that positively impacts communities and individuals."[59]

Espousing Christian social responsiveness to tertiary education in Nigeria, Babatunde Adedibu argues that the intervention of Christian missionaries, especially the Pentecostals, is laudable. According to him, of the 69 non-public universities in the country, 24 are Christian, 4 Islamic. Pentecostal churches have 13 of the 24 universities owned by Christian organisations.[60] But the payment of higher fees than the public universities has raised many questions and criticisms, which some have argued, has not afforded poor members of the churches to access the universities. If the universities were established in response to the failure of the public universities, accessibility and affordability should match with availability, which should be a prime factor in order to

---

[56] Afe Adogame, "'Who are You does not Matter in Europe!': African Diaspora Christianities, the Ethical Politics of Wasting Bodies and Unwanted Immigration in Europe." In Babatunde A. Adedibu and Benson O. Igboin (eds.), *The Changing Faces of African Pentecostalism*, Akungba-Akoko: Adekunle Ajasin University Press, 2018, 50-67.

[57] Richard Burgess, Kim Knibbe and Ann Quaas, "Nigerian-initiated Pentecostal Churches as a Social Force in Europe: The Case of the Redeemed Christian Church of God," *PentecoStudies*, 9/1 (2010): 99.

[58] Burgess, Knibbe and Quaas, 111-116.

[59] See CSR, "Christian Social Responsibility of the Redeemed Christian Church of God," presented at the International Conference on African Pentecostalism (ICAP) organised by and held in the Redeemed Christian Bible College, Redemption Camp, Mowe, Ogun State, on 17th July, 2019, slide 2.

[60] Babatunde Adedibu, "Corruption Conundrum: A Call for Reawakening of the Prophetic Voice of Nigerian Pentecostal Church Leadership," In Benson O. Igboin (ed.), *Corruption: A New Thinking in the Reverse Order*, Oyo: Ajayi Crowther University Press, 2018, 160-161.

effectively reach the target audience. However, one can also argue that some of the facilities in these universities are relatively better than those of the public universities, and that they need money to maintain them, given that the public service in the country lacks maintenance culture. Toyin Falola maintains that COVID-19 pandemic that resulted in shutting down of almost all institutions in Nigeria has shown that many of the private universities have the capacity to run their programmes as scheduled despite the shutdown. These universities, he reveals, taught, conducted examinations and attended convocation using technological devices, feats that no public university could boast of or deploy. He also argues that research has revealed that the profit margins usually associated with these universities are not completely true; some of them are struggling to provide utility at a great expense. Interestingly, these universities are apparently more socially responsible than many public universities in terms of structure, environment, management and responsiveness.[61]

However, the history of Christian social responsiveness to education goes beyond the Pentecostal movement. The missionary (mainline) churches built many schools in the country, especially the southern and central parts. Their attempts to extend mission and schools to the northern part were furiously resisted because mission schools were perceived as a tool for conversion of the Muslims to Christianity, and that they corrupt Islamic education, a perception that is still rife today resulting in the Boko Haram insurgency.[62] Unfortunately, lack of formal education in northern Nigeria continuously makes it vulnerable and backward.

Apart from education, there is evidence of Christian social responsiveness to health, entrepreneurship and empowerment, prison, road construction, employment and so on. For instance, Deeper Life Bible Church (DLBC) contributed to the vision of making Lagos, the 'commercial capital' of Nigeria, a mega city 'plagued' with heavy traffic jams, by constructing roads. The founder, Pastor Williams F. Kumuyi, says that the church has the responsibility of providing social amenities to the people irrespective of their religious or social leaning. In acknowledgement of the road the church constructed in Lagos, the immediate past Governor of Lagos State, Akinwumi Ambode, says: "What the Deeper Life Church [sic] has done is epochal and keys into the overall drive of the state government under my leadership towards the renewal of infrastructure projects all over Lagos in line with megacity ambition of the

---

[61] Toyin Falola, "The Fate of Nigeria's Private Universities," *Premium Times*, 2nd September, 2020.

[62] Olufemi Vaughan, *Religion and the Making of Nigeria*, Durham and London: Duke University Press, 2016.

state. It is my considered view that if all other religious groups and private sector organisations in the state provide similar support to the government, a lot will be achieved in a very short time in improving the quality of infrastructure in Lagos."[63] Bishop David Oyedepo, the founder of Living Faith Church, also committed huge sums of money into road repairs in Ogun state, Nigeria.[64] The Redeemed Christian Church of God whose General Overseer is Pastor Enoch Adeboye has embarked on several social responsibility works; in fact, the church has a unit specifically empowered to deal with matters in that direction.[65]

However, there is the need for a visible Christian social responsiveness to ecological crises around the world. In Nigeria, for instance, there are many ecological crises bedevilling the country, for which the government and the multinational corporations are directly responsible. The consequences are borne by all irrespective of whether or not they caused them in the first place. The case of insecurity engendered by the ecological crises in the Niger Delta region is commonplace. While some Christian leaders have actively preached against it, more need to be done to call attention to further crises that would result from unbridled exploitation. On their own, Christian organisations, particularly Pentecostal ones, have been accused of noise pollution as part of environmental hazard they are causing. A recent study shows that health challenges result from or are aggravated by noise pollution mostly caused by Pentecostal churches that are concentrated in an area. This requires responsiveness from them.[66]

Conclusion

I have argued that corporate social responsibility was borne out of necessity and pressure both from within and outside the corporation. The basis for CSR[1] was social irresponsibility, that is, the inability, unwillingness or crass failure to respond to the demand for better working conditions and healthier and safer environment. The formulation of CSR[1] does not automatically translate into action; it is indeed a set of principles that should

---

[63] Margaret Mwantok, "Deeper Life, Co-builder of Lagos Mega City," https://guardian.ng/sunday-magazine/ibru-ecumenical-centre/deeper-life-co-builder-of-lagos-mega-city/   (Accessed   3rd September, 2020).

[64] Dayo Emmanuel, "Social Responsibility: Winners Chapel commences massive road Rehabilitation," https://dayoemmanuel.wordpress.com/2015/11/16/social-responsibility-winners-chapel-commences-massive-road-rehabilitation/ (Accessed 3rd September, 2020).

[65] Idowu Iluyomade, "RCCG Impacts Lives through CSR," https://www.redemptionlight.org/rccg-impacts-lives-through-csr/ (Accessed 3rd September, 2020).

[66] Caroline O. Adejuyigbe and Amos A. Adediran, "The Consequences of Noise Pollution by Pentecostal Churches in Nigeria." In *The Changing Faces of African Pentecostalism*, 178-186.

guide the actions of corporations towards human and non-human resources. Corporations were and are still not completely faithful to the principles of their CSR[1], hence the need for corporate social responsiveness (CSR[3]) drive. CSR[3] is the measurable, evaluable, tangible deployment of CSR[1]. William I. Sauser Jr. asks: "What might happen if business leaders across the globe viewed their work as a sacred calling in a religious sense? Might not the world be a far better place?"[67]

This question is both a call and standard for Christian social responsiveness (CSR[2]). I have argued in favour of CSR[2] rather than Christian social responsibility (CSR) because, one, like CSR[1], Christians have not fully agreed on the definition and principles on social actions or responses. Two, Christian social intervention is not tangential as in the case of CSR[1], but essential as a call to fulfilling God's love. Three, right from creation, God has made humans a responsive being. In Genesis 2:15, even before the Fall, man was given the task of taking care of his environment, responding to its care, and loving it. The totality of creation thus becomes the constituency of Christians which they must respond to. Four, CSR[2] is viewed as actions that are not altogether strategically oriented towards conversion or evangelism, but ones that accomplish God's command though with eschatological results. Five, CSR[2] is mostly geared towards the common good, that is, the full humanisation of the person and values common to all irrespective of their religious, racial or regional affiliation. Six, CSR[2] also countenances solidarity and subsidiarity, which contrast with utilitarianism of CSR[1]. The question also calls for standard: 'what would happen if Christian leaders take Christian social responsiveness more aggressively than they have done thus far? Might not the world have lesser humanitarian and ecological problems than we have at present?'

Since the wall of partition between the church and the state appears to be crumbling and privatisation of religion is giving way to de-privatisation, there is the need, first, for CSR[2] to guard against the corruption that has pervaded corporate world. Here, Christians need the politics of the dove and serpent to navigate the pressures of the corporate system, which many of them view as being blinded by "the god of this world." This politics requires love and wisdom.[68] Second, there is also the urgent need for other researchers to delve more into areas Christian organisations have responded spectacularly to

---

[67] Pasag, 2.
[68] Benson O. Igboin, "Jothamian Parable and the Democratic Leadership in Nigeria: An Ethical Challenge to Nigerian Christians," *EBSU Journal of Social Sciences & Humanities*, 5/1 (2015): 88-99.

humanitarian and ecological problems to determine where and how they can further respond. This is because the churches do not deliberately promote this aspect of their work, perhaps because of the fear of being misunderstood as being worldly or political. Third, there is also the need for dialogue between CSR[1] and CSR[2] as both can indeed work to make the world a better place. This "art of thinking together" will ensure that areas of interventions are the critical ones that will impact positively on the host communities. Such synergistic co-operation can also result in joint partnership that will birth common good to society.

Chapter 2: Propositioning Elisha's Prophetic Ministry as a Template for Pentecostal Prophets' Civic Roles and Corporate Social Responsibility in Nigeria

Michael Ogunewu and Deji Ayegboyin

Introduction

Pentecostal prophetic ministries (PPM) are sprawling across the continent of Africa. This phenomenon, also known as Neo-prophetism, as a type of Pentecostal Christianity (PC), is relevant to the Nigerian religious context because prophetism reflects an integral part of the religious life of Africans. Nonetheless, neo-prophetism, in spite of its popularity and influence in PC, has attracted much criticisms owing to the fact that a number of prophets who claim to have the ability to reveal hidden things and predict the future are well known for their fallacious forecasts, lack of financial accountability, commercialisation of religion and extravagant lifestyles which are contrary to the teachings of the Lord. As a result of these, instead of making contributions to the regeneration of the nation and her citizens, the excesses and manipulations of some PPM leaders disregard constructive civic and social responsibilities. This chapter, therefore, addresses this anti-climax, using the ministry of Elisha as a template. The study carefully adheres to the principle of epoch and eidetic intuition. The historical and phenomenological methods are employed to evaluate the significance and roles PPM plays in the civic and social life of the Nigerian society. Data sourced from existing literature and personal observation are subjected to qualitative analysis. The study identifies crucial lessons which the contemporary prophets can learn from the life and ministry of Elisha. These include validating life of unpretentious affirmation of divine call (I Kg. 19:19-21), life devoid of materialism (II Kg. 5:15-16); care for the less-privileged (II Kg. 4:1-7); maturity (II Kg. 6:1-4) and demonstration of candour in ministry (II Kg. 3:11-14). The study advocates the discontinuation of various kinds of abuses and financial extortions from the incredulous religious consumers and the sanctioning of questionable characters that compete with one another by commercialising religious products and services. It encourages the PPM leaders to emulate the ancient Hebrew prophets, from whom the prophetic institution developed.

Evidently, Pentecostalism has made phenomenal advancement in Africa, and Nigeria is no exception. Today, this brand of the Christian faith has come to stay at the heart of Christianity in Nigeria. This fact is attested to by virtually all scholars who have had the privilege of writing on the subject.[1] Specifically in Nigeria, from the 1990s the religious scene has witnessed the appearance and relentless expansion of what may be aptly described as neo-prophetism - a genre of Pentecostal Christianity - which constitutes a new manifestation of prophetism in contemporary African Christianity. This development has given birth to various ministries led by individuals who go by such titles as prophets, apostles, bishops and so on. Closely woven into some of these ministries is the phenomenon of "prophetism" with some of the leaders claiming to be prophets. This phenomenon is not new, because it has been a part of Nigerian Christianity since the evolution of the African Indigenous (Aladura) Churches, in the south-western part of the country. Observably, however, it has taken a new dimension since the involvement of the emerging Pentecostal prophets in the practice.

Today, there are many prophets as there are Pentecostal churches, all justifying their ministries as an extension of the Old Testament Hebrew prophetic tradition, when in practice, one could observe a marked departure from it. Naturally, one would expect that the prophetic ministry of the church should contribute significantly to the life of the nation and those of the citizenry. Apparently, however, those of some present-day Pentecostal ministers speak to the contrary. Many have turned the prophetic ministries to instruments of fraud and exploitation. They commercialise the gospel, using it to rob innocent worshippers of their hard-earned wages. Some of these churches have strong financial bases out of which the public benefits little or nothing; a chunk of their wealth being used to service the flamboyant lifestyle of their leaders. In the same vein, their leaders are known for making prophetic utterances, a large percentage of which are never fulfilled. All these in the observation of this paper negate what a veritable prophetic ministry should

---

[1] For details see: R. M. Anderson, "Pentecostal and Charismatic Christianity." In *Encyclopedia of Religions*, Mircea Eliade (ed) Vol. 11, New York: Macmillan Library Reference, 1995, Abamfo, O. Atiemo, *The Rise of the Charismatic Movement in the Mainline Churches in Ghana*, Accra: Asempa Publishers, 1998; J. R. Hackett, "Charismatic/Pentecostal Appropriation of Media Technologies in Nigeria and Ghana," *Journal of Religion in Africa*, 28/3 (1998); Matthews Ojo, *The End time Army*, Trenton: African World Press Inc., 2006.

be from the biblical perspective. This is because the Old Testament prophets as exemplified by Elisha were actively involved in the social (II Kg. 6:1-4), economic (II Kg. 7:1) and political (II Kg. 6:8-11; 9:1-3) lives of Israel. In the light of this assertion, this paper encourages present-day Nigerian Pentecostal prophets to align their ministries with those of ancient Hebrew prophets for maximum benefit of society and the poor masses, using the ministry of Elisha as a prototype.

Civic Roles, Corporate Social Responsibility and the Prophetic Ministry

Citizens and institutions are expected to have certain responsibilities both to the nation and to one another. These are conceptualised under civic roles and corporate social responsibilities. Civic roles focus on responsibilities on the part of the citizens that promote the health and well-being of the community. It could also denote the responsibilities of the government to her citizens. The social responsibility theory holds both the government and the citizenry accountable to each other. While the government is saddled with the responsibility of caring for the masses, they, in turn, are expected to be socially responsible. Both are expected to harness the greatest good for the greatest number, within the community. The ministry of Elisha demonstrated social responsibility in various ways. These include the maturity he demonstrated by accompanying the בני־הנביאים (*bᵉnĕ ha nᵉbî'îm* – sons of the prophets[2]) in embarking on community service of building a residence for the group and healing the waters of Jericho (II Kg. 2:19-2).

Corporate Social Responsibility (CSR) is a business term, which connotes different meanings to different people or institutions. In its broadest sense, CSR is concerned with what is – or should be – the relationship between global corporations, governments of countries and individual citizens. More locally, the term is concerned with the relationship between a corporation and the local society in which it resides or operates. Another definition is concerned with the relationship between a corporation and its stakeholders.[3] Richard Smith, citing Carroll, explains that to some, it conveys the idea of legal responsibility or liability, while to others, it means socially responsible behaviour in an ethical sense; and to still others, the meaning communicated is that of being "responsible for," in a causal manner. Speaking further, he states that many simply liken it to a charitable contribution; some take it to mean

---

[2] The בני־הנביאים (*benĕ ha nebî 'îm*) denotes a community of prophets living, learning and ministering in community similar to contemporary resident seminaries or monasteries.

[3] David Crowther and Guler Aras, *Corporate Social Responsibility*, London: Ventus Publishing ApS, 2008, 10.

social consciousness; while many of those who embrace it most fervently see it as a mere synonym for "legitimacy," in the context of "belonging" or being proper or valid. Yet, a few consider it as a sort of fiduciary duty imposing higher standards of behaviour on businessmen than on citizens at large.[4]

Simply put, however, CSR indicates a situation whereby an economic entity is socially responsible to other stakeholders apart from the entrepreneurs or the shareholders. Business houses are not only set up to make profit, but to maximise it. Their ambition is to make as much ready money as possible. In the process of struggling to do this, some often lose sight of being of any benefit to their immediate environment and people. Therefore, the concept of CSR implies that business enterprises should think beyond profit-making for the shareholders, to include serving the interests of other stakeholders - communities, consumers of products and services and suppliers. Thus, CSR refers to practical involvement of businesses in the life of their host communities and people. Ugwunwanyi and Ekene, citing Freeman , refer to CSR as corporate citizenship, which essentially means that a company should be a good neighbour within its host community.[5] In the same vein, Maimunah Ismail describes CSR as a concept whereby business organisations consider the interest of society by taking responsibility for the impact of their activities on customers, suppliers, employees, shareholders, communities and other stakeholders as well as their environment. It is a departure from the traditional belief in which a corporation is seen as only an instrument for profit maximisation to include that of being socially friendly and responsible to all the stakeholders.[6] The relationship between Israel and Syria as corporate entities would have gone sour if Elisha had not intervened by healing Naaman of his leprosy (II Kg. 5:1-19). In this episode, Elisha did not display materialistic tendencies or greed because he did not collect any monetary or material gift from Naaman. He was more keenly interested in the corporate interest of his nation.

Just as other institutions within society, this paper identifies the Church as a social institution, which is expected to be socially responsible to the

---

[4] Richard E. Smith, "Defining Corporate Social Responsibility: A Systems Approach for Socially Responsible Capitalism," Research Project Submitted to the Program of Organizational Dynamics in the Graduate Division of the School of Arts and Sciences in Partial Fulfillment of the Requirements for the Degree of Master of Philosophy, at the University of Pennsylvania, 2011, 3.

[5] Ananaba Ugwunwanyi and Chukwuka Ekene, "Corporate Social Responsibility and its Implementation in Nigeria: Problems and Prospects," *Global Journal of Human Resource Management*, 4/2 (2016): 61.

[6] Maimunah Ismail, "Corporate Social Responsibility and its Role in Community Development: An International Perspective," *The Journal of International Social Research*, 2/9 (Fall 2009): 199, 201.

community. As expected from other institutions in society, the Church should play significant roles in civic matters and corporate social responsibility. Though the Church right from inception has been actively involved in social development, this study speaks specifically to the posture of some Pentecostal churches whose *modus operandi* seems to be a departure from biblical practice of Hebrew prophets and the age-long humanitarian gesture of the Church such as Elisha demonstrated when he used his prophetic gifts to provide poverty alleviation for the community (II Kg. 4:42-44) and the widow (II Kg. 4:1-7). In both instances, Elisha did not ask for any form of gratification.

A critical study of the biblical account of the ministry of Hebrew prophets as exemplified by Elisha reveals that their preoccupations transcend the mere spiritual exercise of foretelling and forth-telling, to include practical involvement in the social life of the community of Israel. Their ministries impacted positively on the community both individually and corporately. Individually, they helped to better the lot of the people in one way or the other (e.g. the widow – II Kg. 4:1-7; the Shunammite woman - II Kg. 4:11-17; and Naaman - II Kg. 5:9-10), while corporately they helped to reform and develop the nation (e.g. 2K. 6:1-4; 7:1). In the words of Zdravko Plantak, the Hebrew prophets did more than predicting the future; rather their role in the view of the biblical evidence was primarily that of social reformers and prophetic visionaries.[7] Nyasha Madzokere, in a study on Pentecostal prophets in Zimbabwe, encourages present-day Pentecostal prophets to emulate their counterparts of the biblical period. According to him, these served as the voice of the voiceless addressing the evil in society and as bridges helping to link the general populace and the Supreme Being – YHWH.[8] They served as agents of God, speaking against political, social, economic and religious injustices in society to enable people to live holistic lives characterised by peace, love and justice.[9] To him, this is the core duty of prophets in ancient Israel; hence, such is expected of the contemporary Pentecostal prophets for the realisation of development in Africa.

---

[7] Zdravko Plantak, "A Prophetic Community Today: Imaginative Visionaries and Social Activists for the Third Millennium." In *Exploring the Frontiers of Faith: Festschrift in Honour of Dr Jan Paulsen - Congratulatory Edition*, Edited by Borge Schantz and Reinder Bruinsma, Lueneburg: Advent-Verlag, 2009, 139-155.

[8] Jewish Scribal practice does not allow the vocalization of the Divine name; hence the vowels should not be inserted in the Tetragrammaton. The vowels on the Hebrew script is intended to draw attention to the Qere, which could either be "Lord" or "God" depending on whether the second vowel is patah (a) or hireq (i).

[9] Nyasha Madzokere, "Prophets or Profiteer? An Interrogative Study of the Selected Contemporary Pentecostal Prophets in Zimbabwe in the Context of Development," *Journal of Sustainable Development in Africa*, 20/1 (2018): 279.

Madzokere thus advocates a situation where the Pentecostal prophets of Zimbabwe would be practically involved in the social life of the Zimbabwean community as was the case of the ancient Hebrew prophets as exemplified by Elisha. What is true of Zimbabwe is also true of Nigeria. In Nigeria, while some of these so-called prophets could be said to be doing their best to align their ministries with those of the biblical prophets in relation to civic roles and social responsibility, there are many others whose *modus operandi* is quite disturbing. This is because they are riddled with abnormalities, thus foisting series of privation on the populace and sometimes creating tension in the country. Madzokere, speaking from the Zimbabwean experience, explains that it is becoming very difficult to distinguish some Zimbabwean prophets from profiteers,[10] and same could be said of some Nigerian Pentecostal prophets.

Issues in Nigerian Pentecostal Prophetic Ministry

Nowadays, there are many Pentecostal prophetic ministries scattered across Africa in general and Nigeria inclusive. While operating the prophetic ministry is biblical, the *modus operandi* of some African Pentecostal prophets runs counter to the well-being of the people and that of society. The first issue is what Francis Benyah, speaking from the Ghanaian perspective, refers to as the commodification and commercialisation of the gospel. This is a situation whereby the gospel has been turned into concrete economic product and subjected to strict marketing procedures to make these products appealing to members for purchase. He refers to such items as religious products. According to him, Ghanaian Pentecostal/Charismatic pastors-prophets have 'commodified' the gospel by employing various means of marketing to advertise, brand and package religion as a consumer or spiritual product that can be bought to solve life-debilitating issues.[11] He identifies such practices to include the sales of anointing oil, water, wristbands, stickers, honey and anointed handkerchief. In Ghana, there are assertions that some of these prophets do charge in the neighbourhood of $200-300 as consultation fees. These are fees which must be paid by members to be able to access the prophet for prophetic-counselling and other "services."[12] This runs contrary to the model of the ministry of Elisha, who did not receive any gratification for his prophetic services to the people.

These practices are not limited to Ghana; they are rampant among Pentecostal prophets in some other African countries, including Nigeria.

---

[10] Madzokere, 279.
[11] Francis Benyah, "Commodification of the Gospel and the Socio-Economics of Neo-Pentecostal/ Charismatic Christianity in Ghana," *Legon Journal of the Humanities*, 29/2 (2018): 125.
[12] Benyah, 125.

In the Nigerian context, some Pentecostal prophets developed the practice of merchandising the gospel through the sales of religious items, the most prominent being anointing oil and anointed handkerchief, popularly referred to as "mantle." While the use of the anointing oil cannot be said to be out of place, it has been turned into channels of exploitation in some churches. In a Pentecostal prophetic ministry in Lagos, the prophetess does attach expiry dates to the anointing oil being sold in the church. The practice is that the oil must not be purchased elsewhere, but the church; and it carries an expiry date after which it stops being efficacious. Consequently, the purchase of anointing oil has become a ceaseless preoccupation of church members.

Another of such items is the anointed handkerchief, popularly referred to as "mantle." The belief in those churches that use them is that once the "man of God" prays on this, it carries the power of God and so becomes efficacious for the healing of various forms of illness and/or misfortune once the sufferer comes in contact with it. While one is not contesting this claim, the main concern of this paper is the exploitative dimensions woven into this practice by those Pentecostal prophets misrepresenting God through their ungodly praxis. In certain churches, this item must be purchased officially from the church for it to be efficacious. Consequently, there are instances when the product has to carry the official rubber stamp of the church so as to prevent its being procured from other sources, other than the church and there are instances when a mantle may be priced at between ₦10, 000 and ₦25, 000. On the contrary, however, there is no record that Elisha paid money before he received the אדרת (*'aderet* – mantle)[13] that fell from his master Elijah (2 Kg. 2:11-15). These are just few of the ways by which certain Pentecostal prophets have commodified and commercialised the gospel and are using it to fleece the Nigerian public.

Another dimension is the myriads of prophetic utterances by Nigerian prophets that often fail. Annually in Nigeria, it is customary to have prophets reel out prophecies of what, according to them, are God's revelations for the New Year. However, many of these prophecies some of which usually touch on the socio-political fabrics of the nation, had gone off the mark. These often create discontent across the strata of the Nigerian society. At intervals, some have gone international with their prophecies, prophesying events which

---

[13] The Hebrew translated "mantle" in the KJV, RSV and many other English versions means more accurately, a "fur garment" –Holladay, W. L. Ed. 1988. A Concise Hebrew and Aramaic Lexicon of the Old Testament Entry No.158, usually worn as an overcoat or "cloak"- Brown, F., Driver, S. & Briggs C. 1996. The Brown-Driver-Briggs Hebrew and English Lexicon. Entry No.161.

would happen in other nations of the world such as Europe and America, but some of these had also hit the rocks. For instance, at the heat of the American election, a Nigerian cleric predicted a win for Hilary Clinton, but Donald Trump won.[14] All these have negative implications for the Church as it usually presents the Church and her ministers in a bad light before the world. This cannot be divorced from the fact that some prophets speak out of intuition probably to impress their hearers; however, unfulfilled prophecy only portrays the prophet as fake, a man who speaks when the Lord had not spoken.

One of the marks of a true prophet, according to the Bible, is the accuracy and fulfilment of his message. John Neal, citing C. von Orelli, states that from the biblical perspective, a prophet is a speaker for God, because his words are not the creation of his own faculties, but an endowment from a higher power, who is God. The prophet receives power from God, which comes over him through inspiration and compels him to see or hear something which otherwise would have been hidden from him.[15] In this context, therefore, the prophet is expected to speak as an express oracle of God; one whose words cannot fail because they are given by God. However, Alec Motyer, commenting on the issue of prophetic utterances among contemporary prophets, posits that our world today is full of conflicting voices, all claiming to be authoritative pronouncements. Religious opinion varies so widely that quite often there is headlong collision between different views, all of which are put forward in the name of God.[16] He concludes by saying that the biblical proof of ascertaining where the truth lies is that what the prophet prophesies must at all times accord with the Scripture and essentially also it must come to pass. According to Deuteronomy 18:22, "If what a prophet proclaims in the name of the LORD does not take place or come true, that is a message the LORD has not spoken. That prophet has spoken presumptuously. Do not be afraid of him" (NIV).

One other area where some prophetic ministries are wreaking havoc on both the Church and Christians is the level of materialism which presently pervades the church. Some, hiding under the teaching of prosperity, have heightened materialism among Christians. Although as explained elsewhere,

---

[14] For details see: Arukaino Umukoro, Gbenga Adeniji, and Motunrayo Joel, "2016 Prophecies that were off the Mark," *Sunday Punch*, January 1, 2017, 50-51; Gbenga Adeniji, "Failed Accurate Prophecies of 2017" *Sunday Punch*, December 31, 2017, 14; Gbenga Adeniji, "Prophets Who Claimed Nigeria would break Up" *Sunday Punch*, October 1, 2017, 20.

[15] John R. Neal, Sr., "Prophets and Prophetism In the Hebrew Bible", FD 9312 – *Research Methods of Old Testament Criticism*, December 2013, 1.

[16] Alec Motyer, "The Prophets." In *The Lion Handbook to the Bible*, Herts: Lion Publishing Inc., 1986, 370.

the prosperity teaching has both its positive and negative dimensions; however, some so-called prophets have used it more to the detriment of the masses by exploiting it to defraud unsuspecting members of the congregation and the public at large.[17] In the view of some scholars, some of these prophets are continually bringing the office of the prophet into disrepute as they are the only beneficiaries of the prosperity they preach. They are doing nothing to identify with the people in their problems; rather they are manipulating them to enrich themselves. They take advantage of the poor to pursue personal gains. While some of them ranked among the richest citizens in the country, their followers languish in abject poverty.[18] Ihenacho, describing the situation as it obtains within the Nigerian religious landscape, decries the rate at which various atrocities are committed in the name of God by some false prophets, who use delusive prophecies and erroneous interpretation of the Scripture to exploit and defraud the masses, claiming such to come from the Holy Spirit.[19]

As rightly observed by Ihenacho above, erroneous interpretation of the Scripture is rampant among these prophets. One prominent portion of the Scripture often used by them to cajole their members is Isaiah 6:1-8:

> In the year that King Uzziah died, I saw the Lord seated on a throne, high and exalted, and the train of his robe filled the temple. Above him were seraphs, each with six wings: With two wings they covered their faces, with two they covered their feet, and with two they were flying. And they were calling to one another: "Holy, holy, holy is the LORD Almighty; the whole earth is full of his glory." ... Then I heard the voice of the Lord saying, "Whom shall I send? And who will go for us?" And I said, "Here am I. Send me!"(NIV)

This portion of the Bible depicts the call of Prophet Isaiah into the prophetic ministry. The phrase "in the year that King Uzziah died" according to Bible commentators only describes the historical setting in which the call of Isaiah took place. Precisely, Isaiah was called to the prophetic office in the year

---

[17] Michael A. Ogunewu, "The Values, Relevance and Excesses of Prosperity Gospel in Relations to Economic Survival in Nigeria," *Nigerian Journal of Christian Studies*, 2/1 (October 2018): 231.

[18] Kudzai Biri and Lovemore Togarasi, "...but the One Who Prophecies, Builds the Church Nation Building and Transformation Discourse as True Prophecy: The Case of Zimbabwean Pentecostal Women." In Joachim Kugler et al (ed) *Prophets, Profits and the Bible in Zimbabwe*, Bamberg: University of Bamberg Press, 2015, 80, 91.

[19] Ngozi N. Ihenacho, "A Critical Look at Contemporary Nigerian Christianity," *International Journal of Theology and Reformed Tradition (IJTRT)*, 11 (2009): www.academicexcellencesociety.com/critical_look_at_contemporary_nigerian-christianity.html

that King Uzziah died.[20] However, some prophets have taken that to mean that it was the death of King Uzziah that gave Isaiah a breakthrough for the divine call. To them, had Uzziah not died, Isaiah would not have seen the Lord and his call would have been delayed. In this context, they have often told their members that their desire for progress in life may be an illusion for as long as some people remain alive. So certain people must die, if their breakthroughs are not to be an illusion of a lifetime. Consequently, we have situations in some of our churches and prayer centres "when prayers are offered to kill."[21] This type of teaching has created an atmosphere of distrust and suspicion among neighbours, and has adversely affected interpersonal relationships, even among Christians. However, Christian ministries are expected to bring salvation and blessings to people, they are expected to save lives and promote sound relationships, rather than destroying lives and causing disaffection among the populace.

Modelling Elisha's Prophetic Ministry

Contemporary Pentecostal prophets may become involved in the life of their communities and people in the ways demonstrated by Elisha. Christ's call to the believers to be the light of the world and the salt of the earth is an indication that the mission of Christians goes beyond going to church every Sunday and participating in internal church programmes to include taking care of the needy in the community, outside the church. The responsibility entrusted to Christian leaders is holistic, focused not only on meeting the spiritual needs of people but also on helping to meet people's physical, material and emotional needs. These ideals are exemplified in the ministry of Elisha (II Kg. Chapters 2-8) from which the present-day prophets have a lot to learn.

Assurance of Divine Call

The first lesson to be learnt from Elisha's ministry has to do with the fact that he had a definite call from the Lord. Elisha's call is recorded in I Kg 19:19-21. Before then, Elisha was a prosperous farmer, as the number of his family's oxen affirms. Eunice Chung explains that the fact that Elisha was ploughing with twelve pairs of oxen is an indication of his wealth or that of his family, but this did not hinder him from answering the call.[22] Immediately Elijah's mantle was flung on him, he understood what it meant and answered

---

[20] Don Fleming, *Bridge Bible Directory*, Brisbane: Bridgeway Publications, 1990, 193.

[21] Chioma Gabriel, "When Prayers are Offered to Kill," *Vanguard* Newspaper, August 20, 2016, 10-12.

[22] Eunice Chung, "The Focus of Elisha's Ministry on Atypical, Faithful Individuals," A Master's Thesis Submitted to Dr. Gary Yates, Liberty Baptist Theological Seminary, 2014, 9.

the call without question. Divine call was one of the marks of Old Testament prophets for virtually all of them were called into the ministry by God. The sons of the prophets recognised in Elisha's miracles heaven's seal upon Elisha as Elijah's successor and they revered him accordingly. Beyond this, Elisha was faithful to God's calling in his life: he had the interest, energy and ingenuity concerning spiritual opportunities for service. The exemplification of Elisha's brilliant success was manifested in the prophetic insight and wise counsel to kings, individuals, the rich, the poor and the destitute. The call is also essential today because nobody coming into the ministry without a call can make a success of it. To be in the ministry, it is pertinent that one is called into it.

The call is essential because it carries the implication of an encounter with the caller who incidentally is God, the owner of the ministry. Today, however, it is observed that there are quite many people who profess to be called into the ministry but that cannot give specific account of their call or encounter with the caller. Many are in the ministry today because it is becoming prestigious and lucrative in a way. They are not there to serve, but to execute some sort of selfish agenda; hence, the large-scale exploitation which today pervades some prophetic ministries in Africa. Taking a cue from Elisha, it is imperative that those who profess to be called into the prophetic ministry authenticate their call so as to ensure that they are continually operating in the will of God.

Submission to Training and Mentorship

Closely related to the call is the necessity of being trained for the ministry. To be trained is to be guided into the ministry. In ancient Israel, the prophets are trained through a mentor-mentee relationship. The trainee prophets are called "sons of the prophet" (2 Kg. 2:15; 4:1; 6:1), while the mentor is usually called "father" by the mentees (2 Kg. 2:12). According to the trio of Nantenaina, Raveloharismsy and McWilliams, preparation is very important because it is one of the first steps that enable leaders to get ready for the change in behaviour and plan that will usher them into their new assignments. In addition, submission to the training will help the neophyte to be focused and face squarely the many challenges ahead to tackle.[23] Elisha served Elijah as his student, mentee, helper and friend until the older prophet was taken into God's presence. It was only after this that

---

[23] Lollo Zo Nantenaina, Joel Raveloharimisy, and Karen McWilliams, "The Prophet Elisha as an Agent of Change for Community Development," *Journal of Applied Christian Leadership*, (October 2015), https://aujacl.com/the-prophet-elisha-as-an-agent-of-change-for-community-development/

he received the prophet's mantle as a servant of God. He gained a reputation for his service as the man who poured water on the hands of Elijah (2 Kg. 3:11). After his training, Elisha also helped to train and guide the guild of prophets for a long time.

In the same vein, Christ tutored and mentored the twelve apostles throughout the period they were with Him. This enabled them to give the Church the type of exemplary leadership they gave. The Church also realised the importance of theological education from a very early age; hence, the establishment of the Catechetical School of Alexandria in Egypt around 180 AD[24] to ensure maximum training and performance for church leaders of the time. Theological education deals with the study of God. It is the study of the collective and corrective knowledge of God and the things related to Him. Dada describes theological education as an effort to train and improve a person's faculties, judgement, skill and competence through exposure to the revealed truth of God systematically outlined and laid out in the Bible, nature, history and other areas of human experiences.[25]

Today, the importance of theological training for church ministers cannot be overemphasised, because it affords them the privilege of being exposed to broad knowledge about God as entrenched in the Bible, which if embraced enhances maximum performance in the ministry. It also affords the church leader the opportunity of having a mentor, someone to relate with on a continuous basis for steady maturation in the faith. Such training could be accessed through formal or informal platforms. However, today, while one would commend the efforts of various denominations in advancing theological education, there is still the aversion for it among some of the neo-prophetic Pentecostal prophets. They have the misconception that it is not necessary, because all that is needed by the minister for successful ministry would be taught by the Holy Spirit. This, no doubt, is responsible for the large-scale misinterpretation of the Scriptures and the resultant production of half-baked Christians which pervade the Christian landscape in Nigeria.

Exhibition of Stewardship that Glorifies God

A gift is useful and fulfils its purpose only if it is given away, and it should neither be hoarded nor sold. In Elisha, we see a good steward of the manifold

---

[24] Peter Falk, *The Growth of the Church in Africa*, Bukuru: ACTS, 1997, 29.

[25] Adekunle O. Dada, "Theological Education in the Old Testament and Contemporary State of Theological Education in Nigeria," *Orita: Ibadan Journal of Religious Studies*, 1/XXXIX (June 2007): 42-43.

grace of God for the purpose of helping people. A spectacular thing about Elisha which should be emulated is that he expressed his stewardship by giving himself away in the name and for the glory of God. By the performance of his many miracles recorded between II Kings 4:1 and 7:1, he showed that God's grace fits every possible human's need. Elisha's healing of Naaman made the Syrian soldier to recognise the cosmic view of YHWH. Naaman confessed that thenceforth, he was determined to worship no other God except YHWH. Unlike Elisha, many 21st century prophets are self-centred, self-seeking and business-oriented because they are in competition with their rivals and co-contestants. Besides, they would rather take the glory when miracles take place. Elisha's miracles, on the other hand, anticipated the miracle aspect of the ministry of the Lord Jesus.

Shunning Materialism

The ministry of Elisha was devoid of materialism. This could be seen from his refusal to accept the gift brought to him by Naaman after his healing (II Kg. 5:15-16). He made Naaman to learn that the God of Israel was not swayed by riches or status and that any therapy would be wholly God's work in response to faith. On the other hand, Gehazi, his servant who coveted Naaman's gift, and obtained some of it through lies and deceit, reaped the consequences (2 Kg. 5:19-27). Our present crop of prophets has a lot to learn from this. At present, success in Christian life and ministry is being measured in terms of wealth, prestige and power, with less emphasis placed on salvation and spiritual growth. We are in an age where ministers of God crave for valuables at the expense of values. While it may not be out of place for churches teaching their adherents on how to better their lot economically, some preachers have gone to the extreme in the teachings of prosperity to the extent that today, this teaching is fast becoming a bane of Christianity in the country, as many of the prosperity preachers have undermined essential Christian teachings like salvation and holiness and are now in quick pursuit of materialism. It is in this context that Adasu, a Nigerian priest, spotlights prosperity gospel as a phenomenon which has obliterated and diminished the basic teachings and spiritual fervour of the Church in Nigeria.[26]

The flamboyant lifestyles of these prophets cannot be said to be adding any spiritual value to that of their members or society at large. This has continued to attract public criticism in recent time. There are some who

---

[26] Moses Adasu, "Worldliness and Lack of Spirituality in the Church," *News Cathdica*, 19, 1992.

move around in fleet of cars. In the observations of Kitause and Achunike, "some Pentecostal pastors have been accused of being money minded and not preaching pure Gospel and many of them lead flamboyant lifestyle."[27] Similarly, Asaju and Dapo-Asaju, lamenting the pace of materialism among Nigerian Pentecostal churches, are of the view that the selfish and materialistic tendencies of the founders and leaders of some Pentecostal churches inform their exportation of the gospel to Western countries. According to them, many of these leaders do not embark on this venture for the love of missions, but rather are more interested in the foreign exchange which they will accrue from it. Consequently, many of them are not keen on penetrating the indigenous host communities, but minister to an assemblage of Nigerians living abroad.[28]

Consistency and Diligence in Ministry

Elisha demonstrated commitment to his mission right from the beginning. Committed people do not easily give in to discouragement. At the time when Elijah was to leave, the journey was long enough to discourage the most courageous of men, especially when it has to do with crossing the overflown River Jordan, but Elisha would not be deterred. His persistence in accompanying Elijah all through the way before he was taken up to heaven is an indication of Elisha's commitment and consistency in ministry (II Kg. 2:1-15). God calls upon His people to walk with Him in sobriety and holy consistency. Elisha was an epitome of consistency. He was a minister of God both in season and out of season. Similarly, the biblical account reveals that Elisha demonstrated diligence in ministry. Each time his assistance was needed by anyone in the community, he was usually at their service. He never for any reason turned anyone down. However, the dimension which prophetic ministry is assuming in present-day Africa among Pentecostal prophets is highly disturbing with some of them charging consultation fees before attending to those who need their services.[29] This abnormality should be addressed if the prophetic ministry is to benefit the downtrodden masses in Africa, Nigeria inclusive.

---

[27] Rimamsikwe Habila Kitause and Hilary Chukwuka Achunike, "A Historical Discourse on Tithing and Seed Sowing in some Nigerian Pentecostal Churches," *IOSR Journal of Humanities and Social Science*, 18/3 (Nov. - Dec. 2013): 7.

[28] Dapo F. Asaju and Harriet Seun Dapo-Asaju, "Social Obligations of the Church in a Failed Nigerian State." In Mojubaolu Olufunke Okome (ed.), *State Fragility, State Formation, and Human Security in Nigeria*, New York, Palgrave Macmillan, 2013, 201.

[29] Virtually everyone who had conducted studies on Pentecostalism has something to say about the excesses of Pentecostal prophets across the continent of Africa – Nigeria, Ghana, Zimbabwe, South Africa, etc., For details see: Madzokere, 276-289; Benyah, 116-145; Ihenacho, "A Critical Look at Contemporary Nigerian Christianity."

Caring for the Less-Privileged in Society

One of the major preoccupations of Elisha's ministry was its concern for the weak and needy in society exemplified in his intervention in the lives of the widow of one of the sons of the prophet and the Shunamite woman (II Kg. 4:1-36). Elisha's intentional ministry towards the marginalised and outcast members of society reveals YHWH's love for the abandoned, providing both material and spiritual deliverance.[30] An essential value of the Bible is to help the less-privileged in society through the provisions of gainful employment or other meaningful sources of livelihood. Jonathan Sacks explains that God's call to human responsibility pervades the entire Bible, and is, in fact, its overarching theme.[31] In his study of the messages of ancient prophets, Friedman identifies four essentials which the prophets promoted. These are care for the helpless of society; pursuit of truth and justice; leading with integrity; and making the world a better place for all.[32]

The implication of Friedman's assertion here is that church leaders have prominent roles to play in the life of the nation and its people, which can only be actualised out of a heart of compassion for the downtrodden in society. However, rather than caring, some Pentecostal prophets allegedly use their ministries to defraud and exploit the masses. Asaju and Dapo-Asaju reiterate that many churches in Nigeria, especially among the Pentecostal fold, are very wealthy, as they openly boast of their financial assets and capabilities. Some have even purchased airplanes for the use of their leaders, established private universities with extremely high tuition fees, and have foreign investments. However, they conclude regrettably that the materialistic lifestyle displayed by the leaders of these rich Pentecostal churches is more often than not limited to their personal or institutional use rather than contribute generously to the public good.[33] There is, therefore, the need for such people to reposition these ministries for the good of the teeming masses in particular and the nation in general. They should recognise the fact that they have a part to play in furthering civic and social responsibility in the nation.

---

[30] Marsha White, "Elisha," in *Dictionary of the Bible*, ed. David Noel Freedman, Grand Rapids: William B. Eerdmans Publishing Co., 2000, 398.

[31] Jonathan Sacks, *To Heal a Fractured World: The Ethics of Responsibility*, New York: Schocken Books 2005, 28 & 105.

[32] Hershey H. Friedman, "Messages from the Ancient Prophets: Lessons for Today," *International Journal of Humanities and Social Science*, 1/20 (2011): 297-305.

[33] Asaju and Dapo-Asaju, 192.

Elisha was a Prophet of Faith and Power

Elisha is portrayed as one of the greatest prophets of the Old Testament. He emerged from the backdrop of Elijah's ministry, having possessed a double portion of his power. Many miracles attended Elisha's ministry, ranging from multiplying food (II Kg. 4:42-44) to caring for the needy (II Kg. 5:10), healing the sick and raising of the dead (II Kg. 4:18-20, 33-37). The sons of the prophets, the widow in debt, the Shunammite woman, and Naaman, the Syrian General, were all beneficiaries of miracles which characterised Elisha's ministry. All these miracles were products of his faith in God, through the empowering of the Spirit, derived from his close relationship with Him. Rick James avers that faith provides a spiritual fuel for development, because in hopeless situations, it brings hope and perseverance, enabling the work to go forward. Consequently, Christian leaders need faith in God to stand firm in times of adversities. It is then and only then that they could encourage others to be faithful.[34]

Furthermore, Elisha's persistence in accompanying Elijah all through the way before he was taken away implies Elisha's consecration in ministry, and this earned him the double portion of God's endowment on Elijah's life. Consecration means setting apart people or things from the common affairs of life and dedicating them to God. Elisha, no doubt, realised the workings of God's power in Elijah and consecrated himself in order to be a beneficiary of this power. When the opportunity presented itself, he requested twice as much of that power in his own life. Contemporary prophets would do well to emulate Elisha by maintaining a close relationship with God and being patient to be endowed with His power before launching out into the ministry. The close relationship which Elisha had with God through consecration is, no doubt, responsible for the miracles that pervaded his ministry and the fulfilment of virtually all his prophetic utterances. Pentecostal prophets should take a cue from this for the betterment of their ministries. There have been allegations that some of them stage-managed miracles, especially through their television ministries. Here, people are positioned to give testimonies of miracles which never occurred. Rather than continuing in this, they should reposition themselves to experience God's power and maintain close relationship with Him through consecration so as to hear expressly from Him. Hearing expressly from Him will drastically curtail all these abnormalities; if not completely put a stop to unfulfilled prophecies which pervade the Christian environment in Nigeria.

---

[34] Rick James, "Handle with Care: Engaging with Faith-Based Organizations in Development," *Development in Practice,* 21/1 (2011): 113.

Conclusion

The concern of this study is the rise of Pentecostal prophetic ministries across Africa, with special emphasis on Nigeria. It is observed that prophetic ministries are fast becoming a part of many of the Pentecostal churches in Africa. These ministries hold great potentials for the Church, the Christians and the nation. However, rather than use them positively for the good of the nation and the citizens, some of their founders have turned the ministries into instruments of exploitation within society. Anomalies within some of these churches include the commercialisation of the gospel through the sales of religious products. While some of them are very wealthy, the community gains next to nothing from their wealth. However, a study of the lives of ancient Hebrew prophets with Elisha as exemplar reveals that they were actively involved in their communities, contributing immensely to the social life of the people. This paper, therefore, explores how these present-day prophets can emulate their counterparts of Old Testament period, by channelling part of their resources to the development of society and people. It uses the life and ministry of Elisha as a template, hoping that contemporary prophets have a lot to learn from him. In all, it identifies five values to be emulated from Elisha which are divine call, life devoid of materialism; care for the less-privileged; commitment, consistency, and diligence in ministry and the application of faith and power. It is established that if contemporary prophets would incorporate these in their lives and ministries, they would be on the way to leading the ministries to participate actively in civic and social responsibility in their various communities.

Chapter 3: Targeted Evangelism and Knife Crime in London: A Case of Corporate/ Church Social Responsibility by Migrant Pentecostal Churches in the United Kingdom

Bisi Adenekan-Koevoets

'Everybody on the street knows they're going to lose, it's just that we don't know how to win.' (Key Informant KI.07 Waltham Forest in Pitts 2007: 3)

Introduction

It was 11.30on a Sunday morning and the hall was crowded with young people, some sitting, others walking around, all waiting for the commencement of the service. The gathering looked anything but a church set-up, the excitement was electrifying, and the service was about to start. I was attending the Sunday service of a London church, Salvation Proclaimers Anointed Church (SPAC) with an estimated 2000 young people in a rented hall of a hotel in South West London. SPAC is one of the churches that are actively involved in the fight against knife and other forms of youth crime in London. It actively recruits gang members and victims of violent crime through outreach programmes into the church thereby helping to reduce incidents of gang violence. The reported increase in incidents of fatal knife attacks in the United Kingdom especially in London is a public cause for concern. More than 60% of victims and perpetrators are young people aged below 25 who often are residents of some of the most deprived neighbourhoods of London. Academic, governmental and non-governmental institutions have established strong linkages between the occurrence and sustenance of violent crime and membership of gangs or neighbourhood groups. All these point to the need for more intervention by government, civil society and church organisations especially African migrant Pentecostal churches. This article focuses on African migrant churches and makes a case for targeted evangelism as a tool to connect with young people in our neighbourhoods. It collates activities of churches against gang activities and suggests some areas that need more attention.

The service started with exuberant, loud and youthful worship led by a group of young people who were later replaced by some balaclava-wearing men singing 'wrap' music. Later, the pastor (Tobi Adegboyega) mounted the stage to welcome newcomers and make some announcements. First was to let the church know that as of March, the third month of 2019, a total of 1366 young people under the age of 25 years had responded to the altar call. Then he thanked the 'soul snatchers' and 'hope dealers' who went on the street the previous Tuesday and were able to impact the lives of between 2000 and 3000 young people. (The aim of this street outreach is to connect with young people in very creative ways and this time, every young person they came across was invited for lunch and a chat to enable them to connect). He later invited some ex-gang members to the stage for interviews on their trajectory from crime to Christ in a bid to influence new members in the audience who were still involved in gang activities. Finally, he introduced Pastor Tunde Bakare[1] as the father of the house and the guest speaker for the day.

I relate the occurrence at this service because it illustrates some of the themes addressed in this article: gang membership, knife crime and the intervention of Christian and other civil society organisations. In the United Kingdom, the issue of knife and other gang-related violent crimes is a problem confronting the whole society and it requires a multi-pronged intervention. Governmental, non-governmental and faith-based institutions are involved at different levels to proffer solutions. There is a growing research interest in the occurrence of violent crimes, demography of perpetrators and victims

---

[1] Pastor Tunde Bakare, often referred to as the 'pulpit radical' is a Nigerian prophetic apostolic pastor and a former Nigerian vice presidential candidate. He is the overseer of Nigerian-based Latter Rain Assembly and presides over Global Apostolic Impact Network (GAIN) which is a network of churches, ministries and kingdom businesses committed to advancing the kingdom of God on earth. (See http://tundebakare.com/about/)

and solutions by governmental and non-governmental institutions. There are, however, hardly any research publications on the social action of migrant churches in this regard. This article focuses on the case studies of two Nigerian faith-based organisations, SPAC and Freedom Alliance (Revd Nims Obunge), and makes a case for targeted evangelism as a tool to connect with young people in our neighbourhoods. I start with some statistics, the case of London where it is most rampant and some of the activities currently in place to address the problem.

Knife Crime in the United Kingdom: Some Statistics

Knife crime is a crime involving an object with a blade or sharp instrument. It refers to a collection of different offences in which a knife (or other sharp instrument) is used, as well as knife possession offences. This violent crime has become preponderant in the United Kingdom and the police started identifying it as a separate offence in the year ending March 2008 although consistent aggregation of data began in 2011.[2] Figures collated by the Office of National Statistics (ONS) between 2011 and 2018 show that the use of knife in selected violent and sexual offences rose from 36,700 in 2011 to 40,100 in March 2018 though it dipped in 2014 to 25,600 in England and Wales.[3] There are no figures separating street stabbings due to crime gangs from other offences. However, for 2018, 51% of the offences were related to assault with injury and intent to cause serious harm.[4] While a review by officers in the Mayor's Office for Policing and Crime (MOPAC) identifies gangs as the major driving force behind some of the most serious of these violent crimes, the Centre for Crime and Justice Studies (CCJS) identified other causes. Grimshaw and Ford from CCJS find that underlying the familiar themes of 'gangs' and illegal drug markets are some fundamental social relationships such as inequality, deprivation and social trust - as well as mental health issues.[5] Additionally, the interaction between the characteristics of the communities and societies in which people live, the relationships between people and groups, and individual level factors also contribute to the overall levels and rise in knife crime.[6] Of course, with 57% of stabbings featuring serious or fatal injuries

---

[2] R. Grimshaw and M. Ford, "Young people, violence and knives - revisiting the evidence and policy discussions," UK Justice Policy Review FOCUS, Issue 3, (2018).

[3] Office for National Statistics, "Crime in England and Wales: Year ending March 2018," London: Office for National Statistics, 2018a.

[4] G. Allen and L. Audickas, "Knife crime in England and Wales: Briefing Paper," House of Commons Library, SN4304: 9 (2018): 6.

[5] Grimshaw and Ford, 1.

[6] D. Sethi, et al, "European report on preventing violence and knife crime among young people," Copenhagen, Denmark: World Health Organization, 2010.

being gang-related, they are at best a public manifestation of this endemic problem. Apart from street violence, gangs are also involved in other crimes like violence against women and girls, acquisitive crime and drug supply. It is a persistent and worrying concern, especially as it impacts particularly upon young people and children often from deprived, crime-affected backgrounds who frequently have complex needs like mental illness and special education needs.[7]

The case of London: A study conducted by Whittaker et al. finds that there are up to 250 gangs across London with 4500 members.[8] Members range in age between 14 and 24 though there are younger children who look at older peers as role models because of the apparent money, power and status that gang membership bestows on these older members.[9] There are members as young as 12 years in some gangs who are already involved in street crime both as victims and perpetrators.[10] Figures by the Office of National Statistics (ONS) record London as having the highest crime rate of 168 offences involving a knife per 100,000 population in 2017/18, an increase of 26 offences per 100,000 population from 2016/17. In the year ending March 2018, Juveniles (aged 10-17) were the offenders in 21% of cases in possession of a knife or an offensive weapon with a recorded 268 cases of homicide involving the use of sharp instruments such as knives and broken bottles.[11] In actual numbers, according to the MPS, reported cases of crimes due to knife and sharp instruments was 12,000 in 2008/2009 reaching a peak of 14,000 in 2011/2012, decreased to 9700 in 2014/2015 before rising again to around 14,700 in 2017/2018. According to ONS, the increased numbers may be due to improved recording processes and procedures leading to a greater proportion of committed crime being reported.[12] As of April 8, 2019, about 76 people had been victims of knife attacks in London with some of them fatal. These included 26 teenagers and 21 young adults in their 20s which together is about 65% of all attacks.[13]

---

[7] MOPAC report 2018: 4 available at https://www.london.gov.uk/sites/default/files/gangs_matrix_review_-_final.pdf

[8] A. Whittaker, L. Cheston, T. Tyrell, M. Higgins, C. Felix-Baptiste and T. Havard, *From postcodes to profit: how gangs have changed in Waltham Forest*, London: London Southbank University, 2018.

[9] Whittaker, et al, 23.

[10] Whittaker, et al, 26.

[11] Allen and Audickas, "Knife crime in England and Wales: Briefing Paper," 4.

[12] Office for National Statistics, "Crime in England and Wales: Year ending March 2018,"

[13] Data on knife crime present a complex picture in which no one source adequately captures the real levels of these types of offences occurring in the society. This information was obtained from newspaper reports and other internet sources. For more on the report see: The Sun Crime Count: London stabbings 2019. Latest knife crime statistics and attacks at https://www.thesun.co.uk/news/8104412/london-stabbings-latest-attack-2019-knife-crime-statistics/

Gang Membership

Scholars and involved governmental and non-governmental organisations have described gangs variously,[14] in all these identifications, the main typologies are based on criminality, durability, territoriality and structure.[15] The issue of age and ethnicity remains a contentious one with Stelfox declaring his "inability to find a generally agreed definition of a gang which was applicable to the UK situation."[16] He, therefore, gives a broad definition of a gang as: "Any group which uses violence or the threat or fear of violence to further a criminal purpose but excluding football hooligans and terrorists." He challenges the perception that violent gangs are primarily either a youth problem or one which occurs mainly within ethnic communities. Organisationally, most gangs tend towards a loose structure. It has been further argued that the impetus towards gang membership is ultimately determined by the social predicament of gang members rather than their race or ethnicity.[17] Of course, the heavy concentration in social housing of particular ethnicities like Africans and Caribbean dictates that they are predominant in the gangs in those neighbourhoods and that they assume the style and manner dictated by popular, globalised, ostensibly 'Black', street culture.[18]

Demographics: The subject of the demographics of the victims and perpetrators is a difficult one because the two are not often separate.[19] Analysis of Metropolitan Police crime data for 2016/17 indicates that 75 per cent of victims of knife crime are male and frequently aged less than 25 years of age.[20] Almost half of all victims of knife crime were from BAME backgrounds.[21] In that same period, there were 110 homicides across the capital, 57 were fatal knife crimes and 50 of those victims were male. Almost half of these were black male between 15 and 24 years of age. In London, in the twelve months to

[14] W. B. Miller, *Crime by Youth Gangs and Groups in the United States*. Washington DC, US Department of Justice, 1982; Home Office, "Ending gang violence and exploitation," 2016; S. Hallsworth and T. Young, "Getting Real about Gangs," *Criminal Justice Matters*, 55, (2004): 12-13; M. W. Klein, "Resolving the Eurogang paradox." In *The Eurogang Paradox*, Dordrecht: Springer, 2001, 7-19.

[15] J. Pitts, *Reluctant gangsters: The changing face of youth crime*, Devon: Willan Publishing, 2008, 10.

[16] P. Stelfox, "Policing Lower Levels of Organised Crime" in England and Wales, *The Howard Journal*, 37/4 (1998).

[17] J. Short, *Poverty Ethnicity and Violent Crime*, Boulder CO: Westview, 1997; Pitts, J. *The New Politics of Youth Crime Discipline or Solidarity*, Lyme Regis, Russell House Publishing, 2003.

[18] Pitts, 40.

[19] HM Government, *Serious Violence Strategy*, London, 2018.

[20] Sethi, "European report on preventing violence and knife crime among young people;" HM Government, *Serious Violence Strategy*.

[21] Mayor's Office for Policing and Crime, MOPAC, *Review of the Metropolitan Police Service*, Gang Matrix London, (2018):11.

March 2017, there were over 4,400 victims injured due to knife crime – from slight injuries to serious, life threatening wounds. Crime Survey for England and Wales (CSEW) asked respondents aged 10 to 15-year old living in private households about their experience of knife carrying. The data suggest the proportion of 10 to 15-year old who know someone personally who carries a knife has increased since 2011/2012. The ethnicity of offenders is another touchy subject. Home Office reports based on Police data show that for 2017/2018, those who committed knife crime with injury are predominantly described as male and frequently from a Black, Asian Minority Ethnic group (BAME) background.[22] For offenders, almost ninety per cent were male and of those over half were described as black males aged below 25 years of age. Finally, on gender, women are also involved, both as victims and perpetrators though on a smaller scale than men. According to MOPAC knife strategy report 2017, whilst ninety per cent of knife crime offenders are male, 10% are female and interventions and activity delivered through the strategy takes cognisance of the role of women and girls as offenders as well as victims.[23] So, why do young people become members of or form themselves into criminal gangs?

Research has shown that young people join gangs due to a variety of reasons, including poverty, strong or weak familial connections,[24] school communities,[25] places of worship, custodial relationships and geographical boundaries[26] or for cultural or social identity. Associating success with accumulation of wealth, young people see gang membership as a quick path to such wealth[27], while those of them in deprived living conditions express a sense of hopelessness because there was never enough money growing up.

'If you live on an impoverished estate, people have not much money there, we can't get no jobs, so you turn to drugs (Participant 24, young person, focus group 1).[28]

---

[22] 2016/17 accused data shows that almost 88% of knife crime offenders who commit crime resulting in injury were male. Of these, 65% were described as BAME groups.

[23] Mayor's Office for Policing and Crime, MOPAC, *Review of the Metropolitan Police Service,* Gang Matrix London, (2018): 11.

[24] D. Harris, R. Turner, I. Garrett & S. Akinson, "Understanding the psychology of gang violence interventions" Ministry of Justice, 2011.

[25] R. A. Gordon, et al, "Antisocial behaviour and youth gang membership," *Selection and socialization Criminology*, 42(1), (2004): 55-85.

[26] J. A. Densley, "The organisation of London's street gangs," *Global crime*, 13 (1), (2012): 42-64.

[27] Whittaker, et al, 46.

[28] Focus group result by Whittaker et al, 46.

This is especially difficult for boys once they start getting to the age of 16 when they are not boys anymore and yet not men either. As one ex-gang member said, 'you see mum stressing about bills and feel the need to start doing something to help mum pay the bills. If all the people you see around you are selling drugs, you just see it as the easiest thing to make money' (ex-gang member testimony at SPAC nation church service).[29] Income inequality is a significant factor. Several studies show a direct correlation between higher levels of inequality and higher rates of crime in more than 30 high- and middle-income countries. They also reveal closer associations between inequality and certain types of violent crime than others, with stronger correlations between inequality and homicide and assault.[30] Rufrancos *et al.* report that the effect of changes in the level of inequality is something that still requires more conclusive research.[31]

Other reasons for joining include feeling the need for protection from victimisation from other young people or reprisals from neighbouring/rival gangs. A related explanation for youth involvement is increase in the number of vulnerable populations in terms of children in care, children excluded from school, and homeless adults, since 2014 as pointed out by Government's serious violence strategy.[32] Lack of societal trust has been identified as a possible link between income dispersal and violent crime. Some scholars have suggested that those who live in highly unequal societies with low levels of trust may not believe that such societies have the capacity or the willingness to create safe communities for them.[33] Merton's strain theory has been proposed as an explanation for the linkage between the two. Strain theory proposes that people are pressured into achieving socially accepted goals, but lack the means to achieve them, leading to strain which can push them into committing crime.[34] In an interview with Pastor Tobi of SPAC nation and 'testimonies' of ex-gang members, the desire to live up to particular financial status is one of the

---

[29] As part of my research for this article, I visited SPAC nation Sunday service at the ILEC conference centre in Fulham on the 17th of March 2019.

[30] Hsieh and Pugh, 1993; Messner et al., 2002; Elgar and Aitken, 2010; Cribb et al., 2018.

[31] H. G. Rufrancos, M. Power, K. E. Pickett and R. Wilkinson, "Income inequality and crime: a review and explanation of the time-series evidence," *Sociology and Criminology*-Open Access, 1/1 (2013): 1-9.

[32] HM Government, *Serious Violence Strategy.*

[33] F. J. Elgar and N. Aitken, "Income inequality, trust and Young people, violence and knives - revisiting the evidence and policy discussions Centre For Crime And Justice Studies 27 homicide in 33 countries," *European Journal of Public Health,* 21/2 (2010): 241-246; A. Whitworth, "Inequality and crime across England: a multilevel modelling approach," *Social Policy and Society,* 11(1), (2011): 27-40.

[34] R. Merton, "Social structure and anomie," *American Sociological Review,* 3/5 (1938): 672-682.

attractions to get rich at all cost. For the younger ex-members, growing up with role models who rode expensive cars and wore flashy apparels was something to aspire to.[35] For some of these young people, the temptation of making money through drugs appears more attractive than legitimate opportunities.[36]

Finally, there is a research theme that links violent crime and mental health. Abusive childhood in combination with deprived individual predispositions and disadvantaged neighbourhood environments have been identified as factors that increase the tendency towards violent crime.[37] Studies have established links between traumatic experiences and criminal behaviour.[38] Childhood trauma, according to De Zulueta, creates attachment issues which lead to enhanced impulses towards self-preservation at the expense of compassion for others.[39] Violence can emerge from suffering and traumatised minds and societies that systematically engage in shaming and humiliation can experience an epidemic of violent behaviour.[40] Indication of high levels of mental ill-health, with evidence of traumatisation and use of mental health services have been established in a survey of self-described gang members in Great Britain.[41] Finally, online communication characterised by use of social media is another possible factor in the proliferation of violent crime.[42] The use of social media in the negotiation of (youth) identity and reputation is one other issue to further investigate to know the extent of the link to violent crime. This last section looks at intervention by various organisations into knife crime.

Government Intervention in Knife Crime in London

We know we cannot rely on police, or even statutory services alone, to respond to knife crime. Communities, families, faith groups, the

---

[35] Interview pastor Tobi by Dr Richard Burgess and Bisi Adenekan-Koevoets March 2019 and church visit to SPAC nation church where four young people between the ages of 16 and 19 took to the platform to tell their stories. They included three boys and a girl who were involved in gang activities but have now changed their life courses. (March 2019)

[36] Whittaker, et al, 6.

[37] Sethi, et al, "European report on preventing violence and knife crime among young people;"

[38] V. Ardino, "Offending behaviour: the role of trauma and PTSD," *European Journal of Psycho Traumatology*, 3, (2012): 3.

[39] F. de Zulueta, *From Pain to Violence: the traumatic roots of destructiveness*, Chichester: Whurr, 2006.

[40] I. Perry, "Violence: a public health perspective," *Global Crime*, 10/4 (2009): 368–395.

[41] J. Coid, et al, "Gang Membership, Violence, and Psychiatric Morbidity," *American Journal of Psychiatry*, 170, (2013): 985–993.

[42] M. Urbanik and K. Haggerty, "'It's dangerous': The online world of drug dealers, rappers and the street code," *British Journal of Criminology*, 58/6 (2018): 1343–1360.

media and cultural sectors, we all have a responsibility to encourage young people to fulfil their potential and not to carry and use weapons.[43]

Policing and Sentencing: Many young people carry knives not with the deliberate intention to harm, but to protect themselves or to gain respect from peers.[44] Conceptualising these young people only as criminals without considering their wider social context is detrimental. Official punitive measures like stop and search of suspected gang members could be counter-productive pushing young people to act in fear and defiance.[45] It is important to decrease fear, build trust and give young people alternative strategies to build self-esteem. As Grimshaw and Ford argue, interventions which do not seek to address wider social issues such as inequality, deprivation, poor mental health and drug addiction are unlikely to provide long-lasting solutions to knife violence.[46]

Practitioners and scholars have argued that the effectiveness of police stop and search is hard to establish since this is often a responsive police practice,[47] some find non-significant reductions[48] while an analysis of Metropolitan data shows a weak relationship.[49] Quinton and colleagues explain that to have even a small impact on crime rates, the police would have to institute a massive expansion of stop and search to levels which would probably not be tolerated by certain communities. A feeling of discrimination and unfairness against people of colour in the use of stop and search is also well recognised.[50] The use of sentencing, whether prison, cautions or community sentences, has also not served as sufficient

---

[43] Foreword by Sadiq Khan to the London Knife Crime strategy report of 2017 accessed on 20 April 2019 at Mayor of London the London knife crime strategy 2017 accessed 20 April 2019 at https://www.london.gov.uk/sites/default/files/mopac_knife_crime_strategy_june_2017.pdf?redirecting2clickGUID=b3d19483-4aea-41f1-aed8-fac0fb5dd58b&redirecting2campaignID=3298&redirecting2userGUID=6fa73a97-2ed5-459f-bce7-17f6348c502a

[44] D. Shaw, K. Pease, and B. Hebenton, "Possession of a knife and private defence: Dilemmas in the pursuit of personal security in England and Wales," *International Journal of Law, Crime and Justice,* 39/4 (2011): 266-279.

[45] J. A. Densley, and A. Stevens, "'We'll show you gang': The subterranean structuration of gang life in London," *Criminology and Criminal Justice,* 15/1 (2015): 102-120.

[46] Grimshaw and Ford, 10.

[47] Grimshaw and Ford, 11.

[48] R. McCandless, et al, "Do initiatives involving substantial increases in stop and search reduce crime?" *Assessing the impact of Operation Blunt 2,* (2016).

[49] P. Quinton, M. Tiratelli and B. Bradford, *Does more stop and search mean less crime?* London: College of Policing, 2017.

[50] P. Keeling, *No respect: Young BAME men, the police and stop and search,* London: Criminal Justice Alliance, 2017.

deterrent to possession of knife and dangerous weapons.[51] It appears that the criminal justice system has had a limited impact on possession of knives and occurrence of knife violence.

Another thrust of government strategy in the fight against crime has consistently been partnership working, local solutions, early interventions, rehabilitation, and gang exit work with gang members.[52] In 2017, the Mayor of London started the 'London Needs you Alive Campaign' with a six-pronged approach:

- To target lawbreakers
- Keep deadly weapons off the streets
- Stand with communities, neighbourhoods and families against knife crime,
- Offer a way out of crime
- Protect and educate young people
- Support victims of knife crime.

The main thrust of the campaign is to help young people build self-worth and encourage them to truly be part of society. Considering that the primary driver of gang criminality is currently economic, measures that encourage individuals away from gang activities and deter through economic sanctions, could contribute in addressing gang violence. Initiatives to channel the entrepreneurial skills of young people towards legitimate business and where appropriate, deterrent measures like financial investigations to identify illegal funds and money laundering activities should be implemented.[53] Of note is that at the national level, the UK government is investing financially to fight against crimes. It has instituted grants to support community-based activity against knives, instituted actions to target illicit drug markets, welcome initiatives around mental health and trauma-informed practice and controls on knife sales.[54]

Public Health Approach: A New Conversation

The conversation about a public health approach is a relevant one. Can physicians, rather than police officers, devise techniques of violence prevention based on combating epidemic diseases? Can communities and

---

[51] See Ministry of Justice, 2018a; Barnett and Howard, 2018.
[52] Home Office, 2008, 2012, 2014, 2016a; Whittaker et al, 9.
[53] Whittaker et al, 81.
[54] S. Pepin and A. Pratt, *Serious Violence Strategy*, London: House of Commons Library, 2018.

individuals affected by violence be engaged in new ways that address the underlying drivers of violence instead of the surface manifestations? What does a 'public health' approach mean? Is it police-led, albeit with community and multiagency support, as described by the umbrella label 'pulling levers'? Or does it mean the co-ordination of a range of public services, comprising early years interventions, inclusive education, adolescent and family services, community work, and so on?[55]

The 'public health' label is used to describe programmes that deploy deterrence as well as service provision. Research has found the use of such public health procedures as nurse visitation at homes, school-based interventions, schemes for 'at risk' youth, and therapeutic family support programmes for those with known behavioural challenges beneficial in attacking violent crime.[56] Research shows that emerging trends especially in North America point to the need for a change from the historically punitive system of criminal justice to a more preventive public health approach that utilises all the assets of government and civil society.[57] An example is that of the Community Initiative to Reduce Violence (CIRV) in Glasgow. This initiative took place from 2008 to 2011 in the East End of Glasgow.[58] The programme targeted young people averagely aged 16 years and they had to: attend introductory CIRV sessions at the Sherriff Court, participate in a range of services by statutory and voluntary agencies, work with mentors and pledge not to carry a weapon or use violence.[59] However, enforcement was stepped up, including new sentencing powers and police stop and search.[60]

Between 2006 and 2010, there was a large reduction in cases of offensive weapon possession,[61] and rates of conviction for young men also declined.[62]

---

[55] Grimshaw and Ford, 1.

[56] B. Welsh, A. Braga and C. Sullivan, "Serious Youth Violence and Innovative Prevention: On the Emerging Link Between Public Health and Criminology," *Justice Quarterly*, 31/3 (2014): 500-523.

[57] M. Bellis, K. Hughes, C. Perkins, and A. Bennett, *Protecting people Promoting health. A public health approach to violence prevention for England*, Liverpool: North West Public Health Observatory, 2012.

[58] D. Williams, D. Currie, W. Linden, and P. Donnelly, "Addressing gang-related violence in Glasgow: A preliminary pragmatic quasi-experimental evaluation of the Community Initiative to Reduce Violence (CIRV)," *Aggression and Violent Behavior*, 19/6 (2014): 686-691.

[59] Grimshaw and Ford, 21.

[60] J. Crichton, "Falls in Scottish homicide: lessons for homicide reduction in mental health patients," *BJPsych Bulletin* 41 (2017): 185-186.

[61] F. McCallum, Knife Crime, 11, Edinburgh: The Scottish Parliament, 2011.

[62] B. Matthews, *Where have all the young offenders gone?* Edinburgh: Applied Quantitative Methods Network., 2014.

Participants reported positive experiences with their mentors.[63] The formal CIRV evaluation reported a reduction in police-recorded weapon-carrying for the young people engaged with the project. Unfortunately, the project was not sustainable and had to stop when support was withdrawn.[64] A caveat sounded by Cressida Dick, Metropolitan Police Commissioner is that wholesale transfer of the Glasgow model is not advisable as communities vary and there are very different dynamics and very different issues around violence and, indeed, youth violence.[65] Given the widespread availability and use of knives as possible weapons, Grimshaw and Ford opine that there is much to be done to design and implement public health strategies which possess multi-level dimensions and are actively managed and led by skilled health and other social services.[66] They conceptualise violent crime as an epidemic and recommend that the concept of combating epidemic is employed. With epidemics, diseases are mapped and population behaviours that carry the infection are addressed. The more transmission is interrupted, the greater the chances of significant reduction. Reductionist as this may sound, it is suggested that the same principle be applied to violent crime. The key question remains: how to dismantle the fundamental generators of the epidemic like inequality, racism, and discrimination and eliminate them in the future? These are the forces which undermine and destabilise lives and breed traumatised individuals who lash out at society seeking scapegoats to assuage their feelings of oppression and despair.[67] The conclusion from this project is that violence reduction can benefit from the mobilisation and participation of community members in pursuit of positive goals. Next, I will look at interventions by Christian based organisations.

Intervention by Christian and Other Faith-based and Civic Organisations

There are many faith-based organisations across the UK involved in various aspects of social work within their communities. One organisation that attempts to audit these activities is the Cinnamon Network (CN). In 2010, in response to growing social need and public sector reform, 50 Christian

---

[63] L. Burns D. Williams and P. Donnelly, 'A public health approach to the evaluation of the Glasgow Community Initiative to Reduce Violence' in Glasgow's Community Initiative to Reduce Violence: Second year report, Glasgow: Violence Reduction Unit, 2011, 28-32.

[64] W. Graham, Global Concepts, Local Contexts. A case study of international criminal justice policy transfer in violence reduction, unpublished thesis (Ph.D.), Glasgow Caledonian University, 2016.

[65] M. Townsend, "Knife crime needs public health strategy, says London police chief," Guardian, 6 January, 2018.

[66] Grimshaw and Ford, 24.

[67] Grimshaw and Ford, 24.

CEOs and leaders were challenged to consider how the Christian community could deliver more local transformation at national scale and do so at speed. This led to the set-up of CN which is aimed at helping the Church inspire and influence its community. Its mission is to make it as easy as possible for local churches to transform their communities by reaching out and building life-giving relationships with those in need. The CN collates the social impact and the economic value of all that churches and other faith groups do in communities across the UK and releases a report of its research. The report is ecumenical and includes activities of traditional churches like the Anglican, Baptist and Methodist and Pentecostal churches like the Redeemed Christian Church of God (RCCG) and Assemblies of God Church.[68] Churches are already involved, and it is important their involvement in social action is brought to national attention and that their capacity is improved as much as possible. In a foreword, the Archbishop of Canterbury, Most Rev Justin Welby:

> reveals something different. It shows the breadth of commitment across the country, the depth of commitment, and above all the strength of experience and good practice. Thanks to Cinnamon and other bodies like it, this is not mere do-goodery. It is seeking to find best practice and put it into action in the most professional way that can be imagined.[69]

Other organisations include: Synergy Network/Ascension Trust. The two are led by the pair of Bishop Lenford Rowe and Rev. Les Isaac[70] and work to partner with agencies that have specialisms in the three main areas of family and domestic violence, education and mentoring, and gangs and peer-pressure using a holistic approach. There is also Word 4 Weapons, started by Michael Smith MBE and is the UK's Leading Weapons Surrender Charity which is Collecting Knives and Saving Lives. In this final section, I will discuss SPAC and Freedom Alliance and their involvement in mediating knife and gang related crimes.

Peace Alliance: This initiative was launched in 2001 to tackle knife crime. Started by British born Nims Obunge of Nigerian parents, it partners with

---

[68] Cinnamon Audit Report, 2016: 9 See report at https://www.cinnamonnetwork.co.uk/faa-reports/
[69] Most Rev Justin Welby in Cinnamon Audit Report,
[70] Bishop Rowe was the regional overseer of the Church of God of Prophecy in South London area and is the Chairperson of Synergy Network while Rev Isaac (OBE) is the founder and CEO of Ascension Trust who pioneered the Street Pastor initiative in the UK in 2003. (https://www.ascensiontrust.org.uk/synergy-network/about-us/)

churches, the Home Office, the Metropolitan Police, the Borough councils, local MPs and community leaders to promote peace in Haringey. As stated on its website, it also works nationally to advise government on key policies. The Peace Alliance is recognised for its work in tackling gun and other violent crimes through working with victims, their families and other young people to reduce crime in communities.

It has instituted the London leadership and Peace award which recognises members of the community who have been exemplary in helping to build stronger, safer and inclusive communities. Other activities include the London Week of Peace, the Building Relationships Amongst Cultures Everywhere (BRACE) project, enlightenment DVD for schools on violent crime. Revd Obunge chairs the London Criminal Justice Board IAG (Independent Advisory Group) which in partnership with the police, is involved in a project that investigates the geographical origin of convicts with the aim of investing resources, financial and otherwise, into these communities of origin. He is also the pastor at the Freedom's Ark Church in Tottenham which is involved in issues of social justice.

SPAC Nation

Salvation Proclaimers Anointed Church (SPAC) is a church organisation led by Pastor Tobi Adegboyega who migrated from Nigeria to the UK in 2005. It is pro-active on the problem of knife crime across some cities of the UK. In an interview at the University of Roehampton,[71] he stated that he started helping young people off the street since 2006 and into the newly established SPAC Nation. Fourteen years on the church has grown into an organisation that is dedicated to young people, ordaining them into ministry and still getting them off the street, crime and gang life. Although SPAC did not start out to tackle knife and gang crime, it has become some of its main activities. Of interest is how the Church is using evangelism and attributes of gang culture to connect with young people on the streets of British cities. SPAC has also been able to attract young people in corporate world who would ordinarily not want to be part of the Church because of its unorthodox approach to Christian Pentecostal practices.

First is the approach of the Church to evangelism. According to the pastor, the Church has no formal evangelism team but what he calls 'soul

---

[71] Dr Richard Burgess and I interviewed Pastor Tobi for this project at the University of Roehampton in March 2019.

snatchers' and 'hope dealers.' These are church members who have 'hunger for souls', form themselves into groups and go to the streets to meet young people. But unlike the traditional Pentecostal practice of sharing tracts on the street and preaching about Jesus, soul snatchers go to places frequented by young people, dressed in similar fashion to those young people and talk to them about SPAC Nation and what it can offer them. This attracts them to the Church and he then talks to them about Jesus. He explains further in this rather extensive quote:

> On the street we can't {talk to them about Jesus} because they know about Jesus already. Their parents took them to church. Young people idolise people that they see on top of them, whoever that is. What the church wanted them to do is to idolise Jesus, but they don't see him. So, they are not going to have it. I ask my guys, many of them came from prison. My assistant pastor... when he came out of prison, I was saying..., 'why is Islam the fastest growing religion in prison'? He said to me, 'when Christians come, you speak about Jesus, when Islamic people come, they speak about their Imam in their local area ... and they will be excited (they say gassed) to meet the Imam guy. When they meet the Imam, he introduces them to Islam and makes them feel powerful and they love that. You speak about Jesus, but we can't find him, he's not here. When a guy comes out of prison, it's likely, if he is powerful, that he will go towards Islam. So, I understood it and told them to go and talk about the church and all the work we are doing. When they come to me, I have nobody to take them to than Jesus. Young people idolise whom they see, even the girls. If they see Beyoncé singing with a certain hair, they are going to go and do it. What the church has not succeeded in doing...African churches do their own idolising, they put their pastors' faces ...which is falling apart but the world mastered it very well. Like what happened in Brixton just day before yesterday. Three people were stabbed because a guy had come to sing. The moment he started his hit song titled 'Die young' and he was talking about how he wanted to die young, there was a flow of blood. They idolise. When soul snatchers go on the street, they are bringing them the image of SPAC nation and what it can do for them. Some of them are not looking for us to help them financially, they are looking for family, a community. So, I must send people out who look like their community, who look like their

family. They are Pentecostal kids, church kids and Catholics from all faith.[72]

Pastor Tobi believes that this method is bringing them to church because he has recorded an average of 100 responses to 'altar calls' every Sunday in the past one year. There are also those he calls 'Hope Dealers' who go on the streets to speak to young people. Their appearance, language and street life experiences are used as assets in connecting with young people and convincing them to come to SPAC Nation. The Church is also establishing its presence on university campuses across the UK. It sets up 'Revival Houses' on these campuses '*so people who are in SPAC London and are now in Uni just go to start the same thing.*'

Pastor Tobi numbered regular church attendance at around 1300, while church records put membership between 3000 and 3500 with more than 90% of them being young people under the age of 25 years.[73] With this population of young people, the second practice in operation is that of mentoring. Members are grouped into three generations (gen). 1st gen aged between 28-33 (lead pastors); 2nd gen 23-28 (leaders and some pastors) and the 3rd gen (teenage leaders). Discipleship in SPAC is such that the 1st gen disciples the 2nd, then the 3rd and a plan is in the works to create a 4th gen of pupils in the primary school.[74] Some of the 1st and 2nd gen are ex-convicts, so they can guide the 3rd gen appropriately. The fact that the 3rd gen are already in the line of drug dealings or carrying knives makes them potential criminals if there is no intervention to break the circle. This is very similar to mentorship in the gang world[75] where the Elders (16-24) mentor the Younger (12-16) who also mentor the Tinies (below 12 years) on progression in criminality.[76]

One of the criticisms levelled against SPAC by other Pentecostals is the seeming lack of a visible discipleship programme for the teeming population of young people that answer the altar call and join the Church. According to Pastor Tobi, his discipleship style is more about exposing these young people to positive living and the House Fellowship centres turned community units have been instrumental in achieving this. He argues that:

---

[72] Interview with Pastor Tobi March 2019.
[73] Interview with Pastor Tobi March 2019.
[74] Interview Pastor Tobi 2019.
[75] See page 16 for the hierarchy of leadership and their concept of mentorship among gang members
[76] Densley, "The organisation of London's street gangs, 52.

Discipleship is by exposure to our lives and I've trained leaders who are also disciplining them to know about business and money making. They are discipled to know about the Bible. Also, I've taught all of them about the power of God and pray for people to receive the baptism of the Holy Spirit.[77]

Scholars and other intervening organisations on criminal gangs have identified inequality and poverty as some of the driving forces of gangs. During my visit to SPAC Sunday service, I listened to the stories of five young people who used to be gang members and there were two similar themes. One is the lack of positive role models and the other is the poverty that surrounds them and the desire to get out of it. The promise of wealth and the 'good life' is often a strong attraction for young people. A third practice in SPAC is promotion of entrepreneurship. To provide an alternative means of income, SPAC organises various avenues to give them entrepreneurial skills and then helps them set up legitimate businesses and once successful, they then help others from their profits. This way, according to Pastor Tobi,

There is hardly any young person's business in London that SPAC does not have a hand in.[78]

Pastor Tobi, however, does not make the figures public information to protect the people involved and avoid 'exposing those businesses to challenges.' He reiterates though that it is not often just the money. 'At the essence of their pursuit is the search for a family and we provide family. Thereafter, we must spot those who are entrepreneurial and help them because that will only enhance the family they have just found.' Otherwise,

three or four months down the line there is still pressure from outside. Some of these people are under unspeakable pressure from their parents for money, it's everywhere on the streets.[79]

On my visit to SPAC service, there were an estimated 2000 mostly young people at the almost 6-hour service and the question that comes to mind is: how do you oversee such a large population of young people? This raises a second question on whether SPAC is in dialogue with other churches to effect

---

[77] Interview with Pastor Tobi March 2019.
[78] Interview with Pastor Tobi.
[79] Interview with Pastor Tobi.

partnership in helping these young people stay out of crime and remain in church. Pastor Tobi explains that he has been in dialogue with other Nigerian churches in London, including the RCCG. He explains that his leadership style is very unorthodox and difficult for the often-traditional leaders of these churches. For example, trusting young people with power and authority in the organisation of the Church is something that first-generation African Church leaders are unable to do. He maintains that connecting with young people is about:

> Leadership and letting young people know that you believe in them, not by talk but by action. That action is putting them in places of trust. If you can't do that, you can't relate with them. I grew up in Nigeria, I came here at 25, I can't come here and tell people that grew up here and that are always on the street doing their own thing how to reach themselves, so they've got to tell me.

There is also a cultural aspect to this intergenerational gap. According to Pastor Tobi, Nigerian pastors need to cross the cultural divide and relate to young people. The tradition that separates the first generation as the all wise with all the answers is self-defeating because the younger generation cannot relate to that. According to the pastor,

> if I meet a 15-year-old now, I shake them the normal way, we do what we do, and I talk to them as normal, then they can talk to me, they can open up to me. But imagine a 15-year-old looking at Pastor Agu. It's like don't move there. I said, 'if you come down and have lunch with them and talk to them, you'll be shocked how quickly you are going to grow, how fast.[80]

There have been criticisms of SPAC as a Church and Pastor Tobi as the individual leading the Church. These include his alleged ostentatious lifestyle and that of his members as evidenced in his £2.5m rented house and fleet of expensive cars. Secondly, the structure of its leadership mirrors that of gangs and the perceived air of mystery around the Church has resulted in questions about its legitimacy and it being labelled as a "cult". Finally, it allegedly ordains pastors who do not undergo any formal training and encourages its members to flaunt their wealth to make the Church look glamorous to the gang members it wants to attract. The pastor rejects these criticisms. In that £2.5 million house, my wife, two kids and I use only one room and have

---

[80] Interview with Pastor Tobi March 2019 .

14 ex-criminals living with us, he says. In a BBC interview,[81] he admits that critics might think he is dodgy, and he understands it but pleads that people be given the chance to be seen for who they are and given the chance to change including himself. In response to his wealth, he admits to wanting to show the gangsters and young people what they have always wanted to be and have but that they were looking for it in the wrong place. His attempt is to show them legitimate ways to acquire wealth.

> When you check the demographics of the people who attack us most, they are black young Christians while 'the first set of people to love what we were doing were Muslim associations. They came to the church to tell us they love what we were doing and that even though they were not going to change to our religion, they offered to help if we needed any support'. As for the press, he accuses them of making baseless accusations. Pastor Tobi singles out Daily Mail for having 'double mouth' and being racist. They say they write about knife crime and then we realise that for them if they ever see any black person doing well, then it's a problem.[82]

He told us during the interview that he welcomes genuine criticism that seeks to understand why SPAC has certain practices and has suggestions for improvement. In addition to dialoguing with church leaders, he is also in discussions with government agencies. He has been invited by Scotland Yard, Mayor of London, Home Office and No 10 for consultations. While commending some of these efforts, he questions their seriousness, willingness and ability to solve knife and gang crimes, noting that young people are often not involved. He would also like to see things being done rather than the multiplicity of talks going on now. He presently feels overwhelmed because there are lots of young people coming in their 10s and 100s looking for help. He believes that he has some solution to offer to government to help support what SPAC is doing.

Some other organisations targeting knife crime include:

- Rock Christian Centre Sheffield which supports Word 4 Weapons and has a weapon drop point in its Lighthouse centre.[83]

---

[81] N. Phillips, "The church where drugs and knives are left at the altar," (2018) Accessed 29 April 2019 at https://www.bbc.co.uk/news/uk-42887653

[82] Interview with Pastor Tobi.

[83] Visit http://www.rockchristiancentre.org/lighthouse/

- Power the Fight which was set up by Ben Lindsay in 2019 to combat knife crime. He leads two churches, Emmanuel Church London in Greenwich and Emmanuel Church, New Cross. This organisation works with families, churches, faith groups and community organisations that want to be equipped to engage with youth violence issues in their context. This is done through training and workshops, resources like specialist talks and links to helpful websites and toolkits, connecting faith groups, communities and other involved partners and supporting families with therapeutic, financial and legal assistance.[84]

In conclusion, I will like to state the following:

Violent crime has multiple causality and, according to Matt Bird, founder of Cinnamon Network[85], it requires a holistic approach. It requires local churches developing conversation with one another and together forming partnerships across a range of sectors.

Local churches may also benefit from building strong relationships with their communities, local authorities, health services, schools, community organisations and the police to achieve a lasting solution to violent crime.

While these young people are being given spiritual and entrepreneurial skills, it is important to evaluate if there are no mental and emotional needs that should be met by appropriate professionals.

My visit to SPAC Nation showed young people in need of safe spaces where they can go and be with other young people and what better place to do that than the church. This Church appears to provide that, not just for the 6-hour service but through other weekly activities.

There is little academic work, theological or sociological, done about churches like SPAC Nation and their strategies for attracting young people to church. This is an anomaly, albeit understandable considering the lack of visibility and young age of some of these churches. It is pertinent to note that while these young people show little interest in traditional African Pentecostal churches, their membership of SPAC Nation and such new churches, is

---

[84] For more visit https://www.powerthefight.org.uk/about-us/
[85] For more see Cinnamon Faith Action Audit Report 2016 https://www.cinnamonnetwork.co.uk/faa-reports/

on the increase. This raises a lot of questions that need answers both from practitioners and academics.

PS: Clarification of Some Terms

The concept of gangs and its membership have been operationalised earlier in this study. However, equally vital is an understanding of how they evolve. According to some scholars, they evolve through various stages and often start as recreational or peer group, progress to crime, move to the entrepreneurial stage and finally to extra-legal governance stages.[86]

Table 1: The evolution of gangs (Densley, 2012, 2014)

Stage	Features
Recreation	Most gangs start as recreational groups based on friendship and family ties and shared history. Criminal activity is usually opportunistic and rarely acquisitive, for example, fighting and vandalism.
Crime	Crime and violence becoming intrinsic to group identity and a means of supporting gang activities. Members gain respect through these activities, but this attracts attention from the police and rival gangs. As they develop, gangs need to become more cohesive and organised to survive and secure income.
Enterprise	In response to powerful incentives, gangs become more organised and rely more on a goal orientation instead of personal relationships. Crime is no longer a means; it has become the end in itself. Original founding members become de facto leaders, usually with one member who is 'primus inter pares', the first amongst equals, acquired through a combination of a reputation for violence and business acumen.
Extra-legal Governance	Some gangs evolve to be sole suppliers in a given domain (Densley 2012, 2014) and invest in the 'resources' of violence, territory, secrecy and intelligence to embed themselves in an area.

---

[86] J. Densley, "It's gang life, but not as we know it: The evolution of gang business," *Crime and Delinquency*, 60/4 (2014): 517-546; M. L. Storrod, and J.A. Densley, "Going viral and going country: the expressive and instrumental activities of street gangs on social media," *Journal of Youth Studies*, 20/6 (2017): 677-696.

Certainly, it is reductionist to attribute all youth criminal activities to gangs. Sounding a note of caution, Whittaker and his colleagues suggest that the great majority of young people are not necessarily involved in criminal activity[87] and that street crime must be approached with utmost care rather than reducing all crimes to gang activities. As one of the participants in their study warns, care must be taken that the label of 'gang' is not used by government agencies to criminalise young black males who are visible on the street.

A second important operational factor about gangs is that there are strict levels of hierarchy. Though not homogenous across all gangs, Densley identifies three levels of power and authority among gangs in the 'enterprise stage'. There is the higher level or inner circle, the Elders and the Youngers.

- Higher level or inner circle: These are able to make autonomous decisions and sanction individuals in the lower levels. Often founder members with friendship and family ties. Members at this level often share equal authority though there is one at the top of the pyramid who acquires his dominant status through a combination of reputation for violence and business acumen.

- The Middle or Elder level (olders, generals, enforcers): They translate the decisions of the inner circle into action and are the visible face of the gang. A mixture of first- and second-generation gang members usually aged 17-24 years averagely, they direct the day-to-day criminal activities of the Youngers.

- Lower or Younger level: These are directed and groomed by the elders who also reward or punish them. Averagely aged between 12 and 16, they gain entry via the elders who act as gatekeepers. Each younger is attached to a particular elder who gives the Younger a street name or 'tag' that links them to each other. Within some established gangs, even youngers have their own youngers known as Tinies.[88]

County line activities: This is the sale of drugs by urban gangs in other towns and cities. Used by police to refer to urban gangs supplying drugs to suburban areas, rural areas, market and coastal towns using dedicated mobile

---

[87] Whittaker, et al, 38.
[88] Densley, "The organisation of London's street gangs, 52.

phone lines or 'deal lines.'[89] Gangs typically use children and young people as runners to move drugs and money to and from the urban area and this often involves them being exploited through deception, intimidation, violence, debt bondage, grooming and/or trafficking by the gang.

Cuckooing: This is targeting and exploiting vulnerable adults by taking over their homes to use as a local base for drug dealing. These homes are called rat holes and used as places where drug runners or dealers can just crawl in quickly not sell things out of but to bag up their weed.

Drug mules: These are usually children as young as 12 who are used in County line activities to transport drugs to rural areas and other towns from Manchester, Liverpool, Birmingham and London. Gangs use a mobile phone to take orders from customers. They then exploit these young people to move drugs and cash between the urban hub and the county market.

Debt bondage is when a child is sent on county line activity and then set up so that the drug is stolen from him and he becomes indebted to the gang who can then control him.[90]

Grooming: This is a technique for recruiting gang members. It usually starts early, from around the age of 10. It starts with desensitisation where the young person is encouraged to commit petty crime to normalise criminal behaviour. Then the elders play mind games with the potential recruits by telling them 'war stories' of their own criminal exploits to impress the young person.[91]

Former' or 'ex-gang member' describes young people who have had varying degrees of 'embeddedness' in gangs[92] and who either self-identify as gang members and/or who have been identified by gang intervention agencies as being involved with local gangs.

---

[89] National Crime Agency, NCA intelligence Assessment: County lines, gangs and safeguarding, 2015; National Crime Agency, NCA intelligence Assessment: County lines, gang violence, exploitation and drug supply, 2016; National Crime Agency, National Strategic Assessment of Serious and Organised Crime, 2017; National Crime Agency, County lines violence, exploitation and drug supply 2017: National Briefing report, 2017.

[90] National Crime Agency, County lines violence, exploitation and drug supply 2017: National Briefing report, 2017.

[91] Whittaker et al, 48-50.

[92] D. C. Pyrooz, G. Sweeten and A.R. Piquero, "Continuity and change in gang membership and gang embeddedness," *Journal of Research in Crime and Delinquency*, 50/2 (2012): 239-271.

Trap house: A drug house, also known as a trap house, bando, jugg house, or crack house, is a building where drug dealers and drug users buy, sell, produce, and use illegal drugs. Pastor Tobi of SPAC describes trap houses as drug houses where young people go to get high on drugs and can sleep it off. In his attempt to copy street language, the Church has fellowship places called TRAP houses. In their case, it is an acronym for 'Take Risk and Prosper' and is usually filled with young people and managed by young people. It is like community centres but reignited and more focused on business and entrepreneurship trainings.[93]

---

[93] Pastor Tobi, interview, 2019.

Chapter 4: Centrifugal and Centripetal Mission Approaches: Studies in the Corporate Social Responsibility (CSR) of Pentecostal Churches in Nigeria with Emphasis on the Redeemed Christian Church of God

Walnshak Alheri Danfulani
and
Umar Habila Dadem Danfulani

Introduction

This article is a discourse on how urban and suburban religious landscape has been transformed by neo-Pentecostal movements in Nigeria since the 1980s when they appeared. Today, many scholars have measured the quick spread and gargantuan growth of Pentecostalism in Nigeria in particular and Africa in general, together with strategies employed towards achieving the unprecedented growth. They have assessed the social, economic, political and spiritual impacts of neo-Pentecostal movements to the neglect of their Corporate Social Responsibilities (CSR). This neglect nestles against the backdrop of the claim being peddled around that some Pentecostal churches, including the RCCG, are not involved in the development of the communities in which they have been embedded. This paper describes the Progressive-Pentecostal and CSR activities of Pentecostal movements, with emphasis on the RCCG. It articulates the responses of Pentecostal churches to socio-economic and political challenges in Nigeria, focussing more specifically on the CSR responses of the RCCG. The paper assesses the two distinct paradigms of responses forwarded by scholars namely, those churches that they believe have taken a *centripetal*, that is, are socially and politically passive/docile to socio-economic and political needs of their members, while placing emphasis on spirituality, as opposed to those adapting the *centrifugal* approach, which are regarded as confronting head-on these same problems. The paper argues that the RCCG does not warrant inclusion or compartmentalisation into a straight *centripetal* jacket by scholars who actually failed completely in following the trends of its CSR involvement from inception.

This paper examines the concept of Corporate Social Responsibility (CSR) against the backdrop of Pentecostal (*Pente*) paradigms concerning religious engagement with communities within which they are birthed. The paper, in other words, investigates how *Pente* religious organisations manage CSR as a missionary strategy to galvanise and produce an overall positive impact and transformation on society. CSR is a very old concept among mission churches and has been referred to as *Christian Social Responsibility*, a term which most *Pente* churches are more at home with today. In fact, CSR has been so germane in the embedment of Christianity such that the whole materialist theory of Karl Henschel Marx and Freiderich Engels and other works deriving from it, such as the social instrumental theory of conversion propounded by Caroline Ifeka-Moller[1] and other works under the influence of Marxist ideology are solidly hinged on it.

In this paper, two responses of *Pente* to social, economic, political and spiritual challenges on the Nigerian religious landscape are identified: *centripetal* and *centrifugal*. Churches taking a *centripetal* position, according to Gaiya, tend to exhibit a socially docile or passive response to social, economic, and political challenges, emphasising more on the spiritual. Their corrupt leadership rather colludes and compromises with other corrupt leaders and groups to undermine efforts towards political, social, economic and human improvement. They tend, according to him, to focus more of their energies and engagement with society towards offering spiritual solutions to myriads of social, economic and political problems.

> In other words, in spite of the enormous wealth these churches gather from the members, social engagement in the form of political, social and human improvement, such as, political awareness and improvement of living conditions of less endowed members and non-members is almost nil, this genre of charismatic Pentecostal churches is dominated by charismatic Pentecostal mega churches.[2]

On the other hand, he observes that a paradigm shift appears in which churches that develop a *centrifugal* approach tend rather to confront

---

[1] Caroline Ifeka-Moller, "White power: social-structural factors in conversion to Christianity, Eastern Nigeria, 1921-1966," *Canadian Journal of African Studies* 8/1 (1974): 56-61.

[2] Musa A.B. Gaiya, "Social Engagement of Nigerian Charismatic Pentecostal Churches." In: Gideon Ibn Tambiyi and Umar H.D. Danfulani (eds.), *Rethinking Biblical Studies in Africa: Essays in Honour of Danny McCain*, 73-101, Bukuru, Plateau State, Nigeria: ACTS, 2018, 73; cf., Musa A. B. Gaiya, "Charismatic and Pentecostal Social Orientation in Nigeria" Nova Religio: *The Journal of Alternative and Emergent Religions*, 18/3 (Feb. 2015): 63-79.

social, economic and political problems by adapting more proactive empirical strategies through offering help to the needy in society. Giaya, however, maintains that *Pente* churches in this category are relatively few and are located primarily in the Lagos area, although they are growing in influence.

The paper assesses the current general shift of *Pente* churches in Nigeria away from being viewed as solely providing spiritual/salvific solutions towards empirical human problems, such as social, economic and political needs of its members, to more pragmatic strategies. This has elsewhere been referred to by Miller and Yamamori as a part of what they term *Progressive-Pentecostalism*, a concept which this paper will briefly examine.[3] The study points out the need for a more coherent and binding recognition of the CSR principle in all organisations: profit and non-profit alike, multi-national companies and religious organisations operating in Nigeria. This is especially germane since the many indices, principles and benefits of democratic governance, such as the development of much needed civil society, good governance, the rule of law, personal and collective security, basic human rights and the urgent need to get out of abject poverty are still fragile in Nigeria today. This should continually be mainstreamed into implementable national laws and policies.[4]

The paper tackles the following question: Despite the aggressive and robust CSR portfolio of the RCCG in view of its health intervention, civic roles, leadership, media intervention, and economic empowerment programmes, is it right for the RCCG to be categorised as a heavily centripetal movement as M.A.B. Gaiya concludes? The paper closes by saying that for any Church to meet its mandate, whatever genre it may belong to, whether it is orthodox, evangelical, Ethiopian-prophetic, classical-Pentecostal, African initiated, or neo-Pentecostal-charismatic in nature, it must master the game of maintaining an equilibrium between its vertical-centripetal and horizontal-centrifugal paradigms of operation.

---

[3] Donald E. Miller and Tetsunao Yamamori, *Global Pentecostalism: The New Face of Christian Social Engagement* (Berkeley, Los Angeles and London: University of California Press, 2007; see also, Umar H.D. Danfulani, "Popular Religiosities, Corporate Faiths and the Impact of Globalization on the Religious Landscape in Contemporary Nigeria", *Inaugural Lecture: University of Jos Lecture Series 39*, delivered on Friday, 4th December, 2009.

[4] Hakeem Ijaiya, "Challenges of Corporate Social Responsibility in the Niger Delta Region of Nigeria," *Afe Babalola University: Journal of Sustainable Development Law and Policy III*, 3/1 (2014): 60-70, esp. 60.

Clarification of Terms

Pentecostal (*Pente*)

Pentecostalism is not only one of the most dominant Christian expressions in Africa, but it is a most potent and dynamic instrument that is initiating religious change and upheaval on the contemporary African continent. Pentecostalism provides a stimulating and inclusive disconnection from the mission mode of worship, to where prominence and eminence is given to the "Holy Spirit". It is a term defining a 'Protestant charismatic' or 'Catholic renewal' movement within Christianity that places special emphasis on a direct personal experience of God through 'baptism in the Holy Spirit' and 'speaking in tongues' [*glossolalia*]. The term "Pentecostal" is derived from *Pentecoste*, a Greek term describing the Jewish Feast of Weeks, which coincides with "The Day of Pentecost" experience by the early Christian apostles, which is recorded in the second chapter of Acts.[5]

For Christians, this event commemorates the descent of the Holy Spirit upon the followers of Jesus Christ, as described in the second chapter of the book of Acts. Pentecostals also tend to see their movement as reflecting the same kind of spiritual power, worship styles and teachings that were found in the early church.[6]

The emergence of modern *Pente* is associated with religious events experienced at the beginning of the 20th century within two interrelated events: One in Topeka, Kansas on 1 January, 1901 under Charles Parham, and the other, the Azusa Street revival in Los Angeles in April 1906, under the Black charismatic Holiness preacher, William Seymore. These two events that came out of evangelical and puritan traditions have been traditionally recognised as the historical origins of Pente movements worldwide. From

---

[5] Allan H. Anderson, *African Reformation: African Initiated Christianity in the 20th Century*, Trenton, New York and Asmara, Eritrea: Africa World Press, Inc., 2001, 18, Allan H. Anderson, *Bazalwane: African Pentecostals in South Africa* (Pretoria: University of South Africa Press, 1992), pp. 2-6; Harvey Cox, *Fire from Heaven: The Rise of Pentecostal Spirituality and the Reshaping of Religion in the Twenty-first Century*, Cambridge, MA: Da Capo Press, 1995, 3; Jacob K. Olupona, "West Africa". In Stanley M. Burgess (ed.), *The New International Dictionary of Pentecostal and Charismatic Movements*, revised and expanded edition, Grand Rapids, Michigan: Zondervan, 2002, 16-17 and Gotan, C.T., "Paper on the Challenges of Pentecostalism to the Catholic Liturgy and Way of Life: The Nigerian Experience at Our Lady Queen of Nigeria Pro-Cathedral", Presented (by Dean, Faculty of Education, University of Jos) at Our Lady Queen of Nigeria Pro-Cathedral, Garki, Abuja, , on 24.11. 2015, 1.

[6] Gotan, 1f.

here, Pente spread to North America, Europe, Latin America, Africa and Asia.[7]

These charismatic *Pente* or Neo-Pentecostal movements have had a more recent history and origin in Africa emerging from the evangelical-Charismatic renewal of the 1960s and 70s. They are regarded as "Pentecostal" movements because they emphasise the power and the gifts of the Holy Spirit, though they do not always refer to themselves as Pentecostals, in some cases preferring the terms Charismatic" and/or "evangelical."[8] Despite their recent origins, however, some of these churches are already among the largest and most influential denominations in their respective countries, especially in West Africa, with some becoming huge churches in less than a decade after their emergence.[9] Concerning this mesmerising development, Paul Gifford observes that they are found in every major city in Africa.[10]

The emphasis of the *Pente* spirituality on the word [the Holy Bible], Holy Spirit baptism (with accompanying signs of *glossolalia*, that is, speaking in new tongues as social and spiritual identity markers), being born again, prayer, prophecy, dreams, visions, faith healing and the practice of godliness is typical of African Pentecostal churches' way of life, theology and worship.[11] Some of them emphasise prosperity (prosperity gospel or health is wealth movement), others holiness (the holiness or pietist movement) and others still faith and the manifestation of the power of the Holy Spirit in performing signs and wonders (the Faith movement).[12] Even though scholars have claimed that African *Pente* is borrowed in both its structure and theology, founders of Pentecostal churches have vehemently denied this. They state divine authorisation for establishing their religious

---

[7] Afe Adogame, "Introduction." In Afe Adogame (ed.), *Who is Afraid of the Holy Ghost*, ix-xxii, Trenton and Asmara: World Press, 2011, xi; V. Syan, *Century of the Holy Spirit: 100 years of Pentecostal and Charismatic Renewal* Nashville, T.N.: Thomas Nelson, 2001 and Stanley M. Burgess and E.M. Van der Maas (eds.), *The New International Dictionary of Pentecostal and Charismatic Movements*, Grand Rapids: Zondervan, 2002.

[8] Anderson, *African Reformation*, 19.

[9] P. E. Kingsley Larbi, *Pentecostalism: The Eddies of Ghanaian Christianity*, Dansoman, Accra-Ghana: Centre for Pentecostal and Charismatic Studies (CPCS), SAPC Series, 2001, 295.

[10] Paul Gifford, "Some Recent Developments in African Christianity," *African Affairs*, 93/373 (Oct. 1991): 513-533, esp. 515.

[11] Allan H. Anderson, *Introduction to Pentecostalism*, Cambridge: CUP, 2004.

[12] Frederick K.C. Price, *Name it and Claim it! The Power of Positive Confession*, Benin City: Marvellous Christina, 2005.

organisations and for doing so with business sense and fashion[13] and not merely copying North American televangelists or exporting *Pente* from America.

This is the crux of Pentecostal-Charismatic Christian *ummah* or community. Glossolalia, that is, speaking in tongues and 'being slain under the anointing of the Holy Spirit' [either during impartation or deliverance from the influence of demonic and other satanic powers] are the most visible signs of divine, Holy Spirit presence and possession. These are usually followed by prophetic utterances, signs of divine revelation, and other divine giftings from God.

Pente in the early church saw the manifestation of the power of the Holy Spirit filling the apostles and early converts, enabling them to live through three stages of life: First, the testimony of the acceptance of Christ; second, water baptism by total immersion and third, "baptism by the Holy Spirit and by fire", sealed by the eruption of *glossolalia*.[14] This "twice born" *erleibnis* emphasised by Jesus in John 3:3 and 5ff is the initiation into spiritual militancy, leading to revelations in dreams, visions, prophecy, healing and speaking in new tongues. It is the most unique form of religious charismata found among Christian Pentecostals all over the world.[15]

The baptism of Pentecostal-Charismatics is not primarily sacramental, but an emotional baptism in the Holy Spirit; an intense, mystical feeling of contact with God. This feeling is expressed through 'speaking in tongues', which the church witnesses. For Pentecostals, this emotional experience (*erlebnis*) is an element of the religious—the *homo religiosus*. Pentecostalism is a *sui generic* phenomenon resulting from trans-nationalisation.[16]

---

[13] D.R. McConnell, *A Different Gospel: A Historical and Biblical Analysis of the Modern Faith Movement* Massachusetts: Hendrickson Publishers, Inn, 1987, 12; S. Brouwer, Paul Gifford and S. D. Rose, *Exporting the American Gospel: Global Christian Fundamentalism*, New York: Routledge, 1996.

[14] John 1:33, Matthew 3:11 & Luke 3:16.

[15] Nils G. Holm, "Invited Essay-Pentecostalism: Conversion and Charisma," *The International Journal for the Psychology of Religion*, 1/3 (1991): 135-151.

[16] André Corten, *Pentecostalism in Brazil: Emotion of the Poor and Theological Romanticism*, translated by Arianne Dorval, Houndmills, Basingstoke, Hampshire and London: Macmillan, and New York: St. Martin's Press Inc., 1999, 25-26, 37ff.; M. Kelsey, *Tongue Speaking: The History and Meaning of Charismatic Experience*, New York: Crossroad, 1981; Goodman, cited in Mircea Eliade, (ed.), *The Encyclopedia of Religion*, 16 vols. 563-564, vol. 5 (New York: Macmillan, 1987) and Stanley M. Burgess and G.B. McGee (eds.), *Dictionary of Pentecostal and Charismatic Movements*, 334-441 Grand Rapids, Michigan: Regency Reference Library, 1988.

Speaking in new tongues is a gift from God, a language of the Holy Spirit in communication between the *homo-religiosus* and God.[17] It is a divine language; when displayed, it exhibits an exclusive relationship between God and the believer. It is open and available to everyone who desires to have it. It is a sign of Christian *Ummah* or community (*communitas*) as much as a breaking point with the outside world. It is thus viewed by outsiders as 'anti-social', 'anti-clerical' and 'the anti-establishment of Protestantism.'

"Centripetal" and "Centrifugal"

Centripetal move is in line with what Prophet Isaiah [49: 6, NLT] says: I will make you a light to the Gentiles, and you will bring my salvation to the ends of the earth. The light of Christ, which shines in the darkness draws people to it in a centripetal nature. Centripetal mission/evangelism definitely points to churches that are "centre-seeking", since they push towards the centre or revolve around the middle, and are passive. This type of missions was typical of Old Testament times, where Jerusalem, the tabernacle and the Temple were all concentrated in one place. They attract the people with the message: "Come to blessing!"

Conversely, when missions start to push away from the centre instead of pulling towards it, they are centrifugal in their strategy and approach. The term emanates from the Latin root, meaning "to flee from the centre". It is here that the Great Commission given by Jesus in Matthew 28:19-20 takes centre stage. It is an invitation to all the ethnic nationalities of the whole globe to come to the saving grace and relationship with God through his son, Jesus Christ. It calls for a very active participation, exploding in power and performing exploits across borders and entering new frontiers even if it means entering as chaplains without border, as prisoners in chains or as God's smugglers.

If we consider that the Old Testament views missions centripetally, that is, the nation's coming towards Israel as we have done above, and that the New Testament understanding is centrifugal, that is, from the centre, as Israel or the Church and its missionaries move outward, in response to the Great Commission of Matthew 28:18-19, into the world, we may not be having a complete picture. Even though the Old Testament undoubtedly and truly views mission predominantly in centripetal categories, this is, however, not

---

[17] Daniel Brandt-Bessire, *Aux Sources De La Spiritualite Pentecostiste*, Geneva: Labor et Fides, 1986, 174.

exclusively so.[18] Bosch argues for the need of a perfect balance between the two, when he asserts that:

> The metaphor of light in Isaiah 42:6, 49:6, and elsewhere, is particularly appropriate to give expression to both a centripetal and a centrifugal movement. A light shining in the darkness draws, people towards it, centripetally, yet at the same time it goes outward, crossing frontiers, allowing, in the words of Isaiah 49:6, God's salvation to reach 'to earth's farthest bounds.'[19]

Ramon Sarró and Ann Mélice discuss the centripetal and centrifugal dynamics of Kimbaguism, showing how marginal nodes in Kimbanguist networks could easily invert from their peripheral status and become the source of important doctrinal innovations or religious activities.[20]

Progressive-Pentecostalism

Progressive Pentecostalism unveiled a paradigm shift from the stereotype that focuses exclusively on salvation and heaven. Many *Pente* churches, including mission churches in Nigeria, are involved in development initiatives in the face of massive corruption, the 'failed state' status of the Nigerian nation and the destructive nature of anti-establishment movements to Christianity, such as Maitatsine, the Boko Haram movement, and many other fundamentalist groups among others. In propounding the notion of Progressive Pentecostalism, Don Miller and Yamamori, define it "as Christians who claim to be inspired by the Holy Spirit and the life of Jesus [...] seek to holistically address the spiritual, physical and social needs of people in their community."[21] We dare say that non-Christians who live a life of addressing the total/holistic needs of the members of their communities are Progressive Pentecostals by practice.

---

[18] Don Fanning, "The Old Testament and Missions", *Themes of Theology that Impacts Missions*, Paper 1, Centre for Global Ministries Liberty University, http://digitalcommons@liberty.edu/cgm theo/1, 2009:16.

[19] David J. Bosch, "Witness to the World." In: Ralph Winter and Steven C. Hawthorne (eds.), *Perspectives*, 27-33 Pasadena, CA.: William Carey Library, 2000, 60.

[20] Ramon Sarró and Ann Mélice, "Kongo - Lisbon: Dialectics of 'Centre' and 'Periphery' in the Kimbanguist Church." In: S. Fancello and A. Mary (eds). *Chrétiens Africans en Europe*, Paris: Khartala, 2010 and Natalia Zawiejska and Linda van de Kamp (March 2018), "The Multi-Polarity of Angolan Pentecostalism: Connections and Belongings", *PentecoStudies, Electronic Journal*, https://www.researchgate.net/publication/325104599, 2018, 9.

[21] Miller and Yamomoari, 21.

Corporate Social Responsibility (CSR)

Corporate Social Responsibility (CSR) has had and continues to have a plethora of definitions from different scholars, authors, theorists and researchers. Furthermore, the meaning of CSR is variegated depending on societal sectors, regions, countries, businesses and corporations. However, the concept of CSR has acquired broad support in various international fora. While there is no universally accepted definition of the concept, there is arguably a consensus that it implies a demonstration of certain responsible behaviour on the part of governments and the business sector towards society and the environment. For Mallen Baker, "Corporate Social Responsibility is about how companies manage the business processes to produce an overall positive impact on society."[22] The European Commission defines CSR as:

> A concept whereby companies decide voluntarily to contribute to a better society and a cleaner environment. A concept whereby companies integrate social and environmental concerns in their business operations and in their interaction with their stakeholders on a voluntary basis. ...CSR is the process whereby enterprises integrate social, environmental, ethical and human rights concerns into their core 1.[23]

Responsible business conduct (RBC) means that businesses should make a positive contribution.

The World Business Council for Sustainable Development (W0BCSD) defines CSR as "the continuing commitment by business to behave ethically and contribute to economic development while improving the quality of life of the workforce and their families as well as of the local community and society at large."[24] CSR can be defined as the economic, legal, ethical, and discretionary expectations that society has of organisations at a given point in time. The concept of CSR means that organisations have some measure of moral, ethical, and philanthropic responsibilities in addition to their responsibilities to earn a fair return for investors and comply with the law. A traditional view of the

---

[22] Mallen Baker, Definitions of Corporate Social Responsibility-What is CRS? Mallen Baker/ homepage/Clear reflection/mallenbaker.nets/csr/definition, 06 Feb. 2009; http://www.mallenbaker. net/csr/definition.php, accessed March 31 2014, Accessed on 11th July, 2020.

[23] EC Communication 2011, https://ec.europa.eu/growth/industry/sustainability/corporate-social-responsibility_en.

[24] Ijaiya, 62.

corporation suggests that its primary, if not sole responsibility, is to its owners or stakeholders. However, CSR requires organisations to adopt a broader view of their responsibilities that include not only stockholders, but many other constituencies as well, including employees, suppliers, consumers, the local community, local, state, and federal governments, environmental groups, and other special interest groups. Three international institutions have been at the vanguard of underlining the need for governments and companies to adhere to the principles of corporate social responsibility. These are: the World Business Council for Sustainable Development (WBCSD), the Organisation for Economic Co-operation and Development (OECD), and the Dow Jones Sustainable Indexes (DJSGI).[25]

A corporation exists primarily to make profits, according to the traditional view. This money-centred perspective is germane because it also applies to moral dilemmas arising from the struggle for profits. A conception of CSR begins to emerge when people who direct organisations and corporations begin to understand their enterprises not only in terms of profit and loss, but also in ethical ones. When organisations become in a certain moral sense, like persons in society, bound by the same kinds of duties and responsibilities that ordinary folks wrestle with on a daily basis.[26]

CSR can be defined as the "economic, legal, ethical and discretionary expectations that a society has of an organization" which in turn reflects that the "organizations have some measure of moral, ethical and philanthropic responsibilities."[27] According to Helg, CSR refers to the "set of standards to which a company subscribes in order to make its impact on society, has the potential to make positive contributions to the development of the society."[28] For him, CSR in Nigeria is socio-culturally framed even though most CSR activities are commonly accentuated with regard to multinational companies, with far less emphasis on the home-grown organisations and companies.

CSR is a general term for any theory of the corporation that emphasises the responsibilities of money-making and interacting ethically with the surrounding community. CSR is also a specific conception of responsibility

---

[25] Ijaiya, 63.
[26] Book Archive, *Business Ethics:13.2-Three Theories of Corporate Social Responsibility: Learning Objective* (Creative Commons by-nc-sa), Dec. 2012, downloaded by Andy Schmitz, 2012books. lardbucket.org; 5/26/2019.
[27] Ijaiya.
[28] A. Helg, *Corporate Social Responsibility from a Nigerian Perspective*, Goteborgs, Universitet MA thesis, Handelshogskolan Sweden, 2007, 7.

to profit-making, while playing a role in the provision of community welfare facilities.[29]

Theoretical Framework

Mainstream definitions of CSR centre their discussions and definitions along three major contours or prongs, which are economic, environmental and social structures and settings. This is what Helg calls the triple-bottom line.[30] CSR considers the well-being of three major participants or stakeholders relating to an organisation which are the employees, the host community and the broader society by gauging the ability of the organisation to champion or incorporate strategies that tackle and ensuring the sustainable progress, welfare and safety of all but not limited to these three actors.[31] CSR, according to Parast and Adams, "is used in 90% of fortune 500 companies"[32] with varying degrees of failures and successes but tilting far more towards successes.

Ahmadian and Khosrowpour look at two theories of CSR: The first is the *Efficiency theory*, which focuses on improving performance of companies, organisations and corporate entities through quality management by developing trajectories that analyse customers, the surrounding society and the community as a whole, making them all major stakeholders. The second, which is *Institutional Theory*, on the other hand, focusses on social pressures that are mounted by official agents, such as government, industrial regulators, trade or labour unions and citizens or host communities on organisations, forcing them to administer CSR.[33]

Carroll orchestrates that CSR comprises four basic societal obligations encompassing economic, legal, ethical and philanthropic responsibilities. To him, organisations are obliged to make profit as well as comply with set out laws and regulations looking also to indulge in societal norms/values

---

[29] Book Archive, *Business Ethics*.

[30] Helg, 7.

[31] P. Castka and M.A. Balzarova, "Adoption of Social Responsibility through the Expansion of existing Management Systems", *Industrial Management and Data Systems*, 108/3 (2008): 297-309, https://doi.org/10.1108/02635570810858732, cited in Ahmadian and Khosrowpour, 2017.

[32] Mahour Parast and Stephnie Adams, "Corporate Social Responsibility, Benchmarking, and Organizational Performance in the Petroleum Industry: A Quality Management Perspective", *International Journal of Petroleum Economics*, 139/2 (October, 2012): 447-458, DOI: 10.1016/j.ijpe.2011.11.033, cited in Ahmadian, A. and S. Khosrowpour, "Corporate Social Responsibility: Past, Present and Success Strategy for the Future," *Journal of Service Science*, X/1 (2017): 1-12, esp. 3.

[33] Ahmadian and Khosrowpour, 3.

even as they consider engaging in any other activities that are expected of the organisation by society to improve the general quality of life.[34] Thus, as corporations interact with their hosts or surrounding communities and the larger world, they are obligated to provide CSR in these four ways: first is the *economic responsibility* to make money; second, the proactive duty of ensuring that the *legal responsibility* to adhere to rules and regulations is upheld; third, the *ethical responsibility* to do what's right even when not required by the letter or spirit of the law (This is the theory's keystone obligation, and it depends on a coherent corporate culture that views the business itself as a citizen in society, with the kind of obligations that citizenship normally entails.) and fourth, the *philanthropic responsibility* to contribute to society's projects and general development.[35]

Matten and Moon put forward their assertions on CSR in terms of *Implicit and Explicit CSR*.[36] Explicit CSR is associated with procedures and tactics that are "voluntary and self-interest driven", while Implicit CSR are government and non-governmental "corporate policies with the objective of being responsible for what interest society."[37]

CSR connotes the taking up of responsibilities by businesses to society and stakeholders beyond their shareholders as part of a commitment to addressing pertinent societal challenges.[38] According to Wang, corporations now have dedicated branches established to create and run their community commitments, that is, CSR offices.[39] While social and environmental insecurities are at the centre of the deliberations on CSR,[40] they point to the

---

[34] A.B. Carroll, "A Three-dimensional Conceptual Model of Corporate Performance", *The Academy of Management Review*, 4/4 (1979): 497–505; A.B. Carroll, "The Pyramid of Corporate Social Responsibility: Toward the Moral Management of Organizational Stakeholders", *Business Horizons*, 34 (1991): 39–48. http://dx.doi.org/10.1016/0007-6813(91)90005-G; and A.B. Carroll, "The four faces of corporate citizenship", *Business & Society Review*, 100/1 (1999): 1-7. http://dx.doi.org/10.1111/0045-3609.00008.

[35] Book Archive, *Business Ethics*.

[36] Dirk Matten and Jeremy Moon, "'Implicit' and 'Explicit' CSR: A Conceptual Framework for Understanding CSR in Europe", No. 29, *ICCSR Research Paper Series*, International Centre for Corporate Social Responsibility, ed. Dirk Matten, Nottingham University Business School, Nottingham University, Nottingham, UK, 2004 cited in Helg, 20.

[37] Hegl, 20.

[38] Heli Wang, Li Tong, Riki Takeuchi, and Gerard George, "Corporate Social Responsibility: An Overview and New Research Directions", *Academy of Management Journal*, LIX/2 (Feb. 2016): 534-544.

[39] Wang, Tong, Takeuchi and George, 536.

[40] K. Amaeshi, B. Adi, C. Ogbechie and O. Amao (2006). *Corporate Social Responsibility (CSR) in Nigeria: Western mimicry or indigenous practices?* Nottingham University, Nottingham University Business School, Nottingham: International Centre for Corporate Social Responsibility, 2006, 5.

insecurities that poverty manifests in a nation with vast amount of resources, environmental decadence and structural imbalances that allow fraud to become a norm in the entire system.

The European Union's Green paper defines CSR as "a concept whereby companies integrate social and environmental concerns in their business operations and in their interaction with stakeholders on a voluntary basis".[41] McWilliams and Siegel consider it to be "actions that appear to further some social good, beyond the interests of the firm and that which is required by law."[42] Amaeshi, Adi, Ogbechie and Aamao view CSR "as a way for companies to reach out to their host communities by positively impacting on their environ; a way of saying thank you and showing a sense of belonging to the society; philanthropy."[43] Since most firms are an upshoot of their surroundings both socially and economically,[44] this essentially means that they have a responsibility (CSR) to these communities that influence, shape and keep them in business as a way of giving back some facilities to them.

CSR considers businesses to be a part of the community as its actions have intermittent effects on the environment, poverty, employment, education and human development.[45] Citing Miller and Gutherie along with Bénabou and Tirole, Khan *et al.* state that societal issues have mounted pressures on businesses which ultimately led to responses in the form of CSR.[46] They believe that the drivers and possible expected outcomes of businesses overlie and intertwine with the communities they are located in.

There has to be a relationship between these firms/businesses and their immediate environments be it formal or informal, laws or ethics. CSR obliges firms, businesses and organisations to contribute to the improvement of quality of life in their immediate societies in a sustainable manner that can foster long-term sustainable value to the investors and owners creating a win-

---

[41] Amaeshi, Adi, Ogbechie and Aamao, 5 and Ahmadian and Khosrowpour, 3.
[42] Amaeshi, Adi, Ogbechie and Aamao, 5.
[43] Amaeshi, Adi, Ogbechie and Aamao, 23.
[44] Amaeshi, Adi, Ogbechie and Aamao, 23.
[45] M.T. Khan, N.A. Khan, S. Ahmed and M. Ali, "Corporate Social Responsibility: Definition, Concepts and Scope (A Review)", *Universal Journal of Management and Social Sciences*, II/7 (2012): 41-52.
[46] Justin I. Miller and Doug Guthrie, "The Rise of Corporate Social Responsibility: An Institutional Response to Labor, Legal, and Shareholder Environments", *Institutional Determinants of CSR*, 7-22 (Stern School of Business, New York University, 2007; Roland Bénabou and Jean Tirole, "Incentives and Prosocial Behaviour", *The American Economic Review*, 96/5 (Dec. 2006): 1652-1678 and Khan, Khan, Ahmed and Ali, 43.

win situation.[47] They go on to assert that government policies and business strategies reinvigorate and stabilise CSR.

CSR is used as an opportunity to meet the demands and needs of society as well as to profit from the said societies. Businesses and companies thus try to balance the interplay between profit and societal demands to compete in society so as to gain comparative advantage. Ahmadian and Khosrowpour consider the effective execution of CSR by some companies and businesses to lure their rivals to also participate in CSR in what they call pre-emptive CSR.[48]

In Nigeria, though the practice of CSR is yet to take up proper roots, however, pockets of strong clamour for it can be found in some instances around the nation. A prevalent example can be seen in the South-South geo-political zone of Nigeria where for decades now the inhabitants continue to pursue "social justice and environmental protection"[49] in the oil-producing area where the profit-making interests of multi-national corporations are backed by federal government laws, leaving the people with environmental denigration and pollution, diminishing farmlands and low fish producing creeks. In fact, the inhabitants of communities whose homelands are affected suffer huge losses which are not in any way commensurate to the kickbacks that eventually trickle down to a few leaders of devastated communities. The conflict that continues unabated between host communities and the oil firms in the face of government neglect of environmental rights, massive corruption and safeguard of the business interests of the firms involved in oil and gas extraction led to the firms engaging in some form of CSR in the immediate host communities by providing basic amenities such as water, roads, schools, clinics and employment.[50] As part of CSR positive societal impacts on the Niger Delta region of Nigeria, there has been a clamour for oil companies to express the utility of their investments in Nigeria by committing themselves to intensive community development strategies aimed at delivering explicit communal satisfaction to their host communities.[51]

Though CSR is not part of the mandatory laws required to be implemented by companies, Ijaiya argues that the Nigerian law obliges a company to maintain and ensure that air, water and land within its operational

---

[47] Ahmadian and Khosrowpour, 4.
[48] Ahmadian and Khosrowpour, 5.
[49] Amaeshi, Adi, Ogbechie and Aamao, 16.
[50] Amaeshi Adi, Ogbechie and Aamao, 16.
[51] Ijaiya, 65.

community are not polluted. This completely is in contrast to the operations of oil companies in the Niger Delta and also other big, medium and small companies operating in the nation with total disregard of the harm their activities could pose to their host communities with no present or future plans to engage in CSR.[52]

Hegl contrasts the drivers of CSR in the West and in Nigeria. CSR in the West is driven by customer satisfaction as competition to deliver on customer satisfaction fuels the drive for contemporary values as consumer expectations surge towards the responsibility of companies, their products and their principles. CSR in Nigeria, on the other hand, is largely driven by philanthropy when private businesses complement the activities of government in resolving the socio-economic deficits in their societies.[53]

The Interplay between Religion and CSR

Some authors like Chryssides and Kaler trace the history of CSR to the Roman Catholic Church in the medieval period when several facets of society and business were guided by some laws as to what regards "legitimate behaviour."[54] Examples were traced by the authors to the Laws of Moses that required farmers during harvest to allow leftovers of crops for the poor to glean, sabbath rest for servants, and cancellation of debts spanning over fifty years, among others.

Religion has continued to play a major role in compelling businesses and large organisations to take positive conscious actions towards CSR. This drive has largely been driven by the Interfaith Centre on CSR comprising Christianity, Islam and Judaism in establishing principles that could function as parameters for global corporate conduct.[55] They go on to state that "organized religion has sought to play a significant role in establishing and disseminating moral and ethical prescriptions that are consistent with religious doctrines and that offer practical guidance to those involved in business concerning ethical conduct."[56] Brammer, Williams and Zinkin further argue that religiously motivated persons develop a better orientation to CSR as they

---

[52] Ijaiya, 66.
[53] Hegl, 25.
[54] George D. Chryssides and John H. Kaler, *An Introduction to Business Ethics*, 1st ed., London and New York: Chapman & Hall, 1993.
[55] S. Brammer, G. Williams and J. Zinkin, "Religion and Attitudes to Corporate Social Responsibility in a Large Cross-Country Sample," *Journal of Buisiness Ethics*, (2007): 229-243.
[56] Brammer, Williams and Zinkin, 229.

try to demonstrate the link between religion and ethical values especially in managerial decision making.

Some religious bodies have tried and continue to advocate international corporations to utilise their influence to impact the common good through CSR.[57] Finn characterises the CSR of a particular corporation to be a direct reflection of the religion, values and character of the owner of the company or business. He goes on to argue that the debate by communities on the processes to regulate businesses within them is hinged on the impact of religion in such societies. He considers the basic principles of religion such as "honesty, transparency, responsibility, fairness and integrity" to be fully entrenched in social contracts.[58]

Shrestha states that religion and businesses relish in a multifaceted, multi-level and a symbiotic relationship. Shrestha goes on to postulate that religion contributes to business goal accomplishments by regulating the affiliation connecting the quest for physical prosperity and the subsequent subjective gratification which is in turn influenced by the religious values of the actors involved. Shrestha buttresses this point by alluding to how CSR is strongly influenced by adherents of religious values that naturally flow into their moral values compared to non-adherents.[59] Shrestha links CSR to Hinduism based on the *Vedic* and *Veda* philosophy of *Dharma* [moral and all-round duty, vindicated in caste, *varna/jati* duty] and *Sharma* [the feeling of joyfulness, comfort and/or happiness, expressive of the 'good things in life']. This Vedic philosophy as expounded by Shrestha describes business ethics as the "application of the principles of right social behaviour" [*dharma*] based on "prosperity, satisfaction of desires, moral duty and spiritual perfection" [*Sharma*], while the Veda philosophy gives room for the accumulation of wealth through "the right path" [*yoga/marga*] that allows the individual or business to "serve the needs of society."[60]

The *Dharma* concept outlined in the study refers to actions aimed at the long-term uplift of the living standards of all in the community linking work (including businesses) to the benefit of all, without any forms of exploitation and also ensuring sustainability for generations to come rather than just

---

[57] S. Finn, S. *About Us: A. HuffPost Community Publication*, 2011. Retrieved from http://www.huffpost.com
[58] Finn, 1.
[59] B. K. Shrestha, "Religious Ethics and Socially Responsible Behaviors of Small Firms in Nepal," *Journal of Religion and Business Ethics*, III/5 (2017): 1-16.
[60] Shrestha, 2-3.

personal interest and profit. The *Sharma* concept, on the other hand, identifies that "individual and corporate actions should be driven by welfare of all and survival of all."[61] Shrestha also links CSR to Buddhism which enshrines living right as the panacea to build up the ethical standards that ensure good business behaviour. This right living points to "earning a living responsibly and in a righteous way by accepting the *karmic* consequences of one's actions."[62] Moreover, for Shrestha, the Buddhist approach to CSR considers a sustainable way of using the earth's resources, acquiring wealth and conducting business without *ahimsa*, causing harm or suffering to others.

There are opposing notions by other theorists who postulate that religious groups that have a very high penchant for ethics and values have made very minute and peripheral contributions to the discussion on CSR.[63] These discussions they say have filtered through every facet of human life (social, economic and environmental) except for the religious facet which is usually juxtaposed with the social facet. This gross neglect can be paraded as one of the reasons why acquiescence in CSR has not been achieved worldwide despite self, government and international regulations to ensure CSR is mainstreamed and upheld.[64]

Persons working in business corporations have become very conscious of their business actions and inactions in line with their religious and moral ethics. Raimi *et al.* thus posit that "religious ethics and values could be better drivers for strengthening CSR compliance" in the face of "failed or failing regulations."[65] Using the Faith Based Model, Brammer et al. aver that the expectations of religious adherents from a corporation are moulded based on their various faiths. As such Raimi *et al.* posit that "embedding CSR within faith-based systems has the potency of solving the challenges of evasion and non-compliance by corporations owned by faith-based individuals (Muslim, Christian and Jews), because CSR stands on the ethical and theological foundations of the Laws of God."[66] Citing Dasuki, they expound that noncompliance is "an affront to God's will" with repercussions here on earth and in the afterlife.[67]

---

[61] Shrestha, 3.
[62] Shrestha, 3.
[63] L. Raimi, A. Patel, K. Yekini and A. Aljadani, , "Theological Foundation of Corperate Social Responsibility in Islam, Christianity and Judaism: Prospects for Strengthening Compliance and Reporting". *E3 Journal of Business Management and Economics*, 6 (2014): 131-141.
[64] Raimi, Patel, Yekini and Aljadani, 132.
[65] Raimi, Patel, Yekini and Aljadani, 132.
[66] See Raimi, Patel, Yekini and Aljadani, 134.
[67] See Raimi, Patel, Yekini and Aljadani, 134.

Judaism echoes CSR through its Hebrew text and Talmudic laws that encourage love, giving, sharing and benevolence. Here, free will and voluntary compliance to CSR surfaces "as an extension of love to the larger society."[68] Further, Judaism credits the *Tzedakah* system, which is an obligation to provide for the needy no matter your level in society.[69] The community is very central to the Jews as well as family and as such, CSR is very pertinent to their charitable and philanthropic conducts.[70] CSR in Islam is drawn from *Zakat*, *Sadaqat* and *Waqf*, which are all geared towards aiding the disadvantaged in society. These three responsibilities work to solicit obligatory generosity, voluntary generosity and charitable donations respectively from adherents to the Islamic faith.[71] Islamic tenets for corporate and individual entities advocate principles such as *"Tawheed* (unity), *Al'adl wal Ishan* (equilibrium), *Ikhtiar* (free will) and *Fardh* (social responsibility)" with all reciprocally supporting one another.[72]

Mentioning Tounes *et al.* highlight the earliest proponents of CSR to be the Protestants and then the Catholics promoting public service and stewardship to alleviate the plight of the poor in a general concern for public welfare. "The church's philosophy inculcated ethical consciousness among business owners" of the Christian faith. These assertions take root from "Judeo-Christian scriptures, Bible and Hebrew traditions,"[73] which preach against worldliness and pushing faithful ones towards love, brotherliness and selfless service which they opine are far more superior to business success. Victory thus becomes synonymous to "public service, doing of good, love thy neighbour and shunning evil of covetousness" rather than physical quantifiable achievements.[74] Capitalism and giant strides in the growth of businesses globally but especially in Europe and America are also closely linked to the progressive mindsets of Pentecostalism.[75]

---

[68] Lin, C.K.F, "Religion and Corporate Social Responsibility", http://www.cliffordlin.com/religion-and-corporate-social-responsibility (Accessed: 22/02/2014), cited in Raimi, Patel, Yekini and Aljadani, 137.

[69] R.R. Tracey, "Tzedakah: Charity", http://www.jewfaq.org/tzedakah.htm, 2011 (Accessed: 21 Feb., 2014), cited in Raimi, Patel, Yekini and Aljadani, 137.

[70] Raimi, Patel, Yekini and Aljadani, 137.

[71] Raimi, Patel, Yekini and Aljadani, 135.

[72] Raimi, Patel, Yekini and Aljadani, 135.

[73] Raimi, Patel, Yekini and Aljadani, 136-137.

[74] Ryan Wilson, "Business Ethics: Western and Islamic Perspectives", In: K. Ahmed and A. M. Sadeq (eds.), *Ethics in Business and Management: Islamic and Mainstream Approach*, London: Asean Academic Press, 2001; Raimi, Patel, Yekini and Aljadani, 137.

[75] See Raimi, Patel, Yekini and Aljadani, 137.

A Brief History of the RCCG

Even though the RCCG today is in the fastest-growing Church in Nigeria and in Africa,[76] and it is "one of Africa's most rigorously expansionary movements, a homegrown Pentecostal denomination that is considerably becoming a global faith,"[77] it started from humble beginnings. The early stage of the RCCG is thus likened by the Church to the "day of small things."[78] The motto of the RCCG, "Jesus Christ the same yesterday, and today, and forever", is picked from Hebrews 13:8.

Pa Reverend Josiah Olufemi Akindayomi (b. 5 July 1909; d. 2 November 1980), the founding father of RCCG was initially converted in 1927 into Christianity from Yoruba religion, especially Ogun worship, by the CMS in Ondo town. He converted because the Yoruba indigenous religion did not satisfy his spiritual hunger and yearnings. Moreover, he strongly wanted to fulfil the will of God and in the process acquire Western education, which the CMS provided.[79]

He then joined the Eternal Sacred Order of Cherubim and Seraphim (C&S) in Ebute-Metta, Lagos, in 1931. While as a member of the C&S, which was one of the early Aladura movements in Yoruba land, he rose to the rank of apostle and prophet. It was while with the C&S, between 1934 and 1938 that the RCCG appeared mostly akin to the White Garments Churches, under his charismata as pioneer founder and first leader.[80]

---

[76] Asonzeh J.F. Ukah, "Roots and Goals: Nigeria's Redeemed Christian Church of God", *Atlas of Pentecostalism*, January 13. 2014, http://www.pulitzer.org/repository/roots-and-goals-nigeria's-redeemed-christian-church-of-god.

[77] A. Rice, "Mission from Africa", *New York Times*, April 12. 2009, para 5, Retrieved from http://www.nytimes.com/2009/04/12/magazine/12Churches-t-html?pagewanted=all.

[78] See [small pamphlet] Tony Ojo, *RCCG in Prophecy*, 1997 and J.A. Lawanson "Redeemed in Prophecy" *Redemption Light*, 5(10), Nov. 2000, 9 and Asonzeh F.-K. Ukah, *The Redeemed Christian Church of God (RCCG), Nigeria Local Identities and Globalization Processes in African Pentecostalism*, Uni-Bayreuth, Dissertation Bayreuth/Germany 2003, 41.

[79] Moses A Adekola, "The Redeemed Christian Church of God: A Study of an Indigenous Pentecostal Church in Nigeria," Obafemi Awolowo University Ph.D. Thesis, Ile-Ife, Nigeria, 1989, 56; Olusola Ajayi, *Warrior of Righteousness: The Life and Ministry of Rev. J. O. Akindayomi*, Abeokuta: Ordinance Publishing House, 1997; RCCG at 50; Insa Nolte, Nathaniel Danjibo and Abubakar Oladeji, "Religion, Politics and Governance in Nigeria." In *Religions and Development Research Programme, Working Paper* 39, RAD, International Development Department, University of Birmingham, UK, 2009, 55 and Ukah, *The Redeemed Christian Church of God*, 2, 45.

[80] Adebisi R. Tijani, "The Establishment of the Redeemed Christian Church of God in Ilesa." Oyo State College of Education NCE Project, Religious Studies, Ilesa, 1985; RCCG at 50, 16; K.J. Erinoso, "The Life and Ministry of Pastor Adeboye, The General Overseer of The Redeemed Christian Church of God", Long Essay submitted to the Department of Religions, Lagos State University, Nigeria, 1999, 16; Oyelakin Olusegun Babatunde, "The Role of Internet on Evangelism: A Study of Redeemed Christian of God," Long Essay submitted to the Department of Religious Studies, University of Ibadan, Ibadan, Nigeria, 2000, 12, and Ukah, *The Redeemed Christian Church of God*, 42-43.

The RCCG was established as a church by a group of twelve former members of the C&S Church in 1952 led by Revd. Josiah Olufemi Akindayomi. After leaving the C&S, he established a religious group, which became known by a divinely revealed name: the Redeemed Christian Church of God (RCCG). The RCCG began when the Lord established his *Berith*, "Covenant" with the founder, which led to the huge success experienced by the Church. The RCCG started worship services at No. 9, Willoughby Street, Ebute-Metta, Lagos and later moved to the present location of the National Headquarters at 1-5, Redemption Way, Ebute-Metta (formerly 1a, Cemetery Street).[81]

Max Weber's theory of *routinization of charisma* shows a startling achievement in the case of transfer of *charismata* from Revd. Josiah Olufemi Akindayomi to his successor Pastor Enoch Adejare Adeboye, who was a Lecturer of Mathematics at the University of Lagos, Nigeria and Revd. Josiah Akindayomi's interpreter. When the founder and "oil carrier" of the RCCG died in 1980, the RCCG had 39 branches in the southwest of Nigeria. Thus, from the "days of small beginnings", the RCCG has grown into a mega church. When Pastor Enoch Adeboye took over the mantle of leadership (as General Overseer) in 1981, the RCCG expanded rapidly both within Nigeria and outside Nigeria, such that by 2000, the RCCG had over three thousand branches, with close to a hundred of them established abroad.[82]

The RCCG has become a transnational Pentecostal denomination and a mega church organisation, which as of March 2017 is present in 196 countries of the world. Presently, the defining character and action of the RCCG is missionary expansion as a result of its sense of eschatological urgency and its vision of having a member of the RCCG in every family of all nations and to plant churches within five minutes walking distance in every city and town of developing countries and within five minutes driving distance in every city and town of developed cities.[83]

On the international scene, the RCCG is present in Europe, North America, the Pacific, Asia, the Middle East and other countries of Africa, aside from Nigeria. The Redemption Camp at Km. 46, Lagos-Ibadan Expressway plays host to the RCCG Annual Convention that holds for one week in

---

[81] Paul Bankole and Olaitan Olubiyi, "We're Highly Favoured by God," *Redemption Light*, vol. 7/5, June 2002, 21 and Ukah, *The Redeemed Christian Church of God*, 41.

[82] Ukah, *The Redeemed Christian Church of God*, 1f.

[83] W. Bird, *The World's Largest Churches*, Retrieved August 23, 2017, from http://www.leadnet.org/world.

early August of every year, with the 2019 version attracting about 10 million Christians in its new ultra-modern mega auditorium! Former meetings had hosted five million participants for years. The Redemption Camp is also the venue of the Holy Ghost Congress that holds for one week in December. These programmes are replicated in Europe and North America for logistic reasons. The monthly programmes of the RCCG include the Holy Ghost Night, known as the Festival of Life in other locations around the world, Shiloh Hour and Divine Encounter, aside from special Holy Ghost Service that holds in higher institutions of learning. The RCCG events are transmitted live on television, radio and are streamed live on the Internet. The Church runs Bible Colleges and School of Disciples headquartered in Nigeria, with many campuses in the United Kingdom, Europe, Qatar and other continents.[84]

Two major types of parishes exist in the RCCG. These are the Classical and the Model parishes. The Classical Parishes emphasizes holiness, represents an apocalyptical or prophetic movement preparing and waiting for the coming of the end of the world. The Classical parish type largely belongs to the epoch of Revd. Josiah Olufemi Akindayomi the founder of RCCG. But the Model Parishes emphasise modernity, prosperity and rightly see nothing wrong with genuine quest for wealth in line with Exodus 11:2, 12:35, 25:3; Joshua 1:8-9, 2 Chronicles 1:15, 9:1; Job 22:21-30 and Haggai 2:8. The RCCG is Christ-centred and regards Him alone as the index of grace and salvation, as opposed to scholars who erroneously believe that the RCCG emphasises materialism and wealth as the sole indices of grace and salvation.

The model parishes conduct their liturgy mainly in English, accompanied by electronic musical instruments of praise to God. Some members are superrich, mobile middle-and-high class income-earners persons who live in strategic and highbrow suburban areas of cities and operate businesses in city centres.[85] This is so because the RCCG teaches members to develop the correct business ideas and prayerfully pursue their goals with the fear of God, while evangelicals and orthodox churches in Nigeria have tenaciously held on to a theology of poverty. They are highly influenced by the single verse which says: "The love of money is the root of all evil". Even though they also

---

[84] R. Bible-Davids, *Enoch Adeboye: Father of Nations*, Charlotte: Biblos Publishers, 2009; Samuel Oluwatosin Okanlawon, "Churchpreneurship in the Nigerian Socio-economic Space with particular reference to the Redeemed Christian Church of God and Living Faith Church Worldwide," *ASJ: International Journal of Religions and Traditions* (IJRT) Vol. 4/1 (July 2018): 32-41 esp. 34.

[85] Abisoye, "President Buhari Felicitates with Pastor Adeboye at 74," *Channelstv.com*. March 1, 2016, Retrieved from http://www.channelstv.com/tag/general-overseer-of-the-redeemed-christan-church-of-god.

believe they and their members are heaven-bound, they have taught their members the biblical virtue and importance of money. *Pente* churches believe in prosperity and teach their members to prosper, while simultaneously shunning 'materialism.'

The RCCG Corporate/Christian Social Responsibility (CSR) Mission Enterprise

The RCCG refers to Corporate Social Responsibility (CSR) as Christian Social Responsibility. It is clear that the RCCG has been engaged in CRS activities for quite a long time. The RCCG states on its official website that Christian Social Responsibility (CSR) has its root in Christianity, since CSR is a part of the mandate of the Church. The Church is meant to be an example for the world in the area of CSR. The RCCG officially states that:

> We see Christian social responsibility as a conscious avenue for Christians to make visible impact in various key areas of society. Where many see societal challenges and its scale all around the world. We see an opportunity to take decisive effort to creating solutions as we work with people, communities, leaders and governments worldwide. The RCCG has CSR in 196 countries worldwide.[86]

General Overseer of RCCG appointed Pastor Idowu Illuyomade to be his Special Assistant on CSR with an office within the RCCG organisational structure. Thus, there is a Corporate Social Responsibility (CSR) department in each province of the RCCG, aside from the overall office at the headquarters. This unit is saddled with the role of appropriate response to the social, economic, and health concerns of where the province is situated. Therefore, each province of the church, comprising various Parishes, has been mandated to organise empowerment programmes for church members and people residing in their church communities.[87]

The RCCG CSR programmes cover both Africa and the Diaspora, providing an equilibrium between both spiritual and material welfare of Church communities. Its CSR activities cover social welfare, vocational training, orphanages, health institutions, outreaches to drug addicts, street urchins, prostitutes and HIV/AIDS victims, scholarship programmes, free

---

[86] Satcsr@rccg.org

[87] A. Ademigbuji and D. Adejo, "Embracing CSR: The RCCG Example," *The Nation*, January 22, 2016, Retrieved from http://www.thenationonlineng.net/embracing-csr-the-rccg-example.

healthcare services, among others. A huge amount of money is budgeted annually to cover these humanitarian activities worldwide.[88] The RCCG provinces have been mandated to initiate and implement projects within their localities in tandem with their peculiar needs and socio-economic challenges of communities to complement government's efforts in providing basic amenities for the citizens.[89]

Chart 1: Source: The RCCG Website

In fact, the CSR activities of the RCCG presented on its official website cover eight wide areas of interventions. These in include: health, education, media, business, art and culture, governance, social and sports. The CSR projects of the RCCG are located all over the world in places where the church is found (see chart 1).

Health Care: The RCCG provides facilities towards improving primary healthcare, getting doctors to rural areas, reducing treatment costs, and providing follow-up on health checks. The Church encourages its parishes to engage in health advocacy, and in the provision of medical support with drugs and treatment of infected persons, including donation of equipment and ambulances to government-owned hospitals in their communities.[90] It is interesting to note that the RCCG runs the following health institutions:

[88] Okanlawon, 34.
[89] O. Latona, "RCCG Empowers Over 700 People," *Vanguard* Newspaper, April 28. 2013, Retrieved from http://wwwvanguardngr.com/2003/04/rccg-empowers-over-700-people.
[90] N. Ojiego, "RCCG Floats Charity Organisation", *Vanguard* Newspaper, March 6, 2014, Retrieved from http://www.vanguardngr.com/2014/03.rccg-floats-charity-organisation, P. John, "RCCG Region 5 Camp Clinic Begins Skeletal Services", *The Health Post,* July 2, 2017, Retrieved from http://www.thehealthpost.org/rccg-camp-clinic-begins-skeletal-services, T. Olofinlua, "Nigeria Struggles to Shift Maternal Health Care Locally to Tackle Mortality Rate", *Global Press Journal*, May 3. 2013, Retrieved from http://www.globalpressjournal.com/africa/nigeria/nigeria-struggles-to-shift-maternal-health-care-locally-to-tackle-mortality-rate.

Healing Stripes Hospital, Victoria Island, Lagos, Wellspring Rehabilitation Centre, Ojodu; Christ Against Drug Abuse Ministry, Ikeja (CRADAM); House of Joy, Surulere; New Life Drug Addicts Rehabilitation Centre, Lekki; Redeemed Christian Church of God Maternity Centre, Ibadan; RCCG Health Centre, Ogun State, among others.[91] Furthermore, the RCCG has built and managed clinics in many regions lacking healthcare services and personnel around the world. For instance,

> On Friday 10th of May 2019, an ultra-modern 3-bed Intensive Care Unit (ICU) equipment supplied and installed by JNC International Ltd, was commissioned by Pastor E.A. Adeboye, the General Overseer of The Redeemed Christian Church of God at the Plateau Specialist Hospital [PLSH], Jos. The Commissioning had in attendance the Plateau Sate Governor, represented by the Deputy Governor, Prof. Sunny Gwanle Tyoden, the Special Assistant to the General Overseer on Christian Social Responsibility (CSR), Idowu Illuyomade and other senior pastors of the Church.[92]

Furthermore, the PLSH Jos ICU Project of the RCCG, which was named the Folu Adeboye Intensive Care Unit is the second in the series of the RCCG CRS interventions in healthcare in Nigeria, built and equipped in partnership with JNC International Ltd. The first is the Enoch and Folu Adeboye Intensive Care Unit in the Lagos State University Teaching Hospital (LASUTH), which was opened in 2017. The operational Folu Adeboye ICU at the PLSH, Jos was equipped with the following high-tech medical facilities: Servo Air Ventilators, enterprise CR 5000 4-section electric profiling ICU beds, hospital matrasses, portable patient monitors, Volumetric Infusion and Syringe Pumps, Suctioning Machines, bedside lockers, Patient Conveyance Trolleys and Arterial Gas Analysers.[93] The RCCG has also provided water projects across Nigeria, especially in remote communities hosting their missionaries.[94] Further to this, in the wake of the current COVID-19 pandemic, the RCCG was one of the faith-based organisations that joined the effort in supporting the relief measures in Nigeria. The RCCG CSR initiative donated 8,000 hands

---

[91] Okanlawon, 32.

[92] Pastor Adeboye Commissions 3-Bed ICU: Another RCCG CSR Project Completed by JNCI". https//www.jnciltd.com›media›news›pastor-adeboye-commissions-3-Bed-ICU-Friday 10th May 2019.

[93] "Pastor Adeboye Commissions 3-Bed ICU: Another RCCG CSR Project Completed by JNCI". https//www.jnciltd.com›media›news›pastor-adeboye-commissions-3-Bed-ICU-Friday 10th May 2019.

[94] O. Michael, "NGO's Non-Profit and Humanitarian Activities in Nigeria Water Industry", *Hydrate*, July 24. 2014, http://www.hydratelife.org/ngos-non-profit-and-humanitarian-activities-in-the-nigerian-water-industry.

sanitizers, 8,000 Surgical Face Masks and 20,000 hand gloves at Mainland Hospitals Yaba.[95]

Education: In the education sector, the RCCG actively participates in the building of schools in neglected and hard to reach regions of the world by supporting existing schools with building new classrooms, teaching facilities and power generating equipment, aside from organising training workshops for applied and technical skills. In fact, an *Africa Independent Television* report in 2013 titled *Corporate Social Responsibility: RCCG commissions* [sic] *ICT centres in two FCT secondary schools* reports on the RCCG opening of ICT centres in two government secondary schools in the FCT as part of its CSR programmes. The RCCG leadership stated that the gesture was in line with the Federal Government Initiative of Public-Private Partnership (PPP). This intervention was provided by the RCCG, FCT Province 3 to offer internet facilities to the Junior Secondary School, Nyanya II and Government Secondary School, Mpape, all in the FCT. The RCCG did this because while most private secondary schools provide their students with ICT amenities, many public schools lack such facilities.[96]

Chart 2: Source: The RCCG Website

[95] Nifemi Taiyese, "How Faith Based Organizations Support the Containment of COVID 19 in Nigeria", *Proshare-Intelligent Investigating Blog, Health & Religion* 2296 VIEWS, FAITH-BASED, Sunday, April 04, 2020/2.00PM/Nifemi Taiyese for WebTV/Header Image Credit: African Health Science.

[96] Africa Independent Television (AIT) report in 2013 titled: Corporate Social Responsibility: RCCG commissions ICT centres in two FCT secondary schools,

Media: The RCCG has an up to date and well-equipped Media Unit, which broadcasts solely Christian programmes on more than 28 local television channels as well as on satellite/terrestrial television known as the Redemption Television Ministry (RTM). It also runs the Dove Media cable and satellite TV station that disseminates the presence, images and ideas of the Church and its leaders to the global community. Through its media houses, the RCCG continues to create platforms to inform, educate, edify and entertain the public through its Christ-centred programmes. Through its programmes, the Media Unit teaches members to look towards heaven, while living on earth and to exploit the earth, while focusing on heaven.[97]

The RCCG thus feeds the public with alternative spiritual food, aside from its germane and accurate information on vital issues affecting public health, security, climate change and food, such as the current COVID-19 pandemic. In fact, the RCCG operates guest houses and executive chalets opened to the general public, tourists, visitors and members alike, and it has become as a form of "a Christian Disneyland."[98] The Haggai Community Bank owned by the RCCG developed the Haggai Estates, adjacent to the Congress Arena inside the Redemption Camp, comprising semi-detached duplexes, three and four-bedroom apartments and bungalows, aside from numerous other businesses and organisations operating within the RCCG Redemption Camp.

Economic Empowerment: The business wing of the RCCG CSR intervention aims at the creation, funding and growing of businesses of various sizes and to various stages. Its economic empowerment and business education programmes target indigent members of society. The RCCG business project provides aid for advocacy, skills acquisition and for the creation of co-operative societies.

Art and Culture: The RCCG art and culture (including entertainment) intervention project helps to galvanise the bringing of people together to share ideas that will make them better. The RCCG uses this platform to continuously create and support the recreational centres and regional 'talent search' competitions. This same unit continually develops documentaries, TV shows and drama skits for variegated Christ-centred theatres across the world.

---

[97] Okanlawon, 36.
[98] Afe Adogame, "The Redeemed Christian Church of God: African Pentecostalism." In Stephen Cherry and Helen Baugh (eds.), *Global Religious Movements Across Borders: Sacred Service*, 35-60, Abingdon: Routledge, 2016, 50.

Good Governance: At the level of provision of good political governance, the RCCG proactively participates in public engagements with government bodies on how governance and policies could improve society. The Church works with governments on various public engagement projects. While ample funding is provided by the Church for the organisation and participation in sporting events in various communities in different nations. This is because sports are an emotional, mental and physical adventure. It ignites passion within people as well and a sense of collaboration, achievement, self-discipline, talent and team spirit.

Social Welfare and Sports: Finally, the RCCG tirelessly engages and plunges itself into doing a great deal of social works. This is aimed at ending and/or greatly diminishing poverty in all its forms, everywhere by strategically creating opportunities and empowering people of all nations. The Church is working untiringly towards ending hunger, achieving food security and promoting sustainable agriculture to realise high level improvement of nutrition. For example, Aligogo Ugo reports that the RCCG Lagos Province 40 embarked on the feeding of 50 million persons as part of CSR initiative during the Christmas season of 2018. At the occasion, Pastor Peter Olawale, the Special Assistant to the General Overseer of the RCCG in charge of Prayers said:

> Many are out there dying, those who don't have any hope, so we are actually extending our hands to feed and treat them through our medical outreach and through this initiative, this will help to increase their love for Christ and serve him….This initiative has been there for over 30 years, we do it twice in a year, in April during Easter period and December during Christmas period.[99]

Aligogo stated further, the Assistant Provincial Pastor, Lagos Province 40, in charge of CSR, Pastor Tony Agah remarked that:

> We want to support government by rehabilitating Schools, Roads, organize medical check-ups, and other things needed. This will help build a better nation and economy. The government alone cannot do all these things, so the church has to come in to complement the government…. We have renovated three schools so far that were dilapidated. We bring down old structures and build new ones for

---

[99] Ugo Aliogo, "In CRS Initiative, Church Supports Less Privileged," *Life & Style*, Dec. 27, 2018, https://www.thisdaylive.com

students to feel comfortable and learn because they are the future leaders of our great nation.[100]

The National Youth Empowerment Initiative of the National Youth Affairs department of the RCCG empowers youths, while SHIFT introduces Church-oriented entertainment platforms such as choreography, dancing, music, singing, theatre and comedy, RISE a skills acquisition and empowerment package, National Youths Sports Festival, SHIFT Magazine, REACH: outreaches to remote communities with evangelism, CSR programmes in education, distribution of foodstuffs, clothes and urgently needed welfare materials. It is not surprising that in 2016, President Muhammadu Buhari commended Enoch Adejare Adeboye, the General Overseer of the RCCG for the social and humanitarian interventions of the Church in providing healthcare and educational services to complement the effort of government.[101] The social orientation of the RCCG has been influenced by its internal theology, its Pentecostal experience and its external social context.[102]

Conclusion: Is the RCCG Centrifugal or Centripetal?

In fact, the current level of underdevelopment and general lack of provision of social amenities by the churches, is rather, more of a negation of the general principles of Christian missions to say the least, than what is currently obtainable. It should, however, not be forgotten that when both the Protestant and Catholic missionary organisations started work in Africa, they very seldom published all of their social, economic empowerment and political programmes and activities, focusing mostly on the main missionary agenda of numbers of churches built, preaching centres reached, converts made and baptisms conducted, among others that promoted the spiritual aspect of missions. The salvation of their converts was clearly a more urgent need and priority for the church than say the numbers of social amenities provided such as clothes, utensils, and bundles of corrugated iron sheets handed out to new converts or Christian communities. They hardly recorded the numbers of missionary houses built and number of pupils on missionary scholarships though they would place on record the numbers of clinics, hospitals and

---

[100] Aligogo, "In CRS Initiative, Church Supports Less Privileged.
[101] Okanlawon, 36; A. Abisoye, "President Buhari Felicitates with Pastor Adeboye at 74", *Channelstv. com*. March 1, 2016, Retrieved from http://www.channelstv.com/tag/general-overseer-of-the-redeemed-christan-church-of-god.
[102] Richard Burgess, "African Pentecostal Spirituality and Civic Engagement: The Case of the Redeemed Christian Church of God in Britain," *Journal of Beliefs and Values*, 30/3 (2009): 255-273.

schools built. Their records were finer when they were documenting items concerned with the work of the Holy Spirit than when they were providing statistics concerning material issues.

The RCCG started Christian Corporate Responsibility from the time of the founder, Revd. Josiah Olufemi Akindayomi, but the statistics are not available because the Church never recorded them. We remember that they used to meet in those days to pray to God to solve the problems of the Church and those of individuals. In close knit societies such as theirs, we know that there is a high sense of *assabiya*, belongingness and identity as the RCCG members. They certainly would be their brother's keepers as seen in the Church of Acts chapters 2 to 4. When the criticism of the Church became too loud, the RCCG merely made known to the whole world the CSR works it has been carrying out since its inception by transferring them to the World Wide Web.

Furthermore, the centrifugal position of any Church should be counterbalanced by its centripetal posture. This is so because the light of Christ, which simultaneously casts bright rays outwardly, provides a symbiotic balance in its implicatory centrifugal characteristic, while it simultaneously attracts peoples of all races from all over the world to Christ. This is how an anonymous writer puts it: "Our godly character and congregations; full of the power and blessings of God attract the lost. At the same time, we must persist in taking the gospel to where the people are." In fact, both the centrifugal and the centripetal thrusts are urgently needed for Christianity to flourish. The two, therefore, provide equilibrium in a world that is suffering from both abject spiritual and material deprivations. The world, especially Africa, has been relegated to extreme suffering from agents that are promoting 'spiritual-hunger' and 'spiritual death' on the one hand and physical or anatomical death from hunger, disease, natural catastrophes, psychological warfare, social alienation, political marginalisation, economic weakness, chemical warfare, extreme climate conditions and very soon technological warfare and trade-wars.

Chapter 5: Sustainable Development in Nigeria: The Interventionist Approaches to Healthcare Delivery of the Redeemed Christian Church of God, Nigeria

Babatunde Aderemi Adedibu

Introduction

Sustainable Development Goals (SDGs) heralded a new phase in developing strategies aimed at galvanising all principal stakeholders of various communities to be committed to 17 developmental objectives across the globe. The United Nations in 2016 intentionally crafted SDGs to eliminate the inadequacies of the Millennium Development Goals. The SDGs programme since its inception has been lauded for its inclusivity and holistic agenda.

The United Nations and other international development institutions are playing significant roles in initiating and sustaining various discourses on global developmental agenda through their statutory roles and commitment of their stakeholders to development agenda. The year 2015 was the target date for the actualisation of the eight Millennium Development Goals (MDGs) which was the agreement of the member states of the United Nations to halve extreme poverty and its effects. After reviewing the MDGs, the United Nations came to the conclusion that there was need to make a better plan for the future. Gap Task Force undertook "the responsibility of extracting lessons from its monitoring of Goal 8 that may be useful in monitoring the future global partnership for development." [1]Observable lapses identified are:

> lack of quantitative time-bound targets in the five substantive areas, as well as the lack of data to track quantitative and qualitative

---

[1] United Nations, "Taking Stock of the Global Partnership for Development, MDG Gap, Task Force Report 2015," United Nations, New York, 2015, xiii.

commitments adequately and in a timely manner. In addition, some MDG 8 indicators displayed a mismatch between targets set and indicators chosen to identify progress.[2]

However, there were various achievements with respect to the implementation of the MDGs across the globe. For instance, the MDGs "led to great gains in terms of the mean levels of national health-related performance indicators, most of them disease specific."[3]

Sustainable Development Goals (SDGs) came into being through the 2030 Agenda for Sustainable Development which was ratified by all the United Nations member states in September 2015. The agenda for Sustainable Development provides plan for amity and wealth for people and the planet in the immediate and future terms. Sustainable development has been defined from different perspectives. Brundtland Report defines Sustainable Development as "development that meets the needs of the present without compromising the ability of future generations to meet their own needs" which was "popularised in 1987 in the United Nations Commission on Environment and Development."[4]

Sustainable Development Goals are 17 holistic agenda that require prompt attention of development institutions across various frontiers, including the developing and developed nations. The goals deal with six fundamental areas which are: dignity, people, planet, partnership, people, justice and prosperity for many. The holistic nature of the SDGs and the interdependence of the goals on one another have further lent credence to its global significance in its attempt to eradicate poverty, improve education, health and climate change. The holistic and inclusive nature of the SDGs predicated on global partnership as well as mutual responsibility or obligations of stakeholders has been commended.[5] The SDGs heralded a unique approach to development

[2] United Nations, Taking Stock of the Global Partnership for Development, xiii.

[3] Kira Fortune, Francisco Becerra-Posada, Paulo Buss, Luiz Augusto C. Galvão , Alfonso Contreras, Matthew Murphy, Caitlin Rogger, Gabriela E. Keahon & Andres de Francisco, *Health promotion and the agenda for sustainable development, WHO Region of the Americas*, (2018), https://www.who.int/bulletin/volumes/96/9/17-204404/en/ (Accessed June 12, 2019).

[4] Marina Gurbo, "Why Sustainable Development Goals are important: Supporting the Implementation of UN Sustainable Development Goals in Georgia Project," Institute for Development of Freedom of Information, Georgia, US. (2017) https://idfi.ge/en/why_does_sdgs_matter (Accessed June 12, 2019).

[5] Nilsson M. and Costanza, R. "Overall Framework for the Sustainable Development Goals" Review of Targets for the Sustainable Development Goals: The Science Perspective, International Council for Science (ICSU), Paris, (2015) [Web] https://council.science/cms/2017/05/SDG-Report.pdf (Accessed June 12, 2019).

as Western institutions are partnering with indigenous institutions and individuals in the actualisation of the goals of the initiative. It, thus, inadvertently shifts development of these contexts into the hands of the local actors who are principal stakeholders in their respective communities. The inclusive ideals of SDGs are evident in the United Nations Lazy Person's guide to saving the world by being agents of positive change: "Change starts with you. Seriously, every human, on earth even the most indifferent, laziest person among us, is part of the solution. Fortunately, there are some super easy things we can adopt into our routines that, if we all do it, will make a big difference."[6]

The appropriation of local actor's daily routine into the conceptualisation of SDGs facilitates greater level of participation at all strata of society which might lead to actualisation of the SDGs. Some of the daily routines include:

> Save electricity by plugging appliances into a power strip and turning them off completely when not in use, including your computer.... Turn off the lights. Your television or computer screen provides a cozy [cosy] glow, so turn off other lights if you don't need them.... Eat less meat, poultry, and fish for more resources are used to provide meat than plants.... Bike, walk or take public transport. Save the car trips for when you've got a big group.... When you go to a restaurant and are ordering seafood, shop only for sustainable sea foods.[7]

Despite the commendations of SDGs, some scholars have expressed their reservations that SDGs agenda does not in its entirety lead to global transformation. Nunes *et al.* posit that the *modus operandi* of implementing the SDGs is neither robust nor cohesive.[8] However, the thrust of this study is neither to critique the contents of the SDGs nor to argue for or against the initiative but to examine the actualisation of SDG Number 3 in the light of the declining fortunes of the Nigerian health sector in relation to the health delivery services of the Redeemed Christian Church of God through its Christian Social Responsibility (CSR) in Redemption Camp, Mowe, Ogun

---

[6] United Nations, "The Lazy Person's Guide to Saving the World," (2016) accessed at: http://www.un.org/sustainabledevclopmcnt/takeaction/2016 (Accessed 23 March, 2019).

[7] United Nations, "The Lazy Person's Guide to Saving the World.

[8] A. R. Nunes, K. Lee and T. O'Riodan, "The Importance of an Integrating Framework for Achieving the Sustainable Development Goals: The Examples of Health and Well-being," *BMJ Global Health*, (2016): 1-13.

State, Nigeria. The Church over the years has been involved in social concerns through the provision of social amenities, educational and medical institutions to the indigent.

Research Methodology

Research Questions

In evaluating the healthcare interventionist approaches of the RCCG in relation to its contributions to SDGs, the following research questions are imperative:

1. What is the service user's perception of the intervention of the Redeemed Christian Church of God, Redemption Camp, Mowe to the health sector?

2. Do the SDG number 3 and the healthcare deliveries of the Redeemed Christian Church of God, Redemption Camp, Mowe, relate well?

3. Are the healthcare deliveries of the Redeemed Christian Church of God, Redemption Camp, accessible to residents of Mowe?

4. Is the Redeemed Christian Church of God's, Redemption Camp, Mowe healthcare deliveries having any impact on the SDG Number 3?

1.3   Hypothesis

Alongside the above research questions, the following null hypothesis will be tested at 0.05 level of significance.

H0: The healthcare deliveries of the Redeemed Christian Church of God have not led significantly to the achievement of the SDG Number 3 in Mowe, Ogun State, Nigeria.

Health Promotion and the Agenda for Sustainable Development in Nigeria

In 1978, various governments across the globe resolved to initiate and sustain the primary health care concept as the primary focus for health for all by the year 2000. As plausible as the Health For All in the year 2000 was, it was unable to achieve its primary objectives due to the fragmentation of the process which culminated in the creation of selective primary healthcare services characterised by immediate gains. This impeded the focus of the original thought and goal of Health For All by the year 2000. Nevertheless, the global health outcome was enhanced by the MDGs with some nations meeting and exceeding their predetermined expectations although at the end of the target year (2015).[9]

Despite various criticisms of the MDGs and its *modus operandi*, the SDGs aim to address the overall inadequacies of the MDGs. Some of the inadequacies of the MDGs are inherently due to their not inclusive picture as well as silence on human rights and failure to consider the root causes of poverty, gender disparity and holistic nature of development. However, it has been observed that all the SDGs will positively or negatively impact human health except only Goal 3, which is "to promote healthy lives and the well-being for all, at all ages.'" This is a sharp contrast to the MDGs where three of the eight goals centred on human health (MDG3 - To reduce mortality; MD4 - To improve maternal health; and MDG 5 - To control HIV/AIDS, malaria and other diseases). This inevitably raises questions with respect to whether the focus on health is diminishing from the global development agenda as only one out of the 17 SDGs is aimed at addressing health matters explicitly. However SDG 3 provides a much more expansive perspective of health through the direct and indirect functional dependency of the 17 SDGs in relation to the equity, endowing local actors in various communities and defending human rights. According to the United Nations Development, a lot of progress has been made globally with respect to:

Improving maternal health and fighting HIV/AIDS, Malaria and other diseases. Since 1990, there has been an over 50 percent decline in preventable child deaths globally. Maternal mortality also fell by 45 percent worldwide. New HIV/AIDS infectious fell by 30 percent between 2000 and 2013 and over 6.2million lives saved from Malaria.[10]

---

[9] O. O. Oloribe and S. D. Taylor-Robinson, "Before Sustainable Development Goals (SDGs): Why Nigeria Failed to Achieve the Millennium Development Goals (MDGs)," *The Pan African Medical Journal* 24 (2016): 156-161; A. A. Durokila and B. M. Abdul-wasi, "Evaluating Nigeria's Achievement of the Millennium Development Goals (MDGs): Determinants, Deliverables, and Shortfalls," *Africa's Public Service Delivery and Performance Review* (2016): 656-683; W. Easterly, "How the Millennium Development Goals are unfair to Africa", *World Development*, 37/1 (2009): 26-35.

[10] United Development Project, "Good health and Wellbeing" Web: https://www.undp.org/content/seoul_policy_center/en/home/sustainable-development-goals/goal-3-good-health-and-well-being.html#:~:text=New%20HIV%2FAIDS%20infections%20fell,lives%20were%20saved%20from%20malaria.&text=The%20Sustainable%20Development%20Goals%20make,other%20communicable%20diseases%20by%202030. (Accessed 13 March, 2019)

However, there exist huge gaps in the prevailing global health status in relation to the SDG 3 particularly in sub-Saharan Africa, Nigeria in particular, due to the ravaging challenges of inadequate universal basic health care. The UNDP Baseline Report on Nigeria notes that:

> Women [still] die during pregnancy or from child-birth related complications. In many rural areas, only 56 per cent of births are attended to by skilled professionals. AIDS is now the leading source of death among teenagers in sub-Saharan Africa, a region stills severely devastated by the HIV epidemic.[11]

In view of this, it is, thus, imperative to note that the implementation of the SDGs in Nigeria was well received by the Federal Government of Nigeria (FGN) led by President Muhammadu Buhari as a member state amongst 193 countries that signed the initiative under the auspices of the United Nations in September 2015 at New York, United States. The FGN demonstrated its commitment to the SDGs by appropriating human, fiscal and institutional structures to drive the SDGs agenda as well as repositioned the Office of the Senior Special Assistant to the President on Sustainable Development Goals (SSAP-SDGs) as the hub of its implementation in Nigeria. The operational modalities for SSAP-SDGs are broad which include integration of the initiative in Nigeria's development plan, provision of implementation frameworks across the country as well as collaboration with governmental agencies like National Bureau of Statistics and other stakeholders to establish a baseline for the SDG indicators that are domesticated in Nigeria. In Nigeria, the SDGs programme is classified into three phases which are Phase 1: 2016-2020, Phase 2: 2020-2026 and Phase 3: 2026-2030."[12]

Religion has continued to play significant and oftentimes ambivalent role in Nigeria's development. Three major religions dominate Nigeria's religioscape: Indigenous religion, Christianity and Islam. The competitiveness of these religions is well illustrated in the increase of Pentecostal churches in most nooks and crannies of urban cities. This development has redefined the Nigerian social landscape as some of these churches are actively involved in social, educational and health care services in reaction to the moral economy of corruption of past and present leadership of the country. The RCCG is one

---

[11] United Nations Development Project, *NIGERIA, Sustainable Development Goals (SDGs), Indicators Baseline Report (2016)*, Abuja. Nigeria, The Office of the Senior Special Assistant to the President on SDGs, 2017, 1.

[12] J. McDickson, "Sustainable Development Goals (SDGs)-The Nigerian Way," http://sds.gov.ng/sustainable-development-goals-sdgs-nigeria-way/. (Accessed 23 March 2019).

of the several indigenous Nigerian Pentecostal churches that has transnational network of churches led by the General Overseer, Pastor E. A. Adeboye. The denomination can be classified as a "progressive" Pentecostal[13] or "Pentecostal Progressivism"[14] understood as a denomination which contradicts the perception that Pentecostal churches are only heavenly-minded with disregard for earthly concern.

It is, thus, obvious that, scholars and development entrepreneurs are giving attention to the role of religious organisations in international development initiatives.[15] The import of this development is that "social sciences have the particular potential to theoretically and empirically enrich our understanding of the interplay between development and religion."[16] The obvious challenge overtime amongst social scientists is that the concept of development from above is viewed from econometric concept negating the role of religious practitioners in development. Moreover, Adogame argues that "rather than simply foist definitions and concepts on religious peoples and institutions may define, critique, conceptualise and theologise. development, human progress and flourishing not only through abstract, metaphysical and canonical expressions, but also in concrete, prosaic, lived experiences."[17]

The next section of this study highlights the Christian Social Responsibility (CSR) of the RCCG, Redemption Camp as a microcosm of the contributions of the church to the health sector of Nigeria.

The RCCG's Christian Social Responsibility

Scholarly interest in the RCCG, its rituals, leadership and ethos, as perhaps one of the fastest growing Pentecostal denominations across the globe, defies the local dynamics as a result of the church's deterritorialisation.[18]

---

[13] E. Donald and T. Yamamori, *Global Pentecostalism, The New Face of Christian Social Engagement.* Berkeley: University of California Press, 2007, 39-67.

[14] Amos Yong, In *the Days of Caesar: Pentecostalism and Political Theology*, Grand Rapids: Eerdmans, 2010, 34-35.

[15] Afe Adogame, "African Christianities and the Politics of Development from Below," *HTS Teologiese Studies / Theological Studies*, 72/4 (2016): 1-12, doi:10.4102/hts.v72i4.4065.

[16] B. L. Offutt, Probasco & B. Vaidyanathan, "Religion, poverty and development," *Journal for the Scientific Study of Religion*, 55/2 (2016): 207–215. http://dx.doi.org/10. 1111/jssr.12270:

[17] Adogame, Afe. "African Christianities and the Politics of Development from Below," 5.

[18] Babatunde Adedibu, "The Missional history and growth of the Redeemed Christian Church of God in the United Kingdom till date (2015)," *Journal of European Pentecostal Theological Association*, 36, (2016): 80-93; Olufunke Adeboye, 'Arrowhead' of Nigerian Pentecostalism: The Redeemed Christian Church of God, 1952-2005," *Pneuma*, 29/1 (2007): 24-58; Afe Adogame, "HIV/AIDS Support and African Pentecostalism: The Case of the Redeemed," *Journal of Health Psychology*, (2007): 12: 475, DOI: 10.1177/1359105307076234.

The fluidity of the definition of CSR inevitably has limited the use of this concept as an index for decision makers in various organisations.[19] However, the concept of Christian Social Responsibility is biblically-oriented from the RCCG's perspective. The RCCG developed the theoretical framework for CSR as a response to alleviating the social, economic, educational and health challenges of the Nigerian state. The conceptualisation thrives from its attempt to demonstrate God's love to those on the margins of society. The trust of this assertion is the "continuous commitment of an organisation, in this case the church, to behave ethically and contribute to development while improving on the quality of life of its people and their families as well as the community and the society at large."[20] This encompassing definition, within the theoretical framework of the RCCG, resonates with the SDGs 3.

Moreover, it is apt to note the slight modification of the social responsibility initiative of Jesus House, London, United Kingdom with the word Church rather than Corporate Social Responsibility. This might represent one of the heterogeneous notions in nomenclature within the RCCG global brand as diversities are a common feature within the denomination. Irrespective of the difference in the specific area of emphasis of the initiative, we note that the concept of Christian Social Responsibility (CSR) has come under the scrutiny of some scholars due to its multiplicity of usage. The malleability of the CSR concept makes it difficult to operationalise a definition that reveals when a corporation is or is not socially, ethically or politically responsible, or act in accordance with conflicting norms of a society.[21]

However, the RCCG has not limited its CSR deliverables to a locality; it has transnational presence. For instance, within the RCCG North America (NA), network of churches is involved in civic engagements but the website of the organisation reveals the holistic nature of the RCCG CSR in RCCGNA through the Hope for You Initiative launched on the June 7, 2017 by the General Overseer, Pastor E.A. Adeboye. The primary objectives of *Hope for You Initiative* are to end poverty, eradicate social injustice and build healthy communities which are to be based on these four goals:

---

[19] M. Blowtield, & J. G. Frynas, "Setting new agendas: critical perspectives on Corporate Social Responsibility in the developing world," *International Affairs*, 81/3 (2005): 499.

[20] Blowtield & Frynas, 499.

[21] T. Devinney, "Is the Socially Responsible Corporation a Myth? The Good, the Bad, and the Ugly of Corporate Social Responsibility," *Academy of Management Perspectives*, 23/2 (May 2009): 45.

1. build lasting relationships with a cross section of leaders in church, community and society;
2. partner with relevant social agency groups that directly provide services that impact lives of economically challenged individuals and families;
3. Generate a nationwide network of contacts for churches and ministries on our data base.
4. Provide immigrant community with much needed education, capacity building and accumulate assistance to become their best as they integrate into the American culture.[22]

In view of the fact that the purview of this study is on Nigeria, it is imperative to submit that the interpretative framework of RCCG CSR is predicated on the biblical motif (Matthew 25:31-40). RCCG through its multifaceted approaches to CSR is depicted with involvements in eight primary sectors namely: sports, social, education, media, sports, governance, arts and culture, business and health which have redefined the altruistic disposition of the denomination toward human and community development in the Nigerian state. RCCG leadership in Nigeria has since early 2012 incorporated CSR into its organizational structure to reflect the commitment of the denomination to social, economic and empowerment of the Nigerian polity. Adedeji Ademigbaju and David Adejo, quoting Pastor Godwin Obadun, the former Pastor in charge of Lagos Province 58, Ikorodu, Lagos explained the mandate of Adeboye on the RCCG CSR that "Pastor E. A. Adeboye, is the owner of this vision. He [E.A. Adeboye] said: 'Go out, don't only preach the gospel, put something in their hands, let them have a job.'"[23] This is quite commendable considering the social, economic and infrastructural inadequacies in the Nigerian state. Pastor Johnson Funso Odesola, the RCCG Assistant General Overseer (Administration and Personnel) and the pastor in charge of Region One, Ebute-Meta, Lagos chronicled the integration of CSR into the RCCG hierarchical structure to enhance the social, cultural, educational, political and economic development of the various communities in Nigeria. Odesola states that:

About a year ago [2012], the Church in her determination to reach the less privileged across the country, made a move to select Senior Pastors as well as Assistant Provincial Pastors to be in charge of Corporate Social Responsibility both in rural and urban areas. We have been able to cover a lot of places

---

[22] http://hopeforyou.org/Who-we-are/Why-We-care (Accessed 15 March, 2019)
[23] Johnson, Odesola "Cardinal Importance of CSR," *The Good Samaritan*, 1/8 (December 2017): 5.

including Jigawa, Bidda, Katsina, Taraba and Maiduguri, impacted on state schools according to the Lord's command to freely give.[24]

Furthermore, Odesola asserts that the RCCG in Nigeria had spent not:

> less than an approximate sum of N433.3 million [$118.71 million at the exchange of 360 naira to one dollar] between August last year [2012] to date [May 30, 2013] was expended on various activities ranging from digging boreholes, education which include providing books for both primary and tertiary institutions across the country, procurement of drugs, gilt of glasses for those with eyes problems, care-giver for HIV positive and drugs, provision of toilets, libraries, classrooms among others.[25]

This development re-echoes the commitment of religious institutions in Nigeria, particularly the Pentecostal churches to the social, economic and environmental concerns of the Nigerian citizenry. In view of the continued impoverisation of the Nigerian state by the corrupt political class, the emerging trend within the RCCG CSR is filling a gap in its collaborative agenda that seeks not only to provide educational, food and basic necessities of life to the under privileged in various communities in Nigeria, but to the world at large. The collaborative agenda entails strategic partnership with empowerment providers and financial institutions to provide support to young and promising indigent Nigerians to embark on entrepreneurial initiatives which ultimately will reduce employment challenges as well as galvanize many to be employers of labour in a consumer driven economy like Nigeria. For instance, RCCG, Lagos Province 58, Ikorodu, Lagos organised an empowerment programme. After assessing the needs of the attendees, the church paraded high profile human capacity development and empowerment professionals from the Bank of Industry (BoI), Fidelity Bank and Capacity Development and Skills Enhancement agencies to empower the church members and members of the communities as a step to being employers of labour.

In view of the multiplicities of various initiatives of CSR in its foundation years in RCCG, the structure was embedded within the administrative machinery of the church in Nigeria alone. Although, it is quite obvious that churches in United Kingdom have charitable status and are required

---

to demonstrate their commitments based on the requirements of Charity Commission of England and Wales. RCCG parishes in UK are very much into various social, educational and feeding of the vulnerable members of their communities through various projects. The leadership of RCCG Nigeria on the 6th of January 2016 appointed Pastor Idowu Iluyomade as the Special Assistant to the General Overseer in charge of CSR. This newly created office reports directly to General Overseer on the church activities in Nigeria and abroad on the role the church plays in the welfare of the less privileged and the society at large. The continued commitment of RCCG in Nigeria and Diaspora further reinforces previous scholarship with respect to the importance of religious bodies in community initiatives.[26] This development, thus, classifies churches from Africa with trans-Atlantic networks like RCCG as development actors across borders.

RCCG, to a large extent, has been involved in health care delivery in Nigeria for almost four decades particularly through the establishment of Maternity Centres in their churches that provide basic health care for would be mothers and nursing mothers. In the light of deplorable health situation in the country, Pastor Idowu Iluyomade donated medical facilities on behalf of the RCCG Apapa family on June 3, 2017 to Lagos State University Teaching Hospital (LASUTH) which included four CR 5,000 ICU Beds, four Alpha Active 4 Mattresses, B-Braun Infusion Pumps, Syringe Pumps, Multi-Parameter Patient monitors and bedside lockers. The church had also refurbished and equipped the ICU in the Surgical Emergency section of the hospital. Pastor Idowu Iluyomade said that:

We believe that one of the duties of the church is to serve God and humanity; this is just another milestone in our corporate social responsibility projects. We have been serving the state, most especially, in the last 10 years; we have mobile clinics, hospitals and we feed people in the state. We want to ensure that the people are healthy and have good quality healthcare.[27]

Likewise, various medical outreaches are organised by parishes of the RCCG across the breadth of Nigeria that address the immediate social, educational and health challenges of many communities. For instance,

[26] A. Adogame, and C. Weisskoppel, "Introduction." In Adogame, A. & Weisskoppel, C. eds. *Religion in the Context of African Migration*, Bayreuth: Breitinger Bayreuth African Studies Series, 75, 2005, 1-2.
[27] http://www.punchng.com/rccg-donates-icu-equipment-to-lasuth.

Pastor J. F. Odesola, RCCG Assistant General Overseer, Administration and Personnel noted that RCCG, as at 2017, has impacted "460 out of the 774 Local Government Areas which is 54% of all local governments in Nigeria with 609 communities as direct beneficiaries of the CSR activities in Nigeria."[28]

RCCG's contributions to health care delivery are multifaceted ranging from primary care health initiatives to disease prevention and awareness. Some of the para church ministries of RCCG that are involved in healthcare delivery include: Redeemed AIDS Programme Action Committee (RAPAC)[29] that is the RCCG's response to the challenges of HIV/AIDS that is still ravaging the whole of the African continent. The approach of this agency to the challenges of HIV/AIDS is both medical and religious entailing preventative models including abstinence from sexual relationships before marriage, advocacy on HIV/AIDS matters to members of the public to forestall the chances of contracting AIDS/HIV. RAPAC is para- church agency that is evaluated in this research.

RCCG maternity centre, which has its origin as far as late 1970s during the tenure of the RCCG founder, late Rev Josiah Akindayomi at Ebute Meta, has been transformed to be a major RCCG medical outreach as there are several maternity centres situated at Regional or Provincial headquarters of many RCCG parishes. Interestingly, most of these maternity centres make use of qualified medical personnel including doctors, nurses and auxiliary nurses who are trained by RCCG midwife academy thereby providing employment for midwife assistants within the rank and file of the church. At the Redemption Camp, the maternity centre has been transformed to a modern functional medical infrastructure, well ventilated admission and emergency wards. For instance, it was observed that the number of the service users have increased over the years. Van der Haak notes

> when he [Joshua Kayode] took over the [management of] the maternity clinic at the Redemption Camp in 2008, Dr. Kayode had about 40 patients. Five years later, this number has increased to 300.

---

[28] Odesola. 8.

[29] D. Akhazemea, & B. A. Adedibu, "Global Missionary Player: The Redeemed Christian Church of God: Her Message of Human Development." Encounter Beyond Routine, (2011): 53-64, Retrieved from http://www.emw-d.de/fix/files/doku_5_encounter-beyond-routine2011.pdf (Accessed 23 March, 2019) Adogame, "HIV/AIDS Support and African Pentecostalism: 475; Adeboye, 'Arrowhead' of Nigerian Pentecostalism, 37.

Most of them are pregnant women but some are couples struggling with infertility, coming to the clinic for treatment and advice.[30]

Redemption Camp Maternity has modern medical practices, but also uses religious approaches in their health care deliveries. The distinctive Christian ethos entails sessions of praise and worship, prayers and exhortation led by a designated pastor from the Prayer department of the church before consultation with the medical team on ante natal days for pregnant women on every Wednesday of the month.[31] Charges are highly subsidised. For instance, every service user pays the equivalent of $13.9 (5,000 Naira) as registration fee and no other payment is required for child delivery from the clients. Service users pay for their antenatal drugs and injections from the pharmacy section at discounted cost. It was noted that the cost of tetanus injection for pregnant service users at the maternity centre is equivalent to $0.50 cents (200 Naira).[32] Redemption Camp maternity centre is open to the members of the public irrespective of religious or ethnic backgrounds and this has been a major source of healthcare for members of the church and neighbouring communities from far and near who choose to have their babies delivered at Redemption Camp maternity Centre. Nevertheless, complicated cases such as hose requiring surgeries are referred to the Redeemer's Health Centre, Redemption Camp.

Healing Stripes is one of the several hospitals established and managed by Apapa family, a network of churches within RCCG whose members are elites and influential within and outside Nigeria. Healing Stripes hospital according to its brochure:

started its operations in May 2010. It has attended to over 13,403 clients, and has seen 5,482 clients free of charge through the church welfare programme. 24 hours Services to both Private and Insurance Clients with a Resident Doctor available…. In June 2011, we [Management of Healing Stripes] established the Healing Stripes Cancer Screening Centre at Surulere [Lagos], the first faith-based Cancer Screening Centre for Free Screening and awareness. From inception till–date [2015] we have given free Cancer Screening and Therapy to over 17, 542 people in Lagos State… investment

---

[30] Bregtje van der Haak, "Medicine and Miracles at Lagos Redemption Camp", https://pulitzercenter.org/reporting/medicine-and-miracles-lagos-redemption-camp (Accessed 13 June, 2019).
[31] Demilade Oloyede, a registered service user of the Redemption Camp Maternity Centre information provided in her questionnaire, (12 June, 2019).
[32] Oloyede, Demilade. a registered service user of the Redemption.

cost -N250, 188, 819.90 which are donations from highly esteemed Partners.[33]

Healing Stripes hospital has specialist clinics in nephrology, cardiology, obstetrics and gynaecology, paediatrics, urology, general surgery including diagnostic services and dental/eye care.[34] RCCG, through the appropriation of religious capital is harnessing and maximising the professional competencies of her members in diverse professional fields including the health sector to ameliorate the challenges of primary and universal healthcare deliveries in different parts of Nigeria. The manpower appropriated by RCCG is most times through volunteering. This has changed the face of healthcare delivery as most of the volunteers are highly skilled medical personnel who willingly give back to their communities.

Redemption Camp Health Centre is an offshoot of the maternity centre which started in 2008. This is in response to the upsurge in the population of Redemption Camp. Many residents of Redemption Camp Community access the basic healthcare services of this centre. The hospital was previously managed until 2018 by a management committee led by Professor Arije, a medical consultant with the University College Teaching Hospital (UCH), Ibadan, Oyo State and Provincial Pastor in the RCCG. The Health Centre provides basic healthcare services including minor surgeries and cross section surgery for women. The centre has two admission wards, an administrative building, dental clinic and medical laboratory. Redemption Camp Health Centre is now under a new management led by Dr Ileobode. The clinic is open to members of the general public. However, during annual events and monthly national events of RCCG, free medical care is given to anyone who attends the clinic courtesy of Pastor (Mrs) Folu Adeboye, wife of RCCG General Overseer, Pastor E. A. Adeboye.

In the wake of COVID 19 pandemic which largely crippled the global economy Nigeria inclusive, the leadership of RCCG donated "two sets of Ventilators, two Intensive Care Unit (ICU) Beds and other items to the Ogun State government towards the effective curbing of coronavirus (COVID-19)

---

[33] Brochure of formal opening and dedication of the new wing of Healing Stripes hospital (2015), [Web] http://www.cityofdavidng.org/Portals/CityofDavid/Healing%20Stripes%20Brochure- %20September%202015.pdf?ver=2016-12-30-143227-230 (Accessed 12 June, 2019).

[34] Brochure of formal opening and dedication of the new wing of Healing Stripes hospital (2015), [Web] http://www.cityofdavidng.org/Portals/CityofDavid/Healing%20Stripes%20Brochure- %20September%202015.pdf?ver=2016-12-30-143227-230 (Accessed 12 June, 2019).

in the state."[35] The above highlights the multifaceted approaches of RCCG to healthcare delivery in Nigeria. However, the research questionnaires were administered on the following healthcare units of RCCG: RAPAC, The Maternity Centre and the Health Centre all situated at Redemption Camp. The next section chronicles the methodology utilised in this research.

Research Design

In view of the purpose and nature of this paper, the Survey research design was adopted because of its effectiveness in attitudinal and behavioural studies. "Survey research focuses on people, the vital facts of people and their beliefs, opinions, attitudes, motivations and behaviour."[36]

Population

A population is a collection of elements or total group of people which the study is concerned and intends to make an inference from. This refers to a set of all possible cases of interest in a given research activity. The target population for this study consists of personnel and service users of the Redeemed Christian Church of God's healthcare deliveries such as RCCG Health centre, Maternity Centre and Redeemed AIDS Programme Action Committee (RAPAC).

Sample Size and Sampling Technique

A sample size determination is the act of choosing the number of observations to include in a statistical sample.[37] Therefore, to determine the Sample Size for this study, the sample size calculator as developed by the National Statistical Service of Australia was used. The population size of the study as well as the confidence interval of the study was keyed into the calculator while 95% confidence level remains as default. Hence, the sample size for this study was 150. From the identified health care deliveries in RCCG, simple random sampling technique involving the use of the table of random was employed in selecting 50 personnel and 100 service users.

---

[35] Victor Gbonegun, "RCCG donates ventilators, intensive care unit beds, other items to Ogun State" [Web]: https://guardian.ng/news/rccg-donates-ventilators-intensive-care-unit-beds-other-items-to-ogun-state/ (Accessed 16 August, 2020).

[36] E. C. Osuala, *Introduction to research methodology* (3rd ed.), Onitsha: Africana-First Publisher, 2005, 254.

[37] E.S. Asemah, M. Gujbawu, D.O. Ekhareafo, Okpanachi, *Research methods and procedures in mass communication*, Jos: Great Future Press, 2012, 156.

Instrumentation

The research instruments used were questionnaire and structured interview. The instrument was administered to respondents. The researcher designed the questionnaire using the Likert Scale format and close-ended where necessary. Questions were drawn to elicit relevant research data from respondents, first to provide answers on their demographic characteristics, and secondly to the core research questions. The items in the questionnaires were simplified enough to enable respondents understand and answer them correctly. With proper framing of questions, findings are expected to be valid.

Administration of Research Instrument

After the validity and reliability of the research instrument were ascertained, the copies of the questionnaire were administered directly to the chosen sample for the study. A total of 150 copies of the questionnaire were administered for completion and onward retrieval. The possibility of retrieving back the entire questionnaires was achieved through the help of two research assistants.

Method of Data Analysis

For the purpose of this study, two basic statistical methods were adopted as techniques to analyse data collected.

1. Percentage Comparison method

This involved breaking down and ordering of data gathered. The data was coded in simple percentages and histogram presented where necessary in tables with the aid of Statistical Package for Social Sciences (SPSS version 25.0). The interpretations of the responses were used to address the research questions.

Ethical Consideration

The study first got the approval and informed consents from all the authority of RCCG and the management of the selected healthcare deliveries without any form of inducement. They were also informed about the purpose of the study and the information required of them. Based on the nature of the research, all ethical issues were strictly applied in the study ranging from voluntary participation of the respondents through their informed consent which was requested orally before questionnaires were administered, as well as effort to minimize time taken to respond to questionnaire through precise and well-understood questions categories. Also included was the assurance of the respondents of their anonymity, confidentiality as well as avoidance of anything that could cause harm or discomfort to the respondents during or after the study.

Results and Discussion
Results

The results highlighted in this section are in relation to the research questions indicated earlier in this research. Other demographical findings that are not of immediate consideration in this research are excluded in this presentation.

Table 1: **Distribution of Questionnaires amongst sample population**

Group	Frequency	Percent (%)
Personnel	50	33.3
Service User	100	66.7
Total	**150**	**100**

Source: Field Survey 2019

The total sample for this study is 150. About 33.3% of the sample was drawn from personnel of the RCCG healthcare deliveries (Redeemer's Health Centre, RAPAC and Redeemer's Maternity Centre) while the remaining 66.7% of the respondents were amongst the selected users of the RCCG health care.

Table 2: **RCCG healthcare deliveries awareness amongst the sampled population**

RCCG Health Care Deliveries Awareness	Frequency	Percent (%)
All	13	13.0
Redeemer's Maternity Centre	23	23.0
RAPAC	25	25.0
Redeemer's Health Centre	39	39.0
Total	**100**	**100.0**

Source: Field Survey 2019

Table 2 above indicates RCCG healthcare deliveries awareness distribution which reveals that majority of the service users are aware of Redeemer's

Health Centre representing 39% of the entire sample. While 25% is aware of RAPAC, 23% indicated awareness of Redeemer's Maternity Centre and 13% of the respondents were aware of all the identified RCCG health care deliveries.

Table 3: **Service user's perception of the intervention of the RCCG in Mowe to the health sector**

Perception	Frequency	Percent (%)
Fair Extent	10	10.0
Large Extent	40	40.0
Very Large Extent	50	50.0
Total	**100**	**100.0**

Source: Field Survey 2019

Table 3 above shows that 50% of the respondents indicated that RCCG has intervened in the Redemption Camp and neighbouring communities health sector to a very large extent, while 40% of the respondents, who are service users, revealed that RCCG, to a large extent has intervened in the Redemption Camp and neighbouring communities health sector and just 10% of the respondents perceived that the RCCG's intervention to the Nigeria health sector is to a fair extent. Hence, it is evident that the RCCG has visibly intervened in Redemption Camp and neighbouring communities' health sector based on the measured perception of the sampled service users.

Table 4: **Relationship between SDG number 3 and the healthcare deliveries of RCCG**

Sustainable Development	Frequency [38]	Percent (%)
Not At All	11	22.0
Not So Much	7	14.0
Well	18	36.0
Very Well	14	28.0
Total	**50**	**100.0**

Source: Field Survey 2019

---

[38] The frequency distribution utilised in this table is derived from RCCG personnel who are involved in healthcare service of their employers to determine whether there is any congruence in public healthcare policy and the healthcare delivery of the RCCG. Due to the technicality of the question, it was restricted to the healthcare professionals employed by RCCG who are well acquainted with public healthcare policies.

The data in Table 4 presented above portrays that 36% of the respondents agree that there is a relationship between SDG 3 and the healthcare deliveries provided by RCCG at Redemption Camp, in the same vein, 28% of the respondents further supported the position that the relationship between SDG number 3 and the healthcare deliveries of RCCG are very well, while just 22% of the respondents disagreed about the existent of a relationship between the two. The position of the 22% of the respondents is insignificant compared to a total of 64% of the entire respondents who agreed that there is a relationship between the two.

Table 5: **Accessibility of the healthcare deliveries of the RCCG at Redemption Camp**

Accessibility	Frequency	Percent (%)
Not At All	2	2.0
Averagely	14	14.0
Very Accessible	38	38.0
Accessible	46	46.0
Total	**100**	**100.0**

Source: Field Survey 2019

Table 5 above shows that the number of respondents, who have access and rate RCCG's healthcare deliveries to be accessible, surpasses those who indicated that they are not accessible at all. The respondents were asked how accessible is the RCCG healthcare deliveries and 46% said they are accessible while 38% of the respondents rate them very accessible. This means that majority of the respondents are certain that RCCG healthcare deliveries are accessible by the sampled population.

Table 6: **Impact of the RCCG's healthcare deliveries on the SDG number 3**

Impact of RCCG Health care deliveries	Frequency	Percent (%)
No Impact	2	2.0
Undecided	18	18.0
Low Impact	32	32.0
High Impact	48	48.0
Total	**100**	**100.0**

Source: Field Survey 2019

According to the data presented in Table 6 above, it is seen that the percentage of the respondents who indicated that the RCCG's healthcare deliveries have been impactful on the SDG number 3 is 48%. Also from the table, 32% of the respondents are of the opinion that the RCCG healthcare deliveries have low impact on the SDG number 3, this position could have been due to certain factors or uncovered areas identified by the respondents. While 18% of the respondents were undecided in the response to the question, just 2% rated the RCCG healthcare deliveries with no impact on the SDG number 3. Hence, it is evident that the RCCG healthcare deliveries have achieved a noticeable level of impact on the SDG number 3 which could be improved upon to an excellent level.

Discussion

From the foregoing, this research indicates that RCCG Redemption Camp, Mowe healthcare deliveries contribute to the actualisation of SDG 3 by 48% recognising her contributions as high impact. This assertion depicts the contributions of RCCG health care deliveries in the Redemption Camp, Mowe and neighbouring communities. The import of this development is predicated on the accessibility of the healthcare deliveries which is 84% out of which 46% described it as accessible while 36% were of the opinion that it was very accessible. The impact of RCCG Redemption Camp healthcare initiatives is reflective of the forward planning of RCCG leadership as 64% of the sampled population admitted that there is a positive correlation with healthcare deliveries at Redemption Camp and the SDG 3. Interestingly, 90% of the sampled population acknowledged the intervention of RCCG in health care delivery in Mowe, Ogun State. The empirical data realised from this research further corroborates previous scholars' assertions that religious organisations contribute to development in diverse ways. This study also established that local actors such as faith-based organisations like RCCG are major actors in the implementation of the SDGs particularly in relation to the SDG3 as evidenced in this research. This assertion further re-echoes previous scholarship findings with respect to the nexus between religion and development.[39] The implication of the positive correlation between development and religion is that some scholars are now redefining development outside the prism of econometric factors. It is imperative to note that notions of development are contextual as

---

[39] P. Öhlmann, M-L. Frost, & W. Gräb, "African Initiated Churches' potential as development actors," *HTS Teologiese Studies/Theological Studies* 72/4 (2016): a3825. http://dx.doi.org/10.4102/hts. v72i4.3825; Ignatius Swart, and Elsabé Nell, "Religion and Development: The rise of a Bibliography," *HTS Teologiese Studies/Theological Studies* 72/4 (2016): doi:10.4102/hts.v72i4.3862; Offutt, Probasco & Vaidyanathan, 207–215.

such, the western model of development originated from Western discourses which were shaped by theories of modernisation and markedly secular.[40] However, in sub-Saharan Africa, religion is a major factor in development as such Adogame advocates development from below.[41] A corollary to the observation of Adogame is that for SDGs to be a reality in Africa, Nigeria in particularly, faith-based organisations like RCCG have critical roles to play due to state fragility of many African countries. Crucial to the contributions of RCCG Redemption Camp healthcare deliveries to SDG 3 is the appropriation of social and religious capitals that fostered trust and functional networking of members of RCCG who serve as volunteers in providing their professional competencies through their religious membership to the Redemption Camp community and neighbouring communities that make use of the healthcare services of the church.

Conclusion

Although, the research was carried out at the RCCG Redemption Camp, Mowe, Ogun State, international headquarters of RCCG and is the largest private estate in the country with land area estimated to be about 1,687 hectares as at 2016 and 10% water bodies,[42] this research presents a microcosm of the potentials of RCCG to contribute to SDG 3. This is particularly important in view of the commitment of RCCG to her CSR which is driven by biblical mandate rather than global policy drive on SDGs. Policy formulators and implementing agencies might need to have a rethink about the role of religious organisations like RCCG in sustainable development of Africa.

---

[40] Philip Ohlman, Wihelm Grab Hunglinger and Marie-Luise Frost, *Religion and Development: Discussion Paper Series of the Research Programme on Religious Communities and Sustainable Development*. Berlin; Humboldt University, Germany, 1-1-12 2018, https://www.rcsd.hu-berlin.de/de/publikationen/pdf-dateien/discussion.../file (Accessed June 12, 2019).

[41] Adogame, "African Christianities and the Politics of Development from Below," 5.

[42] Redeemed Christian Church of God, *Redemption Camp Master Plan*, Redeemed Christian Church of God, Mowe, Ogun State, 2017 unpublished.

Chapter 6: Ministering Beyond the Pulpit: An Examination of the Impact of the Redeemed Christian Church of God (RCCG) on Healthcare Delivery in Nigeria

Samuel Kehinde Fabunmi
and
Olumuyiwa Olusesan Familusi

Introduction

In sociological context, the relevance of religion extends beyond spiritual illumination. Thus, the church has been proactive in fulfilling her social mandate in various aspects of human existence. It is incontrovertible that the Pentecostal movement has become a major mainstay of Christianity in Nigeria through its creativity and innovations. The Christian faith has become more visible through different channels it has employed to promote its activities. An assessment of the activities of the Pentecostal movement in recent years shows that it has been committed to social development as against the premillennial view which some of them hold tenaciously to in their teachings. Shifting from this standpoint, Pentecostal churches, like other Christian movements, are now involved in national development as part of their social responsibility as evinced in their contribution to the various sectors of society. The focus of this paper is examination of the ways in which the Redeemed Christian Church of God has intervened in or contributed to healthcare delivery in Nigeria as part of its social actions. The emphasis of the Pentecostal churches on divine healing has, no doubt, impacted positively the Nigerian people especially when miracles of healing are advertised as a proof. Moving from this premise, we interrogated the involvement of the RCCG on healthcare delivery through the establishment of hospitals, medical outreaches and programmes such as pre-marital medical screening and counselling. Emphasis was placed on the success story, while recommendations were made towards improving upon the endeavour with a view to having a robust healthcare delivery in Nigeria.

In fact, the Church as an integral part of society has been contributing her quota to the well-being of societies where her adherents are found.[1] This was typical of the first century Church. This obligation was carried out in so many ways; first by taking care of the poor among them and as enjoined by Paul in his epistle to the Romans that Christians should subject themselves to the governing authorities and pay the required taxes, due and revenue (Rom. 13:1ff). In the letter of Paul to Timothy, he urged him and others to pray for all men, kings and all who are in authority, so that they may lead a tranquil and quiet life in all godliness and dignity (I Tim. 2:2). No wonder Tertullian echoes it again in his work that Christians should pray for the emperor and the whole empire on the grounds that the peace and success of the empire were Christians' as well as her disorders and failures.[2] The above sets the foundation for Christian Social Responsibility, and Christianity as a Missionary and Social Movement, had over the centuries deployed the Social Responsibility to drive her mission.

The activities of the Church in the restoration of health to the people had been established from the spiritual perspective in so many ways, and going by available literature that attest to the phenomenon of divine or faith healing among the Pentecostal movement, this position is validated. While the belief in the efficacy of divine healing among the Pentecostals has not diminished, the appropriation of western medicine or orthodox medical practice is being used as part of the ways people could be helped in the restoration of their health. This justifies the need for this research.

Pentecostal Movement in Nigeria

Nigeria has a long and rich history of Pentecostalism. Since its emergence, it has been vocal as far as Christian practice is concerned. Its various manifestations have no doubt contributed immensely to the development of Christianity in the country, challenging the historic churches for relevance in the modern practice of Christianity. It has also traversed Africa down to the Global North as a missionary movement for the re-evangelisation of the Northern hemisphere. From 1918 Braid's prophetic-healing movement to 1930s Pentecostal revival led by Ayo Babalola,[3] to the emergence of Benson

---

[1] Gabriel A. Oshitelu, *The African Fathers of the Early Church*. Ibadan: Safer Books Ltd. 2002, 4.
[2] Samuel A. Fatokun, *History and Doctrine of the Early Church: An Introduction*. Ibadan: Enicrownfit Publishers. 2014, 199.
[3] E. A. Ademowo. *The Growth of the Apostolic Church in Ijesaland 1930-1990*. Lagos: CSS Bookshops, 2010, 64.

Idahosa's[4] of Church of God Mission International and other Pentecostal figures like Pastor W.F. Kumuyi,[5] Pastor E.A. Adeboye, Bishop David Oyedepo,[6] Dr. D.K. Olukoya[7] among others, the Pentecostal movement has continued to make impact on the religious landscape in Nigeria with innovations and creativity. This is seen in their religious networking, effective use of media and blooming tendency through the appropriation of the public space. The utilisation of the public space is becoming an emerging dimension to the practice of Christianity, especially Pentecostalism, in the country. The emergence of this movement in Nigeria has not only impacted Nigerian Christianity in the area of doctrinal practices, but also influenced meaningfully the social and economic life of the people, hence the place of Christian Social Responsibility for the nation's development. A leading Pentecostal Church which has carved a niche for itself as far as Christian Social Responsibility is concerned is the Redeemed Christian Church of God, which was established in 1952 by Revd. Josiah Olufemi Akindayomi as the pioneer of Holiness Movement within the Nigerian Pentecostalism.[8] From 1952 to date, the RCCG has become one of the fastest growing Pentecostal churches in the world.[9]

Christian Social Responsibility and Legacy of Historic Churches in Nigeria

The history of Christianity in Nigeria cannot be discussed without considering the fact that mission and social actions of the missionaries at the beginning are Siamese twins that cannot be separated. The latter became the driver of the former, which became a veritable tool for the successful evangelisation of Nigeria. The pioneer missions like Methodist, Church Missionary Society, Baptist, Catholic, Presbyterian Church and the Seventh Day Adventist used the provision of social services as vehicle for their mission among the host communities. The establishment of these social institutions in Nigeria has become part of the legacies of the established churches. The

---

[4] A. Ukachi. *The Best is yet to Come: Pentecostal and Charismatic Revivals in Nigeria 1914-1990s.* Lagos: Summit Press Ltd, 2013, 131.

[5] M. A. Ojo, "Deeper Life Bible Church of Nigeria." In Gifford, P. (ed.), New Dimension in African Christianity. Ibadan: Safer, 1993,166.

[6] A. H. Anderson. *An Introduction to Pentecostalism.* Cambridge: Cambridge University Press, 2014, 133.

[7] A. Adogame. "Dealing with Local Satanic Technology: Deliverance Rhetoric in the Mission of Fire and Miracles Ministries," *Journal of World Christianity*, 5/1 (2012): 80.

[8] I. O. Olofinjana. *20 Pentecostal Pioneers in Nigeria: Their Lives, Their Legacies*, United States: Xlibris Publishing. 2011, 80.

[9] Babatunde Adedibu, "Redemption Camp, Mowe, Ogun State, Nigeria: A Sacred Space of Religious Innovations and Creativity," *Journal of Religion and African Culture*, 4/1 (Jan-June. 2016): 8.

establishment of schools at various levels and the provision of healthcare services to the people could be seen as the trademark of missionary activities among these churches. In this regard, some people assume that the social actions of the Christians over the years have always been geared towards religious conversion, hence their reservations for these social actions.

A careful observation of the social actions of the Church in Nigeria reveals that Christianity itself is a social movement which does not only focus on the spiritual well-being of its adherents but also shows concern for their material needs. This was demonstrated by Jesus on several occasions in the New Testament. Example of this was the feeding of the five thousand, which shows Jesus' concern for the people (Matt. 14:15-21). Therefore, Christianity as a religion has always been predicated on social needs of the people. In Nigeria, the established churches have demonstrated leadership as regards Christian Social Responsibility as new generation churches otherwise known as Pentecostals churches are taking a cue from them.

The landmark achievement in healthcare delivery by missionary bodies as part of their contributions to the social development of Nigeria is remarkable. Some of the established hospitals had rendered medical services to the people in order to restore health to them and bring about healthy living through some of their medical programmes. Fabunmi argues that

> the missionary healthcare provisions in the real sense were borne out of the need to attend to the people which could make them to be better as regards healthy living. As part of the missionary skills, the early missionary agents equipped themselves with medical knowledge to attend to their medical needs and also attend to the medical needs of their converts. This was exemplary of Thomas Jefferson Bowen who was not medically trained but acquired some medical knowledge for the purpose of evangelisation in the 19th century.[10]

The first healthcare facility in Nigeria was a dispensary opened in 1880 by the Church Missionary Society in Obosi, followed by others in Onitsha and Ibadan in 1886. However, the first hospital by the missionary in Nigeria is the Sacred Heart Hospital in Abeokuta, established by the Society of African

---

[10] Samuel K. Fabunmi, "Historical Appraisal of Missionary Hospitals and Their Impact on Health in Ekitiland," *Ogbomoso Journal of Theology*, XVIII/2 (2013): 18.

Missions of Catholic Mission in 1895.[11] The establishment of this hospital brought about the emergence of organised healthcare services to Nigerians. Familusi notes that the

> Mission churches like Methodist church followed suit by establishing Wesley Guild Hospital in Ilesa and Seventh Day Adventist Church made its mark by establishing its hospital at Ile-Ife. The Baptist Hospital in Ogbomoso has been upgraded to Bowen Teaching Hospital, the Catholic Hospital at Oluyoro in Ibadan is still serving the people well. Many of the missionary hospitals have been taken [over] by the government; however, they still retain the names of the missions that founded them. A good story is that people have become enlightened in the matter of health, hence significant reduction in infant mortality and death resulting from improper diagnosis.[12]

Faith/Divine Healing as Foundation for Pentecostals Impact on Healthcare Delivery in Nigeria

We have argued that the social responsibility to the Nigerian people by the Church in the area of health was an initiative of the foreign missionaries and their African successors, notwithstanding, the emergence of the Pentecostal movement in Nigeria was equally geared towards the needs of the people. The faith healing phenomenon among this strand of Christianity is regarded as one of the social interventions to the health challenges of the people. No wonder scholars of Pentecostal movement refer to them as mass movement because of the creation of happiness to the greater number of people in the aspect of health through faith healing.[13] The social action in the capacity of doctrinal emphasis on divine healing was demonstrated as Christian Social Responsibility as this accounted for their acceptability among the Nigerian people, most especially in the South-Western Nigeria.

Faith healing is one of the major doctrinal tenets of the Pentecostal movement in Nigeria. This phenomenon is also one of the drivers of the

---

[11] www.sacredhearthospital.org

[12] O. O. Familusi, "Christian Conversion as a Tool for Social Transformation in Nigeria." In Opeke R.O., Familusi O. O. & Berekiah, O.O. (eds.), *The Heart of Act: Church Politics and Social Transformation a Festschrift in honour of His Grace Most Rev. Michael Kehinde Stephen*, Ibadan: Ibadan University Press. 2018, 62.

[13] Pentecostal scholars like Deji Ayegboyin, Samson Fatokun, Matthews Ojo, Allan Anderson, Asamoah Gyadu and Olufunke Adeboye have expressed this view in their various works.

movement. Three reasons could be identified for the manifestation of this doctrine among the Pentecostals in Nigeria. The first is that, this doctrine finds its root from the biblical teachings of Jesus' emphasis on faith as an important factor for miracles. References are equally made by the Pentecostals on incidences of divine healing by the apostles through the help of the Holy Spirit. The second reason is that some individuals who cannot afford medical bills resort to faith healing as a veritable alternative. That is why Ayegboyin and Ishola claim that in West African nations where there are very few hospitals and costly medicine beyond the reach of the majority, one would reasonably expect that the promise of *cura divina* (divine healing) would attract a number of people.[14] The third reason is the belief in the African world view. Africans believe that there are spiritual powers that could be used against an individual to cause misfortune which include illnesses that defy treatment except through ritual processes. Faith healing is seen as alternative among these Pentecostals when faced with such challenges. As a result, it has become a regular feature of healing ritual among them. It is on this basis that Ayegboyin lucidly puts forward that the Aladura had given pride of place to healing and wholeness in their ministries right from the beginning of the New Pentecostal Churches (NPCs) and they are only appropriating this which they borrowed from the African Independent Churches (AICs).[15]

Therefore, from the time of the emergence of the AICs to the time of NPCs, faith healing characterised their ministry which also brought about the popularity of this strand of Christian movement in Nigeria. What could be drawn from this development is that faith healing became popular because of its impact on the people in the area of health. As early as 1930s, the impact of faith healing helped in the spread of the Pentecostal revival at Oke Ooye in Ilesa. It was reported that mass healing was the major hallmark of this great revival which drew people from other towns, cities and nations to Ilesa.[16] The revival was so impactful to the extent that the sick in the hospital were reported to have been carried to the revival ground.[17] This revival, with its impact on the generality of the people, especially in the aspect of restoration of health, earned Apostle Babalola a place in the hall of fame of faith healers in Nigeria with the cognomen *Babalola Olomi Iye*

---

[14] D. I. Ayegboyin & S.A Ishola. *African Indigenous Church*, Bukuru: African Christian Textbooks, 2013, 19.

[15] Deji Ayegboyin, "Resonance of African Initiated Churches' Beliefs and Practices in Nigerian Pentecostal Praxis," *Spectrum: Journal of Contemporary Christianity and Society*, 2/1 (2017): 15.

[16] Ayegboyin, Resonance of African Initiated Churches' Beliefs and Practices, 67.

[17] Ayegboyin & Ishola, 67.

or *Woli Onise Iyanu*, meaning Babalola, who has water of life or wonder-working prophet.[18]

As Oke Oye revival spread, the trend of faith healing was not limited to their circle as this was replicated among other Pentecostal churches in Nigeria. This doctrinal platform produced other doyens of faith healing in Nigeria which include Benson Idahosa, William Folorunso Kumuyi, Timothy Obadare, Samuel Abiara, Enoch Adeboye, David Oyedapo, Chris Oyakhilome, Daniel Olukoya, Ayo Oristejafor, Wale Oke, Sola Kolade, Mike Okonkwo, Femi Emmanuel, Paul Adefarasin, Sam Adeyemi, Reuben Adegboye among others. According to Owoeye, the methods of the faith healing activities of these people and other proponents are emphasis on repentance or salvation for anybody wanting to enjoy sound health.[19] It is, however, noted that some of the churches emphasised deliverance as a channel for faith healing and a leading example of this category is Mountain of Fire and Miracles Ministries (MFM). What can be deduced from the foregoing is that faith healing phenomenon has brought tremendous value to the people which is, no doubt, one area they have been contributing to the development of the Nigerian society in their own capacity. The contribution of the Pentecostals to the society could be validated through testimonies shared by those who experienced healing from different diseases.

It is, therefore, often seen among the Pentecostals, wide coverage of testimonies on healing in their religious programme. This could be advertised on the various bulletins or broadcast on live programmes of the church through digital satellites. In some places, special times are allotted for testimonies and careful observation of the Pentecostal religious activities reveals that most of the testimonies centre on healing which could be spiritual or physical. Asamoah-Gyadu recounts that his personal participation in anointing services has brought to his attention such testimonies from people for whom the application of olive oil has worked. He also asserts that the cripples have walked, barren women have given birth, and various tumours have disappeared as a result of the application of oil following prayer.[20] This personal account of Asamoah-Gyadu brings to the fore the significance of testimonies as a means of advertising the Pentecostal churches especially

---

[18] S. A. Owoeye, "Charismatic Prophetic-Healers and their healing activities in Yorubaland." In Ogungbile, D.O. & Akinade, A. E. (eds), *Creativity and Change in Nigerian Christianity* Lagos: Malthouse Press Limited. 2010, 175.

[19] Owoeye, 177.

[20] J. K. Asamoah-Gyadu. *Contemporary Pentecostal Christianity: Interpretation from An African Context.* Oxford: Regnum Book International. 2013,134.

on events relating to healing. When this is done, it often brings about commercialisation of Pentecostal activities, a phenomenon that led to the regulation of the programmes on faith healing and other miracles by the Nigerian Broadcasting Corporation.[21] As plausible as faith healing might have impacted society in regard to health, its abuse among some of the Pentecostals is not deniable.

This contribution of the Pentecostals in this capacity is significant as they made their quota to their immediate society. In the attempt to do more than faith healing as part of social responsibility in the area of healthcare delivery, some Pentecostal churches are now involved in pragmatic and medical approach to healthcare delivery in Nigeria, hence, the establishment of hospital and involvement in para-medical services to the people, church members in particular and the community they are found in Nigeria in general in which the Redeemed Christian Church is a leading example.

Conventional Healthcare Delivery Services as Social Responsibility of the RCCG

Generally speaking, the social activities of the Pentecostals show that virtually all of them are involved in medical services from generalist to specialist perspective. By this, we mean that these churches render medical service to the people in the area of counselling, pre-medical test, medical outreaches and other para-medical services within the church premises which are general, to the establishment of hospitals with special focus. While this is so about the Pentecostal churches in Nigeria, the focus of this study is on the Redeemed Christian Church of God. The Church was founded in 1952 by Rev. Josiah Akindayomi and his successor, Pastor E.A. Adeboye, has over the years demonstrated the leadership that brings the church to limelight across the globe. The provision of medical services by the RCCG is one of the ways the Church is ministering to the social needs of people. This is done in many ways as indicated initially as generalist approach. The inroad of the RCCG into providing medical services to the people started as far back as 1952 when the Church was founded.[22] In this regard, the Church opened maternity centre at Ebute-Metta Church premises to care for the pregnant women who are members of the Church. By 1991,

---

[21] Nigerian Broadcasting Corporation banned the broadcast of miracle in 2004 because of its abuse. At this period, religious programmes aired on national television was limited to preaching and teaching. See https://www.christianitytoday.com/ct/2004/aprilweb-only/4-12-41.0.html

[22] R. Bible-Davids, *Enoch Adeboye Father of Nations: African Legends of Faith* Series Volume 2. London: Biblios Publishers, 2009, 236.

the Church took the healthcare delivery initiative to a new dimension by registering the maternity centre and equipping it. This was done by making provisions for qualified medical personnel, equipment and medications to the hospital.[23] This maternity centre has been sustained and the feat has been replicated in most of the parishes of the Church across the nation with the establishment of maternity or medical centre in an attempt to care for the people regarding their health. Among these parishes, the maternity or the medical centre has been upgraded to serve the people in better capacity considering the health challenges members are faced with.[24] This social intervention is not limited to the parish level as provinces and regions are also proactive through the building of medical outfits. At the national level, healthcare services to the nation have been taken with priority. The upgrading of the maternity centre at the Redemption Camp to Redeemers Health Centre is a good example with medical services rendered to the people from all over the nation especially during the Holy Ghost Services and Holy Ghost Conventions. Apart from the fact that worshippers do gather together for religious programmes in this place, Redemption Camp has equally turned to a city on its own with a lot of socio-economic activities going on there. It is on this ground that Redeemer's Health Centre is seen as medical outfit to improve the health of Nigerians who did not come as worshippers but as individuals working for a daily living. The medical services given to community at the Redemption Camp are best understood from the submission of Adedibu that:

> Redemption Camp has attracted a huge attention from commercial and financial sector with the presence of seven banks and two mortgage banks, property development firms, small-scale entrepreneurs, food hawkers, guest hostels, restaurants, guest chalets of different sizes and shapes to cater for people of different economic statuses.[25]

The foregoing position reveals the impact of this healthcare centre at the Redemption Camp on the people going by commercial and other activities taking place in the Redemption Camp. This means as a city in its own right, those who are in the camp for religious or commercial purpose have access to medical services provided by the Church.

---

[23] Bible-Davids, 236.
[24] Mr Olatunde Akinsanya a member of Redeemed Christian Church of God in one of the Parishes at Abeokuta intimated that medical services are rendered to members with the medical facilities within the premises of the church.
[25] Adedibu, 13.

A good example of the hospital built by the RCCG for the purpose of making medical services accessible to the people is the Healing Stripes Hospital established through His Love Foundation, the Corporate Social Responsibility arm of the Church to offer primary care and community healthcare outreaches. It was reported that since the time of its establishment, the hospital has had 64,000 discharges, while 9,104 free dialysis had been recorded. The hospital equally has out-patient services with 80% of services to be obstetrics and gynaecology. Still Waters Hospital is another example of the RCCG medical facilities built for the common good of the people. This initiative was made by the Province 2 RCCG in Mogboro and Arepo community in Obafemi Owode Local Government in Ogun State. The Province took over the community health centre, upgraded it to ultra-modern hospital for the whole community without religious bias. Medical services at Still Waters Hospital are subsidised with collection of a token amount from patients because it is non-profit establishment. This has greatly impacted the lives of the people who live in the area who did not have enough money to seek medical services in the public or private hospitals.[26]

Different platforms are used by the RCCG to reach out to the people through the Corporate Social Responsibility. These platforms are collaborating with the government and rendering of medical services to the public. In doing this, the RCCG Apapa Family in Lagos for example donated some Intensive Care Unit equipment to the Lagos State Teaching Hospital as part of partnering with Government. Some of the things donated include CR 5000 ICU Beds, four Alpha Active, 4 Mattresses, B-Braun Infusion Pumps, Syringe Pumps, Multi-Parameter Patient Monitors and Bedside locker.[27] Also, the Church refurbished and equipped the Intensive Care Unit in the surgical emergency section of the hospital. At the national level, Intensive Care Unit facilities were donated to Jos Specialist Hospital and recently, during the last 67th Annual Convention, held in 2019, the third Intensive Care Unit named Enoch and Folu Adeboye Intensive Care by the RCCG was commissioned by Governor Dapo Abiodun of Ogun State for the public use.[28] This gesture towards healthcare delivery shows that beyond the pulpit, the RCCG is massively investing in the health sector as part of her social mandate.

---

[26] https//thenationonlineng.net RCCG builds 11 bed-hospital. Accessed on 19/07/2019.
[27] www.punchng.com. Redeemed Christian Church of God Donates ICU equipment to LASUTH. Accessed on 16/08/2019.
[28] https//m.guardian.ng. Governor Dapo Abiodun Commissioned Enoch and Folu Adeboye Intensive Care Unit at the Redemption Camp. Accessed on 16/09/2019.

In areas where there are no financial capabilities to build hospital among members of the RCCG, services on health advocacy and medical support with provision of drugs are rendered to the people. This was demonstrated by Province 37 in Alimosho Local Government of Lagos State where more than 200 residents of Orisunbare received free medical services. As part of social services, the residents of this community were offered free diagnostic tests to ascertain their sugar level, blood pressure and other blood examinations. Beneficiaries were equally offered drugs after detailed examinations have been carried out on their health challenges. The impact of this action was felt with the testimony of Mr. Adeoye Balogun, a Muslim in this community, who stated that the medical services given to them would have been expensive if it were to be acquired in the public or private hospitals around.[29] This shows that most of the beneficiaries are low income earners who could not afford such bills which points to the fact that they needed to be assisted.

The Redeemed Christian Church of God is involved also in counselling services and pre-marital screenings among members throughout the federation. The screenings are usually conducted to determine how healthy family could be raised among members and they are mainly on HIV/AIDS, Genotype and Hepatitis. Not long ago, genital examination for intending couples was added as part of the pre-marital examination to members. This was done to reduce cases of marital crises arising in the case of undeclared reproductive/genital functionality. There is no doubt that this development would have helped a lot of intending couples to seek medical advice and solution to their problems, having realised that they could no longer hide their genital status from the church authority if they are to get married in the Church. This is a step in the right direction. Familusi emphasises that the pre-marital screenings prevent medical incompatibility and will bring about marital stability as against the problems that usually ensue from undeclared health-related issues before marriage, which is one of the factors engendering instability in marital relationship.[30]

It is observed that the RCCG has done much in the area of HIV/AIDS prevention and counselling through what is call the Redeemed AIDS Programme Action Committee (RAPAC) which is part of the social services initiatives of the Church in response to the distress of those who are infected

---

[29] www.Vanguardngr.com RCCG offers medical services. Accessed on 12/09/2020.
[30] O.O. Familusi, "Till Circumstances do us Part: A Socio-Ethical Analysis of Divorce among Christians in Nigeria," *Global Journal of Human-Social Science: Arts & Humanities- Psychology*, 19/5 (2019): 25.

with the HIV/AIDS virus.[31] The objective of RAPAC is to provide detailed and up to date information, training and counselling on HIV/AIDS, sexual and reproductive measures to members. However, the position of Ukah is that RAPAC was created as RCCG response to the influx into the church of people who were looking for miraculous cure for HIV/AIDS.[32] While these people are not discouraged in seeking faith or divine healing, the Church came up with a different platform for the People Living with HIV/AIDS to be assisted. Therefore, RAPAC became the succour to the people who are infected and those not yet infected. This programme equally brings awareness within the Church to let members know that HIV is very real and it is not a respecter of anybody whether or not one is a Christian.[33]

The evidence that the Redeemed Christian Church of God's concern for the healthy living through prayer and advocacy for Nigerians and Christians in particular is beyond the four corners of their parishes was further demonstrated during the outbreak of coronavirus (COVID-19) pandemic that is ravaging the world. The church authority embarked on nationwide public advocacy to preclude the spread of the disease through sensitisation on regular hand washing, keeping social distancing, personal hygiene at the optimum level, wearing of face mask and avoiding large social and religious gatherings, which the Church also demonstrated by asking its members to stay at home with the airing of its programmes on Dove Television. Besides, the Church donated two sets of Ventilators, two Intensive Care Unit (ICU) Beds and other items to the Ogun State Government towards the effective curbing of the coronavirus pandemic in the State.[34] Other equipment donated to the Ogun State Government include two Infusion Pumps, one Vital Signs Monitor and one Suctioning Machine. In addition to the above gesture from the Church towards the State, surgical face masks, gloves and hand sanitisers were distributed for the purpose of preventing the spread of the deadly disease. This medical intervention of the Church is not limited to Ogun State, as Lagos State, which is the epicentre of this pandemic has also benefitted from the Church. In this regard, it was reported that the RCCG and Pastor E. A. Adeboye donated 8,000 hand sanitisers, 8,000 Surgical Face Masks and two hundred thousand gloves to support the efforts of the State government in

---

[31] A.F.K, Ukah. The Redeemed Christian Church of God (RCCG), Nigeria. Local Identities and Global Processes in African Pentecostalism. Ph.D. Dissertation submitted to University of Bayreuth, 2003, 147.

[32] Bible-Davids, 234.

[33] Ukah, 147.

[34] https://m.guardian.ng. RCCG donates ventilators, intensive care unit beds, other items to Ogun State. Accessed on 12/09/2020.

equipping its medical staff with necessary protective wears needed to contain the spread of coronavirus pandemic in Nigeria.[35]

For better service to the people as a result of this social action, the Church works with international non-governmental organisations like International Red Cross, Family Health International (FHI), and the United States Agency for International Development (USAID). From the above activities of the RCCG to prevent the spread of this dreaded virus, its contribution to a productive population in Nigeria is evident. Lastly, the activities of the Redeemed Christian Fellowship among the students during the "rural rugged" where evangelistic outreaches are embarked upon sometimes create opportunities to take medical ministry to the rural dwellers through provision of drugs and diagnosis with the help of medical students among them. The medical services rendered during the 'Let's go a fishing' programme are further steps to expand the scope of the Church social action in the area of healthcare delivery. The RCCG's commitment to Christian Social Responsibility especially in the area of healthcare delivery demonstrates the fact that the Church recognises that it is part of society and as such, it needs to be part of the progress of society, which it has demonstrated and it is still demonstrating by ministering to the health of the people as complement to faith/divine healing.

Conclusion

This paper has identified different channels of healthcare delivery by the Redeemed Christian Church of God, which are building of healthcare centres, embarking on medical outreaches and conducting pre-marital screening and counselling to its members and non-members of society as a good example of faith-based organisation's contribution to the development of humanity. It is probably these activities of the RCCG on healthcare delivery which are seen as one of its oversight functions that made United Nations (UN) seeks partnership with faith-based organisations on achieving its Sustainable Development Goals by 2030. If the UN Sustainable Development Goals on health is to ensure healthy lives and promote well-being for everybody at all ages as stated among other goals, the Church is one of the platforms for achieving this purpose.

There is a need for an aggressive intervention of the Church in the health sector as evident in education, especially in the area of university education. This

---

[35] https://www.thissdaylive.com. Adeboye donates sanitizers, masks, gloves to Lagos. Accessed on 13/09/2020.

could be done by instituting medical schools, which will impel establishment of teaching hospitals in the universities owned by Pentecostal churches as part of the ways to contribute their quota to the development of healthcare delivery in Nigeria. However, the financial capability of the sponsoring churches must be considered in order to ensure standard and quality. This would serve the people better than building Church Headquarters that will not have impact on their lives. The Redeemed Christian Church of God should channel its wealth to further consolidate its efforts on healthcare delivery, while other Pentecostal churches should take a cue from her by contributing to healthcare delivery in Nigeria.

Chapter 7: Nigerian Pentecostalism and Corporate Social Responsibility: The Case of Christ against Drug Abuse Ministry of the RCCG in Lagos State

Rotimi Alaba Oti

Introduction

The Redeemed Christian Church of God (RCCG) under the auspices of corporate social responsibility has in recent times shown interest in the rehabilitation of drug addicts by the establishment of Christ Against Drug Abuse Ministry (CADAM). This is because the Nigerian society is experiencing a lot of violence and high crime rate which may be attributed to drug addicts. In fact, Nigeria has attracted international attention for the criminal activities that emanate from drug addicts.[1] In the country, the most conspicuous drug addicts are the "Area boys/girls" and some "street children."[2] Consequently, the government took several initiatives in the form of promulgation of laws, decrees, public education and drug addicts' rehabilitation to combat the problem. For example, the establishment of National Drug Law Enforcement Agency (NDLEA) in 1989 by the Federal Military Government was to provide public education on dangers of drug addiction to arrest drug traffickers, provide hospital treatment for drug addicts, as well as rehabilitation and aftercare for them.[3]

In spite of all this, not much has been achieved. There are indications that drug addicts and their serious damage to the moral and social fabric of

---

[1] Retrieved from https://www.narconon.org/drug-information/nigeria-drug-addiction.html. Accessed15 January 2019

[2] Area boys (also known as *Agberos*) are loosely organised gangs of street children and teenagers, composed mostly of males, who roam the streets of Lagos and other neighbouring towns and cities. They extort money from passers-by, public transporters and traders, sell illegal drugs, act as informal security guards, and perform other "odd jobs" in return for money to purchase the hard drug.

[3] R. O. Olaniyan, *Drug Abuse and Trafficking Among Nigeria Youths: Dimensions of the problem in a Changing Environment*, Lagos: NIIA, 1999, 87.

the country are on the increase. The implication of this is that the current rehabilitation strategies are not sufficient. Therefore, this chapter examines Christ Against Drug Abuse Ministry (CADAM) of the Redeemed Christian Church of God's (RCCG) drug rehabilitation programme and its implications for drug addicts' rehabilitation in Lagos State, Nigeria.

Drug Addiction in Nigeria

Drug addiction is one of the most serious problems that almost all the nations of the world are facing today. Throughout recorded history and in countries all over the world, a percentage of every population has had serious problems with substance abuse and other types of addiction.[4] There are lots of violent situations and increased rate of crime in Nigerian society which may be attributed to drug addiction.[5] Nigeria used to be a transit point for drugs, but now has assumed the position and destination for hard and illicit drugs, that is, she has gone from being a drug consuming nation to being a drug producing one.

In view of this, some people in society seem to have cultivated the habit that drug use is good because in recent times, drug users openly boast about their habits and skills in taking narcotic drugs unlike in the past when drug addicts hid their drug addiction habits because of the fear of being stigmatised or prosecuted by the law enforcement agencies. Drugs that are commonly used in Nigeria include alcohol (most times illicit gin commonly called *ogogoro* or hot drink), marijuana (cannabis, *Igbo*, etc.), heroine (brown) and cocaine (Charlie, Crack, Italian white, etc.). Others are amphetamines, solvents like glue, paints, fuel, tramadol, etc. There seems to be an increasing number of drug addicts among students, businessmen, labourers, drivers and other professionals in the country although students are mostly affected. Also, it is assumed that drug addiction has contributed to the decline in the standard of education and discipline in schools and caused families to undergo a lot of stress and social stigmatisation.[6] Drug addiction among drivers has caused many road accidents.[7]

---

[4] G. R. Collins, *Christian Counseling: A Comprehensive Guide*, Third Edition, Wheaton, Illinois: Tyndale House Publisher Inc., 2007, 684.

[5] https://www.unodc.org/documents/data-and-analysis/statistics/Drugs/Drug_Use_Survey_Nigeria_2019_BOOK.pdf

[6] Overview of the Drug Addiction Problem in Nigeria, 2010, <http://www.narconon.org/drug-information/nigeria-drug-addiction.html.

[7] Drug Treatment Scene in Nigeria, 2010. http://www.narconon.org/drug-rehab/drug-rehabilitation-program.html.

The devastating effects of the menace of drug addiction on society are enormous. Drug addicts have poor social skills and interpersonal relationships. They seem to be responsible for the highest toll of social breaches like absenteeism at work and schools, irresponsible parenthood or parenting, armed robbery, road accidents, substance-related legal problem, such as rape, wife-beating, broken homes, murder, suicide, violent crime, cultism, prostitution and divorce, among others.[8] Also associated with drug addiction are economic and manpower losses with mortality among the victims.

In Nigeria, the most disturbing health-related phenomenon is the use and abuse of drugs by adolescents. Research on both in- and out-of-school adolescents in Nigeria reveals that majority of the youth ignorantly depend on one form of drug or the other (tobacco, marijuana, cocaine, codeine, heroine, alcohol, rophynol, tramadol, and so on) for their various daily activities such as social, educational, political, moral activities.[9]

There is not much information on how many people are addicted to drug in Nigeria. According to Narconon International, drug addiction and substance abuse figures are largely unavailable in Nigeria, but the most recent figure available is the United Nations report of only 925 addicts that were treated in various rehabilitation centres in 2004.[10] It further reiterates that about 90 percent of them were involved in cannabis addiction, while others were involved in pharmaceutical depressants, inhalants, amphetamine-type drugs, heroin and cocaine. Therefore, it seems that there are many thousands of people who are addicted to narcotic drugs in the country who are not receiving any type of treatment. This is what prompted the Redeemed Christian Church of God to set up drug addicts' rehabilitation centre which is the focus of this study.

The RCCG and Corporate Social Responsibility

Corporate social responsibility (CSR) is a management strategy of companies integrating social and environmental concerns in their business operations and interactions with their stakeholders.[11] It is aimed at

---

[8] S. Momoh, "Social Miscreants Menace," *Businessday* newspaper, 9th January, 2010 www. buisnessdayonline.com/.../3169/social-miscreants-menace.

[9] Drug Addiction in Nigeria, http://www.synapseservices.org/addiction.html 23/09/2018.

[10] Drug Addiction in Nigeria, http://www.synapseservices.org/addiction.html 23/09/2018.

[11] https://www.unido.org/our-focus/advancing-economic-competitiveness/competitive-trade-capacities-and-corporate-responsibility/corporate-social-responsibility-market-integration/what-csr

business self-regulation that gears towards contributing to society through philanthropic, activist or charitable activities by engaging in or supporting volunteering or ethically-oriented practices.[12] Thus, it is the commitment of the RCCG to responding and contributing ethically to economic development of the country by improving the quality of life of the workforce and their families as well as of the local community.

In the RCCG, it is referred to as Christian Social Responsibility and not Corporate Social Responsibility because it is held that CSR has its root in Christianity.[13] The church sees it as a conscious avenue to make visible and lasting impact in various areas of society. Today, there are lots of challenges in society on which the church uses as an opportunity to take effort to creating solutions in conjunction with other people in society. In today's socially conscious environment, some churches place high premium on working for and spending their money to positively affect their environment, the public and the country at large. The Redeemed Christian Church of God is focused on helping through the establishment of Christian Social Responsibility (CSR). It is created to positively effect changes in all sections of society globally by working with peoples, corporate bodies, NGOs and governments to achieve the set goals.

The RCCG's initiative is sub-divided into eight clear sections called SHEMBAGS. The acronym stands for Social, Health, Education, Business, Arts and Culture, Government, Sports, etc. Their targets are active areas that are common to people and societies globally.[14] The RCCG has been deeply involved in the activities which are usually classified under the CSR because of her vision and mission. The Church as an institution is involved in tackling the problem of drug addiction in Lagos State, because social commitment is not just the consequences of the life of the church, but essential element of the life of the church.

In view of this, CADAM is set up to rescue drug addicts so as not to inflict the rest of society with the malaise. In the same vein, the RCCG is performing her moral obligation to society and extending the frontiers of evangelism in setting up this rehabilitation programme. Indeed, as Jesus came for the poor and the lost sheep of the house of Israel, the church also seeks

---

[12] Benedict Sheehy, "Defining CSR: Problems and Solutions," *Journal of Business Ethics,* 131/3 (2015): 625–648. doi:10.1007/s10551-014-2281-x.

[13] https://rccgcovenantsanctuaryuk.org/ministries/christian-social-responsibility/

[14] http://csr.rccg.org/

such people, that is, the drug addicts and the downtrodden instead of giving all the attention to the well-to-do in society,[15] hence, the establishment of the Christ Against Drug Abuse Ministry of the Redeemed Christian Church of God's Corporate Social Responsibility Unit.

Christ Against Drug Abuse Ministry (CADAM)[16]

Christ Against Drug Abuse Ministry is one of the Corporate Social Responsibility-oriented arms of the Redeemed Christian Church of God (RCCG), which is being managed by Acme Parish, one of the RCCG parishes in Lagos State. The programme was founded in 1991. It was then referred to as Drug Addicts Rehabilitation Ministry; however, the present name was adopted in 1994. The programme has three sub-centres which are Ebenezer House in Akute near Ojudu area in Ikeja, Liberty House in Poka (Epe town) and another one in Erodo. They play a complementary role in ensuring adequate rehabilitation of drug addicts. The centres at Poka and Erodo were established as a primary unit for initial drying out process before transferring the clients to Akute (Ebenezer House) for the moral restructuring process.[17] The Akute centre in this regard functions mainly to re-establish drug addicts' faith in order to live a meaningful life thereafter. Through this centre, clients are re-integrated with their families and society at large as responsible citizens. There were 400 clients present in the record of the centre who are attending their correctional programme. It has a total number of 26 workers, 15 at Akute, 5 at Poka sub-centre and 6 in Erodo respectively.[18]

The Parish pastor is the head of all policy administration. Under him, there is a voluntary committee in charge of drug addiction control and vocation. A coordinator to whom the religious, medical, administrative and vocational staff members are answerable in their daily duties heads this committee. The members of staff in the religious unit function as the care staff and field officers who carry out the bulk of the re-socialisation and correctional works. This group of people includes ex-drug addicts who have benefitted from the programmes.

---

[15] S. T. Adetoye, "RCCG: A Planting of the Lord," *The Nation*, 6th August, 2007, 33.

[16] CADAM Pamphlet of advertisement received from the centre during my visitation at various times in April 2019.

[17] Interview held with one of the CADAM beneficiaries named Bro. Prosper on 15th April, 2019.

[18] R. A. Oti, An Ethical Assessment of The RCCG's Rehabilitation Programmes in Lagos and Ogun States, Nigeria. 2001-2011, A PhD Thesis in the Department of Religious Studies, University of Ibadan, Ibadan, 2014.

The Vision and Aim of Christ Against Drug Abuse Ministry (CADAM)[19]

The vision of the programme is to make individuals, families and communities free from the scourge of drug abuse and addiction in Nigeria. It is also structured to combat and eliminate the drug scourge wherever it exists, while at the same time, it aims to identify, combat and overcome the multiple causes and effects of drug abuse through the development of effective programmes and services with the aim of providing absolute freedom for the affected individuals, their families and communities.

Services Rendered by Christ Against Drug Abuse Ministry (CADAM)[20]

CADAM performs in-house programme, that is, development and implementation of the following drug demand reduction programme areas: prevention and early intervention services which involve drug use prevention, drug abuse prevention and early intervention; treatment and rehabilitation services, which take into consideration drug addiction treatment, vocational and educational rehabilitation; and aftercare services which include aftercare (continuing care) and social re-integration of those who have been rehabilitated.

In all, the programme is for 12 months which is sub-divided into 6 months each in the two centres. It is a residential programme with no facilities for visitation by the family members until the end of the programme.

Admission and Accommodation Procedure of Drug Addicts into CADAM[21]

The admission process in the rehabilitation of drug addicts in the RCCG's rehabilitation centre takes the following form: Generally, their admission takes place twice per year. This is in March and September because of the limited accommodation. Admission comes through three means. Firstly, evangelism, which is the preaching of the gospel to the drug addicts; this is conducted at various locations in Lagos, Abeokuta and other towns within and around Southwestern Nigeria because of their proximity to the operational base of the ministry by some of the assigned pastors. Any of the drug addicts that yield positively to the evangelism are admitted into the centre. Secondly, through referral; some drug addicts are referred from other rehabilitation centres and

---

[19] The CADAM centres' official records consulted on 15th June. 2019.
[20] CADAM Pamphlet of advertisement received from the centre during my visitation at various times in April 2019.
[21] Interview held with one of the CADAM beneficiaries named Bro. Prosper on 15th April 2019.

hospitals within or around Southwestern Nigeria. Lastly, some drug addicts come voluntarily after realising their state and the need to change their ways of life. They are admitted and accommodated for treatment through diagnostic and comprehensive assessment procedures which is the basis for a personalised and effective approach to rehabilitation. This includes screening which is to identify individuals with hazardous or harmful drug use or drug dependence, as well as associated risk behaviours (viral transmission via needle sharing and/or unprotected sexual activity, potentially violent behaviour, suicide risk). Standardised tools are used to assess drug use and its severity on an individual which helps in determining the degree of help required. Accurate severity of each individual addict's situation is established before initiating rehabilitation treatment. Furthermore, assessment and diagnosis which are the core requirements for starting rehabilitation are carried out. Here, a comprehensive assessment of each individual drug addicts is performed. This takes into account the stage and severity of their drug addiction, somatic and mental health status, individual temperament and personality traits, vocational and employment status, family and social integration and legal situation. They further consider environmental and developmental factors, including childhood and adolescent history, family history and relationships, social and cultural circumstances and previous treatment attendance. An adequate assessment process creates the environment for the development of a therapeutic alliance to engage the patient into rehabilitation.

Lastly, after the screening assessment exercise, they are accommodated in a temporary hall of residence for at least four or five days for prayers and orientation. Thereafter, they are led to dormitories where they will reside for the rest of their treatment at the centre. Rosters are made for such activities as evening devotion, morning duties, etc. While the morning devotion is handled by the care staff on duty, others are handled by some of the drug addicts.

Mode of Operation of CADAM[22]

The mode of the operation aimed at rehabilitating drug addicts in CADAM takes many forms. Some deal with individual, while others deal with the group. Some seek to alter personality and others only to change behaviour. Some drug addicts are to be provided with vocational skills and educational credentials and others to be the cured of drug addiction or alcoholism. We shall describe some of the methods of operations of CADAM below:

---

[22] Participant observations made to assess CADAM rehabilitation activities on 12th June, 2019.

Moral Instruction

Through moral instructions, all drug addicts are intimated with societal norms and values for their re-integration into society. This is a five-month treatment programme aimed at helping the beneficiaries to recover from drug addict tendencies and associated problems. Classes take place every Monday to Friday, from 9:00 a.m. to 2:00 p.m. The practical aspects take place in their various hostels in the evenings after school hours and during the weekends. In this section, the drug addict is taught moral habits, the standard of behaviour and principle of right and wrong needed to make them conform to the established codes or accepted notion of right or wrong when they leave the rehabilitation centres. In other words, they are taught to develop various moral, civic, good manners in compliant with social order.

Counselling

Counselling is another mode of operation in the RCCG rehabilitation programme. In the centres, compulsory counselling sessions are offered on individual and group bases to equip drug addicts for re-integration into society and reunion with their family and friends.

Skills Acquisition Training

Apart from assisting drug addicts with transitioning into a normal life, they are also empowered to be self-reliant by sending them to various vocational training centres in different parts of Lagos State. At these training centres, they learn skills that will help them after recovery. Each of them is trained according to their skills and capabilities. This is one of the main effects of employment in alleviating poverty which may have been the reason why many drug addicts got involved in criminal activities. The skills acquisition programme involves training beneficiaries as artisans, pastors and social workers for a period that ranges from a minimum of 5 months to two years with the tools and skills for their re-integration into the social and economic schemes of society. This is done to make them become independent and responsible. Through this way, a relapse is prevented.

Follow-up

The follow-up and aftercare phase of treatment takes place in all centres after the drug addicts have completed the rehabilitation process and have been discharged. It is usually done on an outpatient basis and consists of face-to-face visits and communications over the telephone. There are regular contacts with the patient and family over the telephone. During the visitation, patients are evaluated, counselled and provided with other necessary support services. Unscheduled visits are also made if necessary. The aim of the follow-up phase is to provide continuing support to discharged patients, monitoring their post-rehabilitation progress and detect as early as possible any threats or signs of relapse.

Agents of Christ Against Drug Abuse Ministry (CADAM)

The agents involved in rehabilitation in Christ Against Drug Abuse Ministry (CADAM) are Programme Coordinator, Caregivers, Counsellors and Bible study teachers. They are pastors, invited lecturers and spiritual leaders in the RCCG who make themselves available to provide education and counselling for victims for their recovery process. They help them in accepting themselves, getting rid of negative feelings and guilt and living more productively in society.

Impacts and Implications of CADAM for Nigeria

This programme galvanises character reformation among the drug addicts and enhances their resistance to moral compromise. The centre has picked up, treated and rehabilitated many people who had been addicted to drugs and given them a new life. For example, 2,805 beneficiaries from Christ Against Drugs Abuse Ministry (CADAM) with about 70 per cent of them are now living drug-free, independent and productive lives in various professions and vocations all over the world.[23] CADAM has been complementing government efforts in eradicating crime in Lagos State, Nigeria.

It has served as a centre for transformation of youths who suffer drug addiction and are seeking a new life. Today, the centre has both formal and informal relationships with about 12 Nigerian universities whose students are sent for the programme and are readmitted to continue and complete their education upon their certification.[24]

---

[23] RCCG Impacts Lives Through CSR, https://www.redemptionlight.org/rccg-impacts-lives-through-csr/, June 6, 2019.

[24] RCCG's rehabilitation centre gives succour to drug victims, https://guardian.ng/sunday-magazine/ibru-ecumenical-centre/rccgs-rehabilitation-centre-gives-succour-to-drug-victims/ 22 October 2017.

The RCCG through the rehabilitation centres, clothes, feeds and shelters these affected patients and gives them a chance to live again. Many lives that had been compromised as a result of drug addiction have been redeemed, stabilised and given new hope for a better and meaningful future. The centre has assisted more than 2000 beneficiaries, most of whom have become professionals and well-to-do persons in society.[25] The goal of the RCCG rehabilitation programme is not only to help individuals understand why they are involved in criminal activities and why their lives will be better without anti-social behaviours, but also offer them the necessary tools to continue to remain good citizens once they have completed the rehabilitation programme and re-entered into society, which have in any ways reduced criminal activities and immoral behaviours in Lagos State.[26]

Since the inception of CADAM, many drug addicts have graduated from its recovery programme, while 47% have completed the vocational and educational programmes. Skills acquired include catering, barbing, plumbing, auto-spray/panel beating, hairdressing, electrical works, cosmetics, cobbling and poly-nylon works; while educational skills acquired include Secondary School Certificates in Education, theological training, desktop publishing, office information management, computer engineering, and other higher degrees.[27] They are trained as artisans, pastors and social workers in order to incorporate them into the social and economic schemes of society. This is in accordance with Apostle Paul's injunction which says: "if any would not work, neither should he eat." (II Thess. 3:1b). Employment has been identified as an important element in the rehabilitation of drug addicts since the goal of rehabilitation is to help reintegrate them into their community as productive and valued people. Work is a fundamental way in which the contribution of the individual drug addicts to the flourishing of society is recognised and human worth is affirmed. Unemployment is a deeply traumatic experience which could lure them to criminal activities.

Many of the beneficiaries are established themselves and become beneficial to themselves, families, the church, and society at large. They have been helping in sanitising not only Lagos State, but the entire nation, of drug addiction and its problems by preaching to others who are already

---

[25] RCCG commissions drug rehabilitation centre in Epe, https://www.facebook.com/Churchgist.org/posts/rccg-commissions-drug-rehabilitation-centre-in-epethe-rccg-has-commissioned-a-dr/1192516150892254/, 4 October 2017.

[26] Oti, 12.

[27] Participant observations made to assess CADAM rehabilitation activities on 12th June. 2019.

involved and those who may get themselves involved in future.[28] In all, the programmes have offered social, economic and religious benefits to drug addicts in Lagos State, Nigeria.

Challenges Encountered by CADAM

The major challenge of the programme is lack of proper follow-up which results in relapse of some of the drug addicts. This is due to inadequate personnel to match the number of graduands in the various rehabilitation centres and insufficient funding to employ more staff. Relapse is generally considered to be the return to criminal behaviour after a period of abstinence. It may be on a small-scale or large-scale return to any criminal activities. Medically speaking, it is maintained that a relapse is a return to destructive or heavier criminal behaviour. A relapse is a recurrence of a past (typically medical) condition. Relapse, in relation to drug addicts, is "resuming the use of a drug or a chemical substance and accompanied criminal behaviours after one or more periods of abstinence or rehabilitation."[29]

Recommendations

Based on the findings of the study, it is recommended that:

1) in order to avoid relapse of patients, an annual special award event should be instituted where former drug addicts who have consistently kept themselves from deliberate relapse are rewarded in order to boost their morale and self-esteem and challenge others to keep themselves. It is believed that these ex-drug addicts would happily embrace the award system which will, in turn, motivate them to achieve and continue in good character;

2) the church should intensify her social re-integration policy by investing more in the education and enlightenment of the general public, especially church members, and fellow clergy on problems related to the recruitment of rehabilitated or treated drug addicts;

3) the skill training programme of the CADAM rehabilitation centres should be enlarged to accommodate some other new skills in order to

---

[28] Oti, 12.
[29] R. M. Kadden, "Cognitive-Behavior Therapy for Substance Dependence: Coping Skills Training," http://www.bhrm.org/guidelines/CBT-Kadden.

foster more work opportunities. In the alternative, the church should pay proper attention to her centres which are performing below expectation in order to improve their capabilities in handling the rehabilitation programme effectively;

4) in order to prevent them from going back to their former addiction, the church should employ more social workers to regularly monitor drug addicts after rehabilitation. A programme coordinator who will check on the trainees without prior notification should be employed. Trainees should be made to appraise the apprentices periodically. Without that, no realistic evaluation is possible. If there is an objective and honest appraisal, the actual ability of the trainee could be assessed which will lead to further credible skill and be able to affect society better than before; and

5) further research should be geared towards understanding problems and prospects of ex-drug addicts in the larger society after rehabilitation in order to help them to contribute their quota to the progress of society.

Conclusion

This study, therefore, establishes that the Corporate Social Responsibility arm of the RCCG is a factor in the rehabilitation of drug addicts in Nigeria. Hence, there is need to recognise the role the church could play in enhancing social order in Nigeria. With this, the work remains a major contribution to the methods of solving the problem of drug addiction in Lagos State, Nigeria. This paper has shown that CADAM, the RCCG's programme for the rehabilitation of drug addicts, under the auspices of Corporate Social Responsibility has contributed immensely to reducing the cases of drug addiction in Lagos State.

Chapter 8: Nigerien Pentecostalism, Civic Roles and Corporate Social Responsibility

Gabriel Oyevesho Akinlade-Daniel

Introduction

The argument that government alone cannot shoulder the burden of development even though it is its responsibility to provide basic amenities for the people has become a common refrain. It is necessary duty of a responsible government to cater for the people. Some have argued that the church has come in to render some support because of government's failure or inability to provide adequate amenities for the people. In the area of support, Pentecostal churches have been active in playing civic roles and rendering Corporate (or Church) Social Responsibility (CSR) by organising programmes and embarking on projects that cover many areas of social need. The Pentecostal churches stepped in because as rightly observed by Pastor Johnson Odesola, CSR is the heart of the gospel of Christ. CSR is all about giving to others (Jn. 3:16). For him, the church is established to continue the work of Christ and to walk in it. So, by its very nature, the church is a people-centred institution and should naturally care for the people in the community from where it draws its membership (Matt.19:19). Consequently, a church must think within and without by following the examples of Christ. Thus, this chapter examines the emergence of CSR in different Pentecostal churches as a strategy of preaching the gospel and overall development of the Nigerian state.

The Concept of Corporate Social Responsibility

The concept of Corporate Social Responsibility (CSR) is not a new one as discussions about it started as far back as in the 1950s. It has since continued to grow in significance as a way to improve society in one way or the other. It has been subjected to lot of debates and research. In spite of the seeming endless discussions about CSR, it has brought a lot of development in both academic, societies and practitioners in the communities all over. CSR is a concept whereby organisations commit themselves to improving their environmental and social performance in society. Panwar and his colleagues conceptualise it as "a unique, context-specific and wholesome business philosophy, translated into corporate strategy and fused with organizational culture, aiming at ethically-guided initiatives that sustainably protect and promote the interests of the ever-changing components of a corporate eco-system."[1]

Bowen proposes that Corporate Social Responsibility (CSR) is an obligation to pursue those social responsibility policies to make those decisions, or to follow those lines of action that are desirable in terms of the objectives and values of our society.[2] For corporations, social responsibility includes economic, legal, ethical and discretionary expectations that society has of them at a given point of time in the context of their operations.[3] Furthermore, CSR is "the commitment of business to contribute to sustainable economic development, working with employees, their families, the local community and society to improve quality of life. It goes beyond the legal, technical, and economic requirements of the company and is viewed differently by people having different values."[4]

Accordingly, CSR strategies encourage the company to make positive impact on the environment and stakeholders, including consumers, employees, investors, communities and others. In other words, CSR is concerned about an organisation's mission as well as a guide to what the company represents for its consumers and environment. It also aims to ensure that companies conduct their business in a way that is ethical. This means taking account of their social, economic and environmental impact and consideration of human rights. It also evolves a range of activities such as working in partnership with local communities, socially responsible investment (SRI), developing relationships with employees and customers as well as environmental protection and sustainability.[5]

However, in the religious sphere, CSR is often partly geared towards reducing improving the moral standard of society.[6] Thus, most observers

---

[1] R. Panwar, T. Rinne, E. Hansen and H. Juslin, "Corporate Responsibility: Balancing Economic, Environmental and Social Issues in the Forest Industry," *Forest Product Journal* 56/2 (2006): 5.

[2] H. R. Bowen, *Social Responsibility of Business*, New York: Harper and Row, 1953.

[3] B. B. Carroll, "A Three-Dimensional Concept Mode of Corporate Performance," *Academy of Management Review* 4/4 (1979): 497-505.

[4] H. Juslin, and E. Hansen, *Strategic Marketing in the Global Forest Industries*, Oregon: Authors Academic Publishing, 2003, 610.

[5] Juslin, and Hansen, 611.

[6] See Francis cited in "Impact of Corporate Social Responsibility on Church Growth", June 29, 2018 https://www.modishproject.com/csr-church-growth

agree that religious institutions are woven deeply into the physical and social fabric of the community. In nearly every neighborhood and suburb, we find temples and churches. Churches are perhaps the oldest and most ubiquitous form of urban community.[7] As a result, the church also acts as an organisation whose social intervention could yield some profits. It is from these perspectives that the church is assumed to carry out social responsibility as a business strategy.

Emergence of CSR in Churches

Globalisation has influenced churches to be more committed to the social, economic, health and environmental concerns of their members and communities due to government's failure to address some social needs. Thus, Corporate Social Responsibility (CSR) is crossing the border of corporate organisations and perching on the altar of religious institutions. By implication, churches have found it worthwhile as a strategy to impact on society without losing their primary objective of preaching salvation and making heaven.[8] Today in Nigeria, with the growing 'army' of unemployed graduates, poverty among other issues who seek solutions from God, churches are beginning to explore CSR as buffer for their congregations. To enhance better coordination of what some religious scholars also term Christian Corporate Social Responsibility (CCSR), some churches, especially those with large congregation, now set up CSR/Sustainability departments to bind both faith in God and work for the betterment of society, which anchors on faith without work is dead. The Church is expected to be a social pioneer in its social responsibility needs. As part of its pioneering social role, the Church is designed as part of the human community to respond first to God-in-Christ. Going by the nature of the Church, it ought to be the most sensitive and responsive entity in every society. The Church hears the Word of God, sees His judgments, and has the vision of resurrection. This unique role of the Church makes it the pioneer part of society that responds to God on behalf of the whole society.

For example, the Israelites were chosen by God to lead all nations to Him. Jesus also displays the same responsibility in his obedience to God by sacrificing himself for the redemption of humankind. In the same vein, the General Overseer of the General Overseer of the Redeemed Christian Church of God,

---

[7] O. McRoberts, *Street of Glory, Church and Community in Black Urban Neighbourhood*, Chicago: University of Chicago Press, 2005.

[8] A. Ademigbuji, and D. Adejo, "Embracing CSR, the RCCG example," *The Nation*, January 22, 2016, https://thenationonlineng.net/embracing-csr-the-rccg-example

Pastor Enoch Adeboye, has keyed into making the Church socially relevant to the community. The Church has projects spread over 353 communities in 255 local government areas and local council development areas of the nation. Geared towards increasing CSR, projects included construction of community schools, provision of potable water, and scholarship for indigent students and patrol vans for the police, among several others. Nevertheless, CSR's activities are not done as charitable events but tools for boosting positive image of an organisation. According to Misam, the concept of churches has changed from only spiritual activities to social welfare activities where churches are not only responsible to its members but also to the immediate society.[9] Thus, Maigan and Ferrell describe corporate social responsibility as "an instrument to increase organisation's legitimacy in the eyes of their stakeholders and to develop positive social responsibility images to burnish their reputations."[10] That is why the foundations and emergence of CSR in our churches today can also be alluded to what the Scriptures say. For example, Micah 6:8 and Luke 4:18 do not only give a rationale for engaging in social responsibility and doing justice but also providing foundation for understanding the nature of social relationships and the form and content of society to which Matthew 5:7 and Romans 12 :15 attest as well as defining our responsibility towards the whole of creation (Rom. 8:19-25). Hence, the Pentecostals Christian churches' social responsibility policies are in accord with evangelical, reformed and orthodox teaching concerning social relationships.

CSR as a Tool for Spreading the Gospel

In Nigeria, as a result of the political and social economic circumstances, the Church has stepped up measures to reach out to surrounding communities through such activities as social welfare programmes to the homeless, poor, providing spiritual and economic empowerment to social misfits and drug addicts, road construction, and building of schools from elementary to university level. CSR has a deep background in the Bible. For instance, Deuteronomy 15:11 emphasises this mandate when it says: "For the poor shall never cease out of the land: therefore I command you saying, you shall open your hand wide unto your brother, to your poor, and to your needy, in your land." The Church is expected to be a social pioneer. That is why social responsibility of the Church needs to be considered as part of pioneering efforts of the Church to provide succour.

---

[9] Misam (2012) cited in "Impact of Corporate Social Responsibility on Church Growth", June 29, 2018 https://www.modishproject.com/csr-church-growth

[10] Isabelle Maigan, O.C. Ferrell (2004), Corporate Social Responsibility and Marketing: An Integrative Framework, Jan. 1, 2004 https://doi.org/10.1177/0092070303258971

Corporate Social Responsibility is a tool for fulfilling of God's purpose for establishing the Church on earth. CSR allows the Church to authenticate what the Lord did when he was on earth physically and helps the believers to represent Jesus physically in the community. Right from the onset of the ministry of Jesus, his preaching was greeted with astonishment and judged to be authoritative (Matt. 7:28-29). Jesus' transforming messages began to alter existing "traditions of men." Jesus' teaching about the Beatitudes in Matthew 5 and 6 actually eroded existing cultural norms and brought in kingdom teaching that changed lives. The book of Acts is the culmination of the foundations of the Gospels of Matthew, Mark, Luke and John. By now, the gospel message had spread through Jerusalem, Samaria, and Judea; it was now time for the word of life to be diffused round the world. The experience of the day of Pentecost demonstrated the love of God for humanity (Jn. 3:16). He loved humans beyond their man-made systems and civilisation.

The main motivations leading to the change that resulted in that adoption of CSR include to: (i) make the Church relevant to the community by putting in place corporate social responsibility initiatives; (ii) pursue the Church's goal of raising professionals and supporting entrepreneurial initiatives in the community. One theme that stands out for the purpose of CSR is missions. The outreach segment of the Church focuses on how to make the Church in each community relevant and adaptable to the needs of the community in which they are located. One way to approach this task is to educate the Church membership by laying emphasis on discipleship and community involvement. The teaching of Jesus in the Sermon on the Mount (Matt. 5:13-14) is that the community of saints is not just light in darkness but a city on a hill which cannot be hidden. This places social responsibilities on the churches to help the community of faith and beyond.

The huge social impact on the community can allow the Church to harness social resources in the community for the common good. As churches bring people together during religious programmes, they have opportunities to inform, educate and give fresh orientations towards attitudinal change on vital community subject matters. Faith communities can collaborate with outside organisations for improvement in the areas of technology, sanitation and hygiene, education and crime reduction to effect practical changes in the community. For instance, the issue of water and sanitation is common to several religions. Understanding cultural interpretations and religious behaviour around water can have an important impact on water projects in any community. So also, the creation of faith-based projects in any community can have (in)direct connection with the faith of the community.

In faith communities that value work, the dignity of labour, reducing economic inequalities, and equal distribution of wealth, projects like faith-based job creation are likely to receive community backing and patronage.[11] In what follows, I shall give a synopsis of how some Pentecostal churches in Nigeria have contributed to their communities through their Christian social responsibility activities.

The Redeemed Christian Church of God (RCCG)

It all started 24 years ago when Pastor Enoch Adejare Adeboye, General Overseer of the Redeemed Christian Church of God, mandated 50 workers to go to Surulere to find people like themselves and give them a church they would want to worship in. Unable to get a suitable venue in Surulere, they started out at Roxy Cinema, Apapa. It was from this erstwhile notorious centre of seedy activities that the Apapa Parish grew into what is now known as the Apapa family. Over the years, the Apapa family has consistently delivered on her mission. Not only are parishes in the family well founded spiritually, their impact and effectiveness manifest in every neighbourhood where they are located as the light of the world and a city set on the hill that cannot be hidden.

The CSR initiative of the Redeemed Christian Church of God is anchored on the acronym SHEMBAG which is sub-divided into eight identifiable sections. This acronym stands for Social, Health Care, Education, Media, Business and Economy, Arts and Culture, Entertainment, Government and Politics. These sections specifically target active areas common to people and societies globally. The CSR of the RCCG is anchored on Apapa Family headed by Pastor Idowu Iluyomade who is currently the Special Assistant to General Overseer on Christian Social Responsibility and Pastor-in-Charge of Region 20. The aim of the RCCG CSR is to positively effect changes in these sections of society by working with people, corporate bodies, NGOs and government to achieve these goals. As one of the leading religious Pentecostal churches in Africa, the Redeemed Christian Church of God (RCCG) has over the years established different platforms through which it touches the lives of people in different parts of Nigeria and beyond. CSR has thus become the heartbeat of the RCCG. For example, through RISE – an acronym for Redeemed Initiative for Skills and Empowerment – the church has trained over 5,000 students in various skills since 2011 when the scheme started. This is apart from its support for drug addicts through Christ Against Drugs Abuse Ministry (CADAM),

---

[11] Akvopedia, "Faith Groups As Agents of Social Change," December 11, 2013, http://www.akvopedia. org/wiki/faith-groups-as-agents-of-social-change

widows, orphans and underprivileged persons across the country in various ways. The religious organisation has also supported dozens of schools, hospitals and even security agencies with equipment to aid performance over the years. In a recent interview with *The Guardian Sunday Magazine*, Pastor Johnson Odesola, Assistant General Overseer, Admin/Personnel and Pastor-in-charge of Region 1, said that despite government attitude on the issue, the RCCG has a solid programme that covers many areas of corporate social responsibility. According to him,

> we have dug boreholes; provided books for schools as well as renovated public toilets. We have even gone to the extent of providing police stations for convenience of members of the force. The church also offers scholarships to students. RCCG has an elaborate programme, when it comes to giving back to the people or what is known as Corporate Social Responsibilities in the various areas of our operations. The Church does not limit its construction of roads and provision of amenities. The Church also empowers members of the church. For example, not long ago, one of the provinces in RCCG, organised an empowerment programme for members in demonstration of care for the people, perceived to be confronted with economic challenges. After assessing their needs, the church paraded high profile human capacity development and skills enhancement agencies to empower the members to be job creators. Every province in RCCG has a robust CSR programme as ordered by the General Overseer, Pastor Adejare Adeboye. Corporate Social Responsibility entails giving back to the society by adding value to people's lives. Not only blessing the people spiritually but also ensuring that their physical lives also have a meaning.[12]

The Mountain of Fire and Miracles Ministries (MFM)

Impacting lives both spiritually and physically in the communities where it operates is not the exclusive preserve of the RCCG. Other churches in Nigeria have also raced to the frontline of societal development in recent times. The Mountain of Fire and Miracles Ministries falls in this category. Led by Dr. Daniel Olukoya, the Church has gone beyond organising deliverance services for Nigerians to touching their lives in ways that make daily living easier

---

[12] Johnson Odesola, "Clerics on Churches and Social Responsibility" November 5, 2017 https://guardian.ng/sunday-magazine/ibru-ecumenical-centre/clerics-on-churches-and-social-responsibility/

and interesting. For example, in March 2019, the Productivity Enhancement Forum, a cell in the Church, trained over 300 persons in different skills, while also empowering several others with tools and items that could help them establish thriving businesses, including award of scholarships. This initiative, which started in 2002, according to the coordinator of the Forum, Pastor Olakunle Shiwoniku, is aimed at lifting people out of poverty. Those living around MFM's campground along the Lagos/Ibadan Expressway have also testified to the impact the Church has had on them and their environment. In 2019, Dr. Olukoya rewarded 306 members of MFM under the "Dr. D.K Olukoya's Academic Award of Excellence" who graduated with first-class honours from their various universities which is one of his 70-point agenda to reach out to the youth.[13]

Deeper Christian Life Ministry (DCLM)

Located in the heart of Gbagada, a quiet neighbourhood in Lagos, Deeper Christian Life Ministry headquarters sits imposingly on Ayodele Oke-Owo Road – some metres away from the Gbagada General Hospital. What is now a melting pot for thousands of worshippers from across the country wore a magnificent look in 2018 after it was rebuilt. Estimated to have cost about N5 billion, the edifice, which is described as the fourth largest in the country boasts of 45,000-capacity hall and a multi-layered car park. Remarkably, the significant transformation of the Church has also impacted positively on the road network of its host community, on one hand and commercial activities in the area, on the other. For instance, the overhead bridge constructed by the Church on Oduwaiye Street has put an end to the perennial traffic the route was notorious for in the past. The link bridge built by the Church has greatly eased vehicular traffic in this community. Aside from the bridge project, the Church has equally embarked on the construction of Twins Obasa Road in the community to provide an alternative route for linking the Gbagada-Oshodi Expressway. The multiple projects executed by the Church, which included a link bridge, traffic lights and 600-capacity multi-level car park, would improve the quality of life of the people in the community.

Living Faith Church a.k.a. Winners Chapel

It is the same thing in Ota, Ogun State, where the presence of Living Faith Church Worldwide has not only splashed renewed hope across the town

---

[13] Kayode Makinde, "Are Churches the Hands of God in Nigeria?" *Newswatch*, (International Edition) vol.2, no 1, December 2015, 14-35.

and beyond but also lifted a growing number of individuals and households out of poverty. The Church's intervention in road development and electricity distribution has changed people's lives for good. A lot of the development strides that Ota has witnessed so far can be credited to the efforts of the Living Faith Church, popularly known as Winners' Chapel. According to some Ota residents, there was a time the entire Ota was in total darkness; it was the Church that brought electricity to this community. "The development Ota is enjoying today can be attributed to the church. Bishop David Oyedepo brought the community into the limelight. When our transformer packed up, it was Oyedepo that gave us a transformer; he brought us from physical darkness to light. Furthermore, things changed when the Winners' Chapel repaired this major roundabout and they have continued to maintain it from time to time."[14]

Christ Apostolic Church (CAC)

CAC is not left out of the CSR activities as the Church is deeply involved in reaching out to the people in the communities where it operates. The Retired General Evangelist of Christ Apostolic Church, Prophet Samuel Abiara, observes that "empowerment is one of the core responsibilities of churches." He states that the Church had intervened in some areas by providing help for those affected by natural disasters: "We empower people by giving them money – between N100, 000 and N500, 000 – to start their business. The church also assists in fixing houses affected by natural disasters such as rainstorm." He added, "The church has bought sewing machines, grinding machines, tricycles and cars for some members of the public for them to have stable sources of income. These are things churches are expected to do to benefit people in the communities."[15]

Four Square Gospel Church (FSQC)

Four Square Gospel Church has a major presence in Nigeria. It entered Nigeria in 1955 through the ministry of Rev. and Mrs. Harold Cutis who established LIFE Theological Seminary at Herbert Macaulay Road, Yaba-Lagos. Corporate Social Responsibility (CSR) of the Church has impacted

---

[14] Eric Dumo, Afeez Hanafi and Timileyin Akinkahunsi, "Adeboye, Oyedepo, Olukoya, others rescue Nigerians from poverty," June 1, 2019 https://punchng.com/adeboye-oyedepo-olukoya-others-rescue-nigerians-from-poverty/

[15] Dumo, Hanafi and Akinkahunsi, "Adeboye, Oyedepo, Olukoya, others rescue Nigerians from poverty," June 1, 2019 https://punchng.com/adeboye-oyedepo-olukoya-others-rescue-nigerians-from-poverty/

the lives of the people in greater measures through the humanitarian and community-based activities. The Church's activities are classified under the following schemes: CLAW-Create Love Activities Window; SNAP-Sick Needy Assistance Project; ISAP-Indigent Students Assistance Project; AVAP-Accident Victims Assistant Project; WAP-Windows Assistant Project; DPAP-Displaced Persons Assistance Project. All these are embarked on by the Church because of its belief that CSR is the heart of the gospel. For instance, thousands have benefitted from their health programmes managed by professionals, where consultations and free drugs are given to participants. The Church has also provided potable water for its immediate communities as well as bursary for students to attend public primary to tertiary institutions. It also embarked on road repairs and maintenance.[16]

Christ Embassy Church (a.k.a Believers' Loveworld)

Christ Embassy founded by Pastor Chris Oyakhilome is not just only for winning souls for God but also impacts greatly on the people by providing employment for thousands of people in its businesses across banking, publishing, broadcasting, entertainment and hospitality industries. The Church operates "like a conglomerate with no fewer than 10 subsidiaries. The major money-spinning arms of the ministry include Love World Cyber ministry, Love World Television, Love World Christian Network, Love World Multimedia ministry and Love World Publishing ministry. There is also Love World Record Limited." The company "has produced many talented music artistes who are members of the church" and the "studio operates a distribution network that facilitates the selling and marketing of records within and outside Nigeria." The Church helps to reduce unemployment in Nigeria by employing some of its graduate members on full-time basis in the various companies

Conclusion

To achieve the goal of integrating CSR into the church, the maxim of Shalom as codified by Jeremiah, "Also, seek the peace and prosperity of the city to which I have carried you into exile. Pray to the Lord for it, because if it prospers, you too will prosper" (Jer. 29:7) must be the primary focus. Any gospel or theology that does not include this biblical piece is merely daydreaming. Religion that preaches salvation, holiness, and how to get to heaven but does not care about the social and economic emancipation of people is no religion. This is why the Pentecostal churches embrace diversity,

---

[16] Makinde, 14-35.

step out of their comfort zone, and launch out into the communities using the CSR framework. In the end, collective efforts will generate positive and tangible outcomes that will bring desired peace and prosperity to Nigerian cities.

At the community level, Pentecostal churches should, with assistance and collaboration with community agencies, seek to utilise the skills, talents, people of all professions - health and allied, educators, business people, policy makers, government leaders, community stalwarts, agricultural experts, and artists to galvanise their inputs and resources to confront the menace created by the apparent failure of government. Generating a web of interaction, mutual consulting, and awareness among various sectors of society through communication and goal setting should be taken seriously. They should take the advantage that globalisation offers to facilitate and deploy the pragmatic ideas that will promote CSR and make it a greater success.

Chapter 9: An Examination of the Catholic Social Teaching

Deborah Doyinsola Adegbite

Introduction

This paper explores the relevance of the Catholic social teaching in the encyclical of Pope Leo XIII in 1891. The methodology is purely historical. In Matthew 25:31-46, the basis of individual and Christian social service appears in Jesus' depiction of the King, welcoming the righteous and the blessed into his kingdom because they gave food to the hungry and they took care of strangers. The case of the Samaritan in Luke 10:29-37 also depicts what is expected from good neighbourliness. Since the papacy of Pope Leo XIII, the Roman Catholic has a body of official teaching on social issues the most significant of it being economic ethics. Pope Leo XIII first addressed these questions in his 1891 encyclical Rerum Novarum. This Rerum Novarum deals with the right of workers and later became what opened the doors for subsequent encyclicals. The documents reveal authoritative teaching of the Church. Curran notes three most important aspects of the teaching as: the "Ethical methodology, the content and the binding force of the authoritative teaching."[1]

The ethical aspect can be deduced from their moral theology as seen in major category of their doctrine which includes medical ethics, sexual ethics, and various doctrines on individual moral virtue and moral theory. The Catholic social teaching also involves the Catholic doctrine that deals with human dignity and common good in society as against oppression and all forms of social injustice which includes wealth distribution.

Falconer notes from Pope Leo XIII's declaration of 1891 that:

"Class war is strong", and religion teaches the labourer and the artisan to carry out honestly and fairly all equitable agreements

---

[1] C. E. Curran, *Official Roman Catholic Teaching, in Christian Ethics*, J. Macquarie and J. Childress (eds.), London: SCM, 1995, 44.

freely entered into; never to injure the property, nor to outrage the person, of an employer; never resort to violence in defending their own cause, nor to engage in riot or disorder and to have nothing to do with men of evil principle. Christianity teaches that labour for wages is not a thing to be ashamed of but it is to a man's credit, enabling him to earn his living in an honourable way; and that it is shameful and inhuman to treat men like possessions to make money by, or to look upon them merely as so much muscle or physical strength.[2]

Later the encyclical goes on to emphasise the fact that the Church is not concerned with the soul alone and that it exercises duty to succour the poor just as the state must remove the causes of strikes, riot and regulate the condition of civil servants. Apart from the fact that the concepts are presented in the Bible, and the culture of the Ancient Near East (ANE), it could also be traced back to Thomas Aquinas and Augustine of Hippo. This is also opined by Pope Leo XIII who asserts that Thomas Aquinas was the patron of Catholic theology and philosophy.[3]

Quadregesimo Anno

Quadragesima Anno (QA) is an encyclical which was issued by Pius XI on the 15th of May, 1931 to celebrate the 40th anniversary after Leo XIII's encyclical Rerum Novarum (RN). This work is not like that of Leo XIII which addresses the condition of workers; it states in the QA that it was the right and duty of the Pope to deal authoritatively with social and economic problems and the first thing that had to be laid down was the right of property which has been so well defended by Leo against the teachings of the socialists of his time. Just like what is experienced in the 21st century Nigeria, the state grew rich by the labours of the working class. We are called to the uplifting of the working class to enjoy the fruits of their labours. Just wages must be fixed so that a working person could maintain his family.

Principles of Social Teaching

Ethic could be generally defined as the study of moral standards and how they affect conduct. Debbie Adegbite also deploys it to describe human

---

[2] A. D. Falconer, *Human Dignity*, London: SCM, 1995, 270.
[3] http://www.usccb.org/beliefs-and-teachings/what-we-believe/catholic-social-teaching/life-and-dignity-of-the-human-person.cfm (1st June,2019).

character.[4] Therefore, Social Ethic and Social Responsibility is what makes an individual accountable for fulfilling their civic duty; it is a belief that the actions of an individual must benefit the whole of society. The principles of Catholic Social Teaching (CST) are rooted in the Old Testament jubilee custom in conjunction with the late 19th century system of encyclical letters and which Falconer attests that has been in use since then to develop better the life of the Church.[5] Catholic Social Teaching argues that human beings are fulfilled in community and family; they believe that all humans have the responsibility to participate in society and promote the common good, especially for the poor and vulnerable.

The Catholic Social Teaching

Jesus' life and teaching are influential on his followers till date; he lived a life of morality with great fidelity. His pattern of life has become the standard for Christian living. Jesus taught his followers to live for the Kingdom here on earth, a life that cares for the poor, the oppressed and the vulnerable. In the social teaching of the Catholic Church, it is obvious that Pius XI was trying to interpret Jesus' teaching while he presented the seven themes in the CST:

i.   The first of the CST is Life and Dignity of the Human Person. This teaching is based on the biblical teaching that asserts that the Lord is the maker of both rich and poor (Pro. 22:2) and that the act of the good Samaritan in Luke 10 shows that he recognised the dignity in the man that was attacked on the Jericho road. Most importantly, Jesus broke the societal and religious customs intentionally to honour the dignity of the Samaritan woman in John 4:1-42.

The Catholic Church also proclaims that human life is sacred and that the dignity of the human person is the foundation of a moral vision for society. the Church used this as a medium to speak against abortion, cloning, euthanasia, and death penalty during that period but now dressing should be added for the modern Christian girls. This is a decade when dignity has been redefined in terms of wealth instead of morality.

The teaching also calls for the avoidance of war. Nations must protect the right to life by finding increasingly effective ways to prevent conflicts and

---

[4] D. D. Adegbite, *A Concise theological & Philosophical Dictionary*, Gbongan: BIP, 2015, 130.
[5] Falconer, 271.

resolve them by peaceful means.[6] If the Fulani herdsmen, Boko Haram and all the terrorists hold that every person is precious, they will go out of their way to protect human lives rather than wasting them. They should understand that people are more important than anything else, including cows.

ii. The second is the Call to Family, Community and Participation. Man is sacred being. It is argued that the organisation of society (that is, the economics and politics, in law and policy) has a direct effect on human dignity and the capacity of individuals to grow in the community.

The family is thus an agent of pastoral activity through its explicit proclamation of the Gospel and its legacy of varied forms of witness, namely solidarity with the poor, openness to a diversity of people, the protection of creation, moral and material solidarity with other families, including those most in need, commitment to the promotion of the common good and the transformation of unjust social structures, beginning in the territory in which the family lives, through the practice of the corporal and spiritual works of mercy.[7]

It is noted that marriage and the family are the central social institutions that must be supported and strengthened, not undermined. They have the right and a duty to participate in society and together seek the common good and well-being of all, especially the poor and vulnerable. This is also firmly supported by the Scripture which negates being a lone ranger: "woe to him who is alone ..." (Eccl. 4:10). Also, Jesus' commandment was that his followers should love one another. 1 John 4:21 asserts that we cannot claim to love God without loving one another.

Rights and Responsibilities: The Catholic tradition teaches that human dignity can be protected and a healthy community can be achieved only if human rights are protected and responsibilities are met. Therefore, every person has a fundamental right to life and a right to those things required for human decency. To them, human dignity can only be protected if all human rights are protected and responsibilities of all human beings are met.

Every person has a fundamental right to life and a right to the basic needs of life. The Catholic Church teaches that every person has a duty and

---

[6] http://www.usccb.org/beliefs-and-teachings/what-we-believe/catholic-social-teaching/life-and-dignity-of-the-human-person.cfm (1st June,2019).
[7] Pope Francis, *On Love in the Family*, Amoris Laetitia, www.usccb.org (15th May,2019).

responsibility to help fulfil these rights for one another, for our families, and for the larger society.[8] The Catholic Church proclaims that the basic moral test of a society is how the most vulnerable members are faring. The Scripture is so passionate about this and Prophet Isaiah spoke about justice: rescue the oppressed, defend the orphan, and plead for the widow (Isa.1:16-17). In the ministry of Jesus, he commended those who fed the hungry, clothed the naked, visited the sick, etc. and he added that inasmuch as they have done it unto one of the least of the people, they have done it unto him (Mt. 25:40). It was also practised by the apostles because Acts 4: 32-35 indicate that everyone had things in common, meaning none of them is richer or poorer than the others.

The fourth principle is the Option for the Poor and Vulnerable[9], while the fifth is the Dignity of Work and Rights of Workers. Work is one such essential human responsibility which shapes and fulfils human dignity by providing for the needs of oneself and one's family. Work is considered to be the central reality of human existence and as soon as there is division of labour, it becomes a basic social reality. The OT clearly states that the idle soul shall suffer hunger (Pro.19:15) and in the NT James says that faith without works is dead (2:20), while Paul also warns that Christ followers should not be idle in God's business. Work done is more than a way to make a living; thus, the marketplace should not take precedence over the rights of workers who must be given decent and fair wages. Respecting these rights promotes an economy that protects human life, defends human rights, and advances the well-being of all.

The Catholic Church proclaims that every human being has a responsibility to one another. We must be our brothers' and sisters' keepers. We are called to protect people and the planet by living our faith with respect for God's creation. In a society with controversy over environmental issues, the Catholic Church believes it is a fundamental moral and ethical challenge that cannot be ignored.[10]

iii. Solidarity. This has to do with mutual agreement and support or living in harmony of interests and responsibilities among individuals in a group. To them:

---

[8] L. Rice, Catholic Social teaching: Rights and Responsibilities, www.saintstephenhinesville.com (15th May,2019).

[9] https://www.loyolapress.com ›...› Scripture and Tradition › Catholic Social Teaching, (1st June,2019).

[10] https://www.loyolapress.com ›...› Scripture and Tradition › Catholic Social Teaching, (1st June,2019).

Christian revelation shines a new light on the identity, the vocation and the ultimate destiny of the human person and the human race. Every person is created by God, loved and saved in Jesus Christ, and fulfils himself by creating a network of multiple relationships of love, justice and solidarity with other persons while he goes about his various activities in the world. Human activity, when it aims at promoting the integral dignity and vocation of the person, the quality of living conditions and the meeting in solidarity of peoples and nations, is in accordance with the plan of God, who does not fail to show his love and providence to his children. ...

Inextricably linked in the human heart are the relationship with God — recognized as Creator and Father, the source and fulfilment of life and of salvation — and openness in concrete love towards man, who must be treated as another self, even if he is an enemy (cf. Mt 5:43-44). In man's inner dimension are rooted, in the final analysis, the commitment to justice and solidarity, to the building up of a social, economic and political life that corresponds to God's plan.[11]

In conclusion, it is noted that our society often stresses individualism, indifference, and sometimes isolationism in the face of international responsibilities. The Catholic Church proclaims that every human being has a responsibility. This virtue is described by John Paul II as "a firm and persevering determination to commit oneself to the common good; that is to say, to the good of all and of each individual, because we are all really responsible for all."[12] The seventh RC teaching is the "Care for God's Creation". The Catholic tradition insists that every human being show respect for the Creator by stewardship of God's creation. This encompassing teaching is still relevant to contemporary society as it engages in social responsibility.

---

[11] http://www.usccb.org/beliefs-and-teachings/what-we-believe/catholic-social-teaching/life-and-dignity-of-the-human-person.cfm (1st June,2019).

[12] Sollicitudo Rei Socialis, no. 38.

Notes on Contributors

Babatunde Adedibu holds a Ph.D. in Missiology from North West University, South Africa. He is Associate Professor with the Department of Christian Religious Studies, Redeemer's University, Osun state, and Provost, Redeemed Christian Bible College, Nigeria. He is the author of *Coat of Many Colours*, co-editor, *The Changing Faces of African Pentecostalism* (2018) and also co-editor, *African Pentecostalism: Probity and Accountability* (2019). He is the Editor-in-Chief, *Spectrum: Journal of Contemporary Christianity*, and the initiator of the International Conference on African Pentecostalism (ICAP) held annually at the Redeemed Christian Bible College since 2016.

Benson Ohihon Igboin, Ph.D. is a professor of Philosophy of Religion, Adekunle Ajasin University, Nigeria. He is also Academic Associate of the Research Institute of Theology and Religion, University of South Africa. His areas of interest include philosophy of religion, African cultural values, African Pentecostalism among others. He is the editor, *Corruption: A New Thinking in the Reverse Order* (2018), co-editor (with Babatunde A. Adedibu) *The Changing Faces of African Pentecostalism*, and co-editor (with Jacob K. Ayantayo and Babatunde A. Adedibu), *African Pentecostalism: Probity and Accountability* (2019) and "Nigerian Pentecostalism, Alternative State, and the Question of Accountability," *Studia Historiae Ecclesisasticae*, 46/3 (2020).

Bisi Adenekan-Koevoets, Ph.D. Researcher, University of Roehampton, United Kingdom, is a sociologist of religion focused on the 'reverse mission' agenda of Nigerian-led Churches in London and Amsterdam. A developing interest is the impact of Nigerian Pentecostal spirituality on 'second and subsequent generations of Nigerians and white indigenous Europeans. Email: debisiade@yahoo.com

Deborah D. Adegbite, Ph.D. is Associate Professor of New Testament Theology and History at Bethel Institute of Theology and Biblical Research, an affiliate of Olabisi Onabanjo University and Ajayi Crowther University, Nigeria. She has contributed to many local and international journals in Theology and Religious Studies.

Gabriel Oyevesho Akinlade-Daniel holds B.A and M.A degrees in Philosophy from both the Ambrose Alli University, Ekpoma and the University of Lagos, Nigeria respectively. He also holds a Master degree in International Relations and Strategic Studies (MIRSS) from the Lagos State University and a Diploma in Journalism from the Nigerian Institute of Journalism, Lagos. He has published in learned and academic journals and currently a Doctoral student in the Department of Philosophy, Lagos State University.

Isaac Deji Ayegboyin, Ph.D. is a retired professor of Church History of the University of Ibadan, Nigeria. His areas of interest include African Pentecostal and Charismatic Churches, Sociology of Religion among others. He is a Fellow of the Nigerian Academy of Letters and Chairman, Baptist Accreditation Council for Theological Institutions in Nigeria (BACTSIN) since 2015. He is currently with the Bowen University as a Visiting Professor.

Michael Adeleke Ogunewu, Ph.D., served as senior lecturer in Church History and the Director of Museum and Archives at the Nigerian Baptist Theological Seminary in Ogbomoso. He holds a Bachelor of Arts in Religious Education from the University of Lagos; a Master of Arts in Religious Studies and a Ph.D in Church History from the University of Ibadan as well as a Postgraduate Diploma and a Master of Science degree in Mass Communication from the National Open University of Nigeria. His specialization is in the area of Pentecostalism and African Christianity.

Olumuyiwa Olusesan Familusi, Ph.D. is a Senior Lecturer in the Department of Religious Studies, Faculty of Arts, University of Ibadan, Ibadan, Nigeria. He specialises in Social Ethics and the Sociology of Religion.

Rotimi Alaba Oti, Ph.D. obtained his doctorate degree from the Department of Religious Studies, University of Ibadan, Ibadan, Nigeria and lectures at The Redeemed Christian Bible College, Main Campus, Redemption Camp, Ogun State. He is a Pastor in the Redeemed Christian Church of God. His research area is Christian Ethics.

Samuel Kehinde Fabunmi, Ph.D. lectures in the Department of Christian Religious Studies, Federal College of Education, Abeokuta, Ogun state, Nigeria. His area of specialisation is Church History and Doctrine. He is a member of learned societies, notably Nigerian Association for Christian Studies and African Association for the Study of Religions.

Umar H.D. Danfulani, Ph.D. Uppsala, Sweden, is Professor, *History of Religions*, Department of Religion & Philosophy, University of Jos, Nigeria, where he has served as Dean of Students (from 1999-2006), Head of Department (2006-2008), & Dean, Faculty of Arts (2010-2014). His fellowships, include: Alexander von Humboldt fellow Bonn Germany (1996), Uppsala STINT Fellow (2000), Global Scholar, Kansas-Missouri, USA (2010), Fellow - Academy of Religion (2012), and National Academy of Letters (NAL, 2019) among others. He has published over 100 works and the most recent include: *Juju vs Christianity: An African Dilemma* (Ipaja, Lagos: WATS, 2019; co-written with Gary Maxey), *African Healing Shrines and Cultural Psychologies* (Oxford, UK: Regnum, 2020; co-edited with Matthew Michael), and "Waging War on Peace in Jos Plateau Communities: Traditional Strategies of Conflict Resolution and Management", in A. Adogame, O. Adeboye and C.L. Williams (eds.), *Fighting in God's Name: Religion and Conflict in Local-Global Perspectives* (Lanham, Boulder, New York and London: Lexington, 2021).

Walnshak Alheri Danfulani, MSc. is a lecturer at the Centre for Conflict Management and Peace Studies, University of Jos. He is presently a PhD Student in Politics and International Studies, Girne American University, Turkish Republic of Northern Cyprus. His recent publications include: "Trends and Dynamics of the Libya Conflict", *IOSR Journal of Humanities and Social Science*, 25(10) series 8, October 2020 (co-authored with Ersoy Onder); "Governance, Human Security and Development in Nigeria", *PACEM Journal of Peace and Development*, 2(1), 2019 among others.

#CFP

Call for Papers

Publish with us! As an international Berlin publishing house we are offering a professional publishing enviroment. As international scientific booksellers we have more than 30 years of experience in the book market.

Do you have African or Asian Studies to publish?
We are mainly interested in the humanities, arts and law.
Works devoted to country or territory specific topics will receive most interest. We do not publish Medical and Scientific works with the exception of endemic studies.

English, French and German manuscripts are welcome. With regard to other languages, we offer a professional translation service.

To discuss your proposal please email us at **contact@galda.com** and our editorial team will reply in return.

G Galda Verlag
Academic publisher of books
especially in African and Asian studies

www.galda-verlag.de